THIS Volume is Presented by the Newcastle and Gateshead Incorporated Chamber of Commerce to commemorate the services of

with the 18th Battalion Northumberland Fusiliers (1st Tyneside Pioneers).

1914—1919.

HISTORICAL RECORDS
Of the 18th (Service) Battalion Northumberland Fusiliers
[1st Tyneside Pioneers]

HISTORIES OF THE NORTHUMBERLAND FUSILIERS

Hon. General Editor: Alfred Brewis.

Vol. I.   9th SERVICE BATTALION (in Preparation).

Vol. II. 16th SERVICE BATTALION (in Preparation).

Vol. III. 18th SERVICE BATTALION: Pioneers.
  Lieut.-Col. J. Shakespear, c.m.g., c.i.e., d.s.o.

Vol. IV. 19th SERVICE BATTALION: Pioneers.
  Captain C. H. Cooke, m.c.

[The larger portion of the narrative in this volume has been written by Colonel Shakespear, the rest of the narrative is by "various hands," whose identity may be recognised by those who have served in the Battalion, the honorary editor being responsible for Rolls, Itinerary, etc.]

Historical Records

✤ of the ✤

18th (Service) Battalion

Northumberland Fusiliers
(Pioneers)

✤ By ✤

Lieut.-Colonel John Shakespear
C.M.G., C.I.E., D.S.O.

✤ ✤ ✤ ✤ ✤

Printed for Private Distribution by the Council of the Newcastle and Gateshead Incorporated ✤ Chamber of Commerce_____
The Guildhall, Newcastle-on-Tyne.
✤ 1920 ✤

The Naval & Military Press Ltd

Reproduced by kind permission of the Central Library,
Royal Military Academy, Sandhurst

Published by
The Naval & Military Press Ltd
Unit 10 Ridgewood Industrial Park,
Uckfield, East Sussex,
TN22 5QE England
Tel: +44 (0) 1825 749494
Fax: +44 (0) 1825 765701
www.naval-military-press.com
www.military-genealogy.com
www.militarymaproom.com

In reprinting in facsimile from the original, any imperfections are inevitably reproduced and the quality may fall short of modern type and cartographic standards.

TO
OUR·COMRADES
WHO·FELL· IN·THE· GREAT·WAR
1914   1918

Their Name
Liveth for evermore

WE welcome back our bravest and our best!—
Ah me! not all! some come not with the rest,
Who went forth brave and bright as any here!
In these brave ranks I only see the gaps,
Thinking of our dear ones whom the dumb turf wraps,
Dark to the triumph which they died to gain:
   Fitlier may others greet the living,
    For me the past is unforgiving;
     I with uncovered head
     Salute the sacred dead,
Who went, and who return not. Say not so!
'Tis not the grapes of Canaan that repay,
But the high faith that failed not by the way;
Virtue treads paths that end not in the grave;
No bar of endless night exiles the brave;
    And to the saner mind
We rather seem the dead that stayed behind.
Blow, trumpets, all your exultations blow!
For never shall their aureoled presence lack:
I see them muster in a gleaming row,
With ever-youthful brows that nobler show;
We find in our dull road their shining track;
   In every nobler mood
We feel the orient of their spirit glow,
Part of our life's unalterable good
Of all our saintlier aspiration;
   They come transfigured back,
Secure from change in their high-hearted ways,
Beautiful evermore, and with the rays
Of morn on their white Shields of Expectation!

                                    RUSSELL LOWELL.

"THE PIONEER."
From a drawing by Lieut. A. K. Lawrence, 19th Battalion.
(To face Introductory Note.)

INTRODUCTORY NOTE

I HAVE not yet had the opportunity of reading this book, but I know that a history of the 18th Northumberland Fusiliers could not be in better hands than those of the man who raised and trained the Battalion and commanded it throughout almost the whole of its service on the Western front.

The work of a Pioneer Battalion during the long months of trench warfare was arduous beyond words, dangerous and, in a sense, continuous, inasmuch that it was rarely if ever relieved as a complete unit. Some part of it was almost always in the line throughout the period during which I had the honour of commanding the Division to which the 18th Northumberland Fusiliers belonged. I have never known it fail to complete any task given to it, and not only complete it, but complete it up to time and with a thoroughness that I personally have never seen equalled.

Frequently, in the offensive operations in 1916 and 1917, and more especially in the hard and bitter fighting of the enemy's attacks in March and April, 1918, the rôle of the Battalion was purely combatant. In that rôle, which was always most congenial to it, it behaved with magnificent valour and steadiness, and fully maintained the reputation of the old Fifth Fusiliers.

C. L. Nicholson. Maj-Genl.

late Commdg. 34th Division.

18*th June*, 1919.

CONTENTS

		PAGE
	DEDICATION.	
	INTRODUCTION: MAJOR-GENERAL SIR LOTHIAN NICHOLSON, K.C.B., C.M.G.	
I.	THE BIRTH	1
II.	ROTHBURY	7
III.	CRAMLINGTON	12
IV.	SALISBURY PLAIN	18
V.	FRANCE: SHAKING DOWN	23
VI.	ALBERT	33
VII.	1ST JULY, 1916	43
VIII.	WANDERERS	50
IX.	ARRAS	59
X.	"WIPERS"	66
XI.	ON THE DEFENSIVE	74
XII.	CLEARING UP	95
	EXTRACT FROM ARMY LIST	101
	34TH DIVISION, INFANTRY BATTALIONS, 1916 AND 1918	102
	EMBARKATION ROLL OF BATTALION	104
	ITINERARY	164
	ROLL OF HONOUR	170
	HONOURS AND AWARDS	174
	APPENDIX A. EXPERIENCES OF A PRISONER OF WAR	176
	„ B. NOTES ON APRIL, 1918, RETREAT, ETC.	183
	„ C. 18TH COMRADES' LEAGUE	186
	„ D. WORK OF MILITARY COMMITTEE	188
	ACKNOWLEDGMENTS BY THE EDITOR	194
	GENERAL INDEX	197
	INDEX TO ROLLS	204

ILLUSTRATIONS AND MAPS

Lieut.-Col. J. Shakespear, C.M.G., C.I.E., D.S.O.	*Frontispiece*
	FACING PAGE
Dedication	ix
Drawn by Lieut. A. K. Lawrence, 19th Battalion	
"The Pioneer"	xi
Drawn by Lieut. A. K. Lawrence, 19th Battalion	
Headpiece to Chapter I	1
Drawn by Lieut. A. K. Lawrence, 19th Battalion	
Officers of Battalion, Cricket Field, December, 1914	6
From a photograph by Jas. Bacon & Sons	
The Sergeants, Rothbury	8
From a photograph by Jas. Bacon & Sons	
Officers of Battalion, December, 1915	22
From a photograph by Elliott & Fry, Ltd.	
La Boisselle: Looking East from our Lines along Bapaume Road. Showing Crater of "Y" Sap	42
From a photograph, taken in 1919, by Lieut. Webb, M.C., 18th Battalion	
Orderly Room and Battalion Head-quarters, St. Catherine, Feb.–April, 1917	60
From a photograph, taken in 1919, by Alfred Brewis	
Roclincourt from Arras-Lille Road	60
From a photograph, taken in 1919, by Alfred Brewis	
Mission Junction: Ypres Salient	68
From a photograph, taken in 1919, by Lieut. Webb, M.C.	
Erquinghem, 1919	80
From a photograph, taken in 1919, by Lieut. Webb, M.C.	
New Bridge at Nieppe, 1919	80
From a photograph by Alfred Brewis	
Lieut.-Col. J. A. Methuen, D.S.O.	96
Presentation of Colours: May 2, 1919	98
The Colours of 18th, 23rd and 25th Battalions at Guildhall, June 12, 1919	98
From a photograph, Newcastle Chronicle	
"A" Company, 1915	108
To the Gallant Men of the 34th Division: La Boisselle	170
From a photograph, taken in 1919, by Lieut. Webb, M.C.	

MAPS

Map—I. Somme Sector: 1916
    II. Arras Sector: 1917
   III. Lys Sector: 1918
   IV. General Map
      Drawn by Captain J. B. Nixon, M.C., Adjutant

} At end of Volume

HISTORICAL RECORDS
OF THE EIGHTEENTH (SERVICE) BATTALION NORTHUMBERLAND FUSILIERS

CHAPTER I

THE BIRTH

THE 16th Battalion having been raised within a week, the Newcastle and Gateshead Chamber of Commerce started at once to raise another Battalion for the Northumberland Fusiliers. The North-Eastern Railway Battalion having been numbered 17th, we became the 18th, and the birth, childhood, youth, manhood and untimely end are herein described. This is a family record, a tale primarily intended for ourselves, our relations and our intimate friends, and if others read it, as we hope they will, and find some of the details petty and uninteresting, we trust they will skip them and pass on, remembering that even trifles are of interest to those of the baby's family.

The record is the joint product of more hands than one, and no names or initials will be inserted, so that the reader may not recognise and point the finger of scorn at the authors.

The necessary permission to bring us into being was issued by the War Office on the 14th October, 1914, and addressed to the Lord Mayor, who was our nominal parent; but our real parents were the Military Committee of the Chamber of Commerce, and no infant ever had kinder, wiser and more generous parents. Well, having received the authority on the 15th, no time was lost, and on the 16th October the 18th Battalion saw the light. Like all babies, it was but a small thing to start with ; but its Commanding Officer, Major R. Temperley, T.D.,[1] felt as proud of it as any parent could be, and was confident that the growth and development of the 18th would soon challenge that of its elder brother, the 16th.

At 2 p.m. on the 16th October, 1914, a small gathering of thirty or forty civilians assembled at the County Cricket Ground. They had enlisted and had taken the oath, and were now come to do their first drills.

They were provided, by some person in the pavilion, with a piece of yellow window cord, and this mystic symbol they jealously guarded and carried home. The recruit was very proud of it : his best girl sewed it on the right shoulder of his coat. He was slightly annoyed when some passer-by in Grainger Street made the remark, with regard to the yellow sign, " Yes, he's tried to enlist, but has been marked medically unfit." The yellow cord afterwards became well known as the " uniform " of the " Second Commercials."

Promotion was quick in those early days, and marked was the man who had seen service in the Territorials, Cadet Corps, Boy Scouts, or Boys' Brigade. The sergeant was privileged to wear a piece of red ribbon, and the corporal a piece of white ribbon, round the right arm. Then were explained and performed the mysterious moves—form fours, right and left turns, and that almost impossible " H'about turn." Free discussions took place between instructor and instructed as to the various movements necessary for the " Right turn " and the " Stand at ease." One old soldier insisted that the hands were clasped in front at the " Stand at ease " ; that was what they did when he was with the Colours.

About noon a sergeant, a corporal and six men were told off for guard duty. The guard mounted at 5 p.m. and was quartered in the pavilion. Then the poor sergeant began night manœuvres in earnest, teaching the wretched six " Slope arms," " Present arms " and " Order arms," to be ready for the morning's inspection. How awful it was staying out all night for the first time, and that next door to a cemetery. Strange night noises were reported, and the tread of a passing policeman was listened to behind the hoarding—he might possibly attempt to steal that important piece of " His Majesty's Property," the pavilion. They were good friends who sent the maid at 10 p.m. with hot coffee to the sally-port. Then came the terror of the morning's inspection by the C.O., when each one of the guard " presented " in his own style and his own

[1] Late of our 6th Battalion.

time. And can anyone forget the terror of that memory test—" To guard all His Majesty's property within vision "; " In case of fire, alarm the guard and ring up Major Temperley," etc. The Pelmanists were few.

Colonel Finlay[1] arrived and began to make a selection of officers and N.C.O.'s. Some transfers were made from the 16th Battalion; they had " trained " material from which we might draw. At night, after work, and on Sunday mornings, the Colonel proceeded to " put the wind up " the select few, in lectures on outposts and fire control. Platoons and then companies began to take form.

The " leave question " soon made its appearance even in those early days. As a matter of fact, the private didn't apply for leave. He boldly walked up to the officer, without the necessary introduction by an N.C.O., and told him that he wouldn't be attending drills for a day or two as he was having a " few days off." Was there any difference between an officer and a " deputy " or a foreman ?

Squad drill from 9 a.m. till 12 noon and from 2 p.m. till 5 p.m. began to get monotonous. One morning an officer received a deputation to protest against squad drill. " When are we going to learn something else than forming fours ? We joined to fight Germans ! "

Quaint orders were heard from the newly promoted. Awful was the dismay of the squad which received the order " At the halt—quick—march ! "

Route-marching was much in favour and much better sport than squad drill. The favourite marching songs were, " Who's your lady friend ? ", " I joined the Army yesterday " and " Ragtime Cowboy Joe." Of course, there were always the " bloods " who persisted in shouting " I had a good job, but I *left*." The Colonel damped our ardour by calling the officers together and warning them that route-marching would cease if the men did not stop " making eyes " and passing remarks to passing nursemaids.

Then there was the Officers' Squad, which was marched one day by a sergeant to a quiet corner of the ground and told, " Now then, you fellows, you must remember we're all pals and must get on well together." The sergeant had mistaken them for recruits.

We soon learnt the discipline of the bugle. Two blasts were blown by a stout sergeant-major. At the first call everyone " stood fast," and the second was the order to " get fell in."

In a few days the splendid turf of the cricket ground began to have a brown appearance, and by the end of the stay it developed into quagmire. To the dismay of the civilians around, Colonel

---

[1] Late O.C. Rangoon Rifles.

Finlay ordered ashes to be laid down. Business was not as usual; there was a war on.

Rainy mornings were spent in lectures at neighbouring church halls and Sunday-schools. Nervous subalterns talked for ten minutes, in a cold sweat, on such subjects as "The History of the Regiment," "Drill, Dress and Shaving" and "Outposts." Strict orders were issued for every man to produce a moustache forthwith. The intervals between lectures were filled in by sing-songs, when the "talent" of the company was discovered in artistes who sang, "Don't go down the mine, Daddy," and the ever popular "Blaydon Races."

Occasionally platoons were marched down to the baths. There was much amusement over the miner's dirty back, left dirty purposely to prevent him perspiring. And, of course, there was always the fool who couldn't swim and persisted in falling in at the "deep end."

On Monday morning (November 16th) there was great excitement at the cricket ground. There were rumours of great movement and stir at Kiel and Hamburg. The Germans were going to make an invasion, and Blyth was probably one of their chief landing points; from there they would close on Newcastle and Elswick works. Had not the Zeppelins been reported over Hull? The Battalion was to provide fighting men at once. The Colonel paraded the whole Battalion, and all the men who had ever fired a rifle, or handled one, were drafted into one company. Feeling now ran high, and men whose only experience of shooting was that gained at the penny shooting gallery, where they "potted" the celluloid ball, boldly stepped forward. The Colonel's test was to see a man take aim over the sights of a D.P. rifle. There were many disappointments, some men held the rifle to the wrong shoulder, and others closed the wrong eye. As the Colonel came along the line one could see likely candidates receiving their first instructions in aiming from pals who had been in the Territorials, or had been markers of a civilian rifle club. The selected—the élite—began to feel bloodthirsty as they handled their rifles and tied their bayonets to their waist with pieces of window cord. The new company was organised into four platoons, and given a few hours' leave to collect the few necessaries before going into billets. Two platoons went to the Sunday-school in College Road, and the remainder were billeted in the Co-operative Stores in Fern Avenue, and were afterwards occasionally referred to as the "Store" men. No man was allowed to leave his billet. A guard was mounted and blankets distributed. Subalterns busied themselves about Standing Orders, fire buckets and answering questions. Questions ranged from, "Am I allowed to wear two pairs of socks?" to "Do you want a mascot?"

producing a dirty mongrel. Full dress consisted of rifle, bayonet on window cord and a white canvas haversack, worn over civilian clothes. Bowler, felt hats and caps were worn. The effect on parade was not smart.

The following day the Emergency or Composite (pronounced composight) Battalion paraded under Colonel Stockley[1] on the Town Moor, the four companies consisting of Tyneside Irish, Tyneside Scottish, 16th Battalion and our own. Musketry instruction on D.P. rifles was commenced, and a short skirmish of 500 yards carried out. The object was an imaginary railway embankment which had to be " lined."

On Saturday, the 20th November, there was cause for alarm. The company paraded as usual on the wet Moor to be sent back immediately to billets for emergency rations and ball ammunition. It really did look as if we were going to man trenches and fight. But we did none of these things ; instead, we " stood fast " in billets, and religiously "stood to " each morning from 6 a.m. until 7 a.m., coughing and spitting, watching stars, or being wetted through.

A further development occurred on the 23rd. The company marched to Gosforth Station to pick up shovels and picks, and then trekked in the Benton direction. It was a long march for those early times and " heavy going," as each man carried, besides his rifle, a pick and a shovel. Where were we going ? One man suggested that we were going to the Gosforth race-course to " pick " winners. Another objected that we couldn't be expected to use the pick or the spade, as we hadn't been taught the " parts " yet. The teaching of the parts of the rifle had been somewhat laboured during the week previous.

From that day we marched each morning from billets to Benton to dig. It was there that we conceived our first idea of trenches. During the first day the work was competitive, the expert miner got down to 4 feet 6 inches in an hour, while the novice managed painfully to remove the turf in the same time. The " shift " system was adopted—two hours' work and two hours' easy. The days were cold and wet, and mufti was still being worn, but football during the " easy " kept our spirits up. There was always a spirit of rivalry between the " Store " and the " Chapel " men, the latter were on starvation diet, while the former fed well at the Minories.

Aeroplanes were still a novelty in those times and attracted much attention as they passed over daily in the direction of Blyth.

Later, uniform and kit began to be issued. The first issue was the grey cap, and a toothbrush followed quickly. There was a

---

[1] C.O. 21st Battalion, 2nd Tyneside Scottish.

shyness at first in wearing the cap, as the wearer was liable to be mistaken for a tram conductor.

The Benton trenches began to look business-like, with a proper parapet and machine-gun emplacements. A reserve line and communication trenches were being dug. Each general as he inspected them (and there were many inspections) gave instructions for further alterations, so that at one time the fire trench had a parapet, then the parapet was removed, to reappear again a few days later. On the 7th December we marched from Benton to the hymn tune " Count your blankets, Count them one by one," and the following day the Composite Battalion disbanded. No one was sorry.

In the meantime the Battalion at the cricket ground had filled up, " D " Company had been completed and " E " was forming. N.C.O.'s were being selected and the rudiments of company drill were being taught. They, too, had come under the " Defence of the Tyne Scheme." A party of cyclists, under O.C. Road Hogs, slept nightly in the pavilion, ready at a moment's notice to dash off into the country and call up the Battalion. Each cyclist was given a district with a list of names and addresses, and was responsible as " knocker up."

The band must not be forgotten. It came into being with a nucleus of two or three bugles, two kettle drums and a " big " drum, the gift of Mrs. George Renwick. It made a noise in the drill field along the Benton Road. There was a hazy idea at first as to whether the drums " set " the step for the Battalion, or the Battalion for the drums. The climax was reached one day when the Captain of a company, marching over Armstrong Bridge, moved it from the head of the column to the tail. Of course, all this happened before the time that the band became recognised as " A " Company's band.

On the 21st December, the ground covered with snow, the Battalion, with the band at its head, marched to the Central Station and entrained for Rothbury.

OFFICERS OF BATTALION: CRICKET GROUND.

KEY.

TOP ROW: 2nd Lieuts. Robson, Dodsworth, Fortune, Wood.

SECOND ROW: Sergt.-Maj. Lovett, Q.M.S. Turner, 2nd Lieuts. Francis, Vasey, Ray, G. A. M. Hall, Wells; Major and Q.Mr. Liddle.

THIRD ROW: Captains Sweet, Bell, Needham; Lt.-Col. Sir Kirkman Findlay, Lt.-Co. J. Shakespear, Major Stephenson, Captain Renwick.

FRONT ROW: 2nd Lieuts. Wilson, Worthington, McQuillen, Drury, R. O. Hall.

OFFICERS OF BATTALION, CRICKET GROUND, DECEMBER, 1914.

Photo *Jas. Bacon & Sons.*

CHAPTER II

ROTHBURY

WE may now be said to have outgrown long clothes. Our equipment, though far from complete, was getting on. Our uniform was neat and serviceable (not khaki, of course, that was to come later, at present there was not enough to clothe the crowds who clamoured for it, but good stout cloth of a dark grey colour). We knew a bit, too, and thought we knew a good deal more, we also had arms, not enough to go round, and not of the latest pattern, still good enough and numerous enough for us to learn with, provided they changed hands often enough. We no longer lived at home or slept in beds, we found ourselves billeted in bare rooms in the County and Station hotels, the schools and elsewhere. Companies and platoons had become more than names, and we quickly began to feel that we were no longer irresponsible individuals, but members of a brotherhood; first the platoon spirit stirred us, later, our company became an object of pride, and still later, when we had met other Battalions, we felt that though compared with our platoon every other platoon in the 18th was not up to much, yet we would not allow anyone outside the 18th to hint at such a thing. Then, too, we heard that we belonged to the 122nd Brigade, in which were also our 16th and 19th Battalions, our elder and younger brothers; for no sooner had we reached our full strength than our Raisers started on recruiting for the 19th Battalion, of which Major Temperley took command until a permanent commanding officer could be found. The 4th Battalion in the Brigade was the 18th Durham Light Infantry. However, we did not come in contact with these Battalions just yet.

Sir Kirkman Finlay had been busy, while we were in Newcastle preparing for us in Rothbury. Assisted in every way by our Raisers he had cook-houses and other necessary buildings erected, so that on our arrival we had not much to complain of.

On the 22nd December Sir Kirkman Finlay handed over command to Lieut.-Col. John Shakespear,[1] and left, much to our regret, to take up more important work. He was shortly followed by Sergeant-Major Lovett and Quartermaster-Sergeant Stone, whom he had

[1] Lieut.-Col. J. Shakespear, C.I.E., D.S.O., retired Indian Army; late Political-agent Manipur State.

brought with him and who had worked unceasingly. Bereft of these trusted guides, we perhaps felt a little doubtful of the future, but we soon found our feet and went bravely forward. Our Brigadier, General J. G. Hunter, C.B., an old Indian like our new C.O., lost no time in coming over to inspect us, in fact, some of us, who were recalled from their Christmas leave, thought his visit rather premature.

We were welcomed most kindly by the people of Rothbury and the neighbourhood who, from Lord Armstrong downwards, did their utmost to make our stay among them comfortable. The Rector, Canon Blackett Orde, gave us special services on Sundays and placed a reading-room at our disposal, of which we made free use. Our Raisers, too, paid us frequent visits and spared no expense to increase our comfort and provide us with all necessary outfit and appliances. A miniature rifle range equipped with moving and vanishing targets enabled us to show how we were improving under the instructions of Major G. A. Renwick and Colour-Sergeant Nixon. (Major Renwick was soon taken from us, the first of many good men similarly haled away, first to the Brigade staff and then to be second in command of the 19th Battalion. Colour-Sergeant Nixon left us on a week's leave and reappeared as 2nd Lieut. Nixon.) Practice on the range was a very popular change from musketry instruction on the wind-swept Haugh. How we hated that standing load.

Among the many kindnesses done us by the good people of Rothbury, not the smallest was allowing us the use of their fully equipped hospital, in which when sick we were ably and kindly attended to by Dr. Barrow and Sister Webber. We heard a rumour that a complete Voluntary Aid Detachment was prepared to come and look after the welfare of our sick, but, fearing that the susceptible young subalterns might be distracted from their work, our C.O. gratefully declined the offer, much to the regret of some. Our own Medical Officer, Lieut. Joseph Graham, R.A.M.C., soon arrived and relieved Dr. Barrow. When we first saw him in khaki we understood why there was a shortage of that cloth.

Our numbers steadily increased and we soon outgrew the accommodation available in Rothbury, and "E" Company, under command of 2nd Lieut. C. Francis, was located in Wreighburn at Thropton, which was placed at our disposal by the owner, Mrs. Hawthorne.

On the 29th January we were informed that the War Office wished two out of the Battalions raised locally in Newcastle to become Pioneers. In those days there were no Pioneer Battalions in the British Army, but they existed in the Indian Army, and our

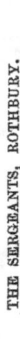

Photo THE SERGEANTS, ROTHBURY. Jas. Bacon & Sons.

C.O. was able to explain to us what was required of Pioneers. Two of us only objected to the proposed change. One asked for more pay and the other objected on principle, being always against every proposal made by anyone above him. So from the 8th February, 1915, we were known as the 18th (S.) Battalion Northumberland Fusiliers (1st Tyneside Pioneers). We were pleasantly surprised to find this change brought with it twopence a day extra pay, so one of the objectors withdrew his objection. We have only heard of one man who regretted our decision, and he, after an experience of pioneering in the sloughs near Armentières, requested a transfer to one of our Infantry Battalions, saying he had enlisted to fight the Germans, not to make mud pies. He was transferred to the 25th Battalion of the Regiment, in which he won first the M.M. and then his commission.

Some people have a mistaken idea of a Pioneer, and seem to think that he sits in a cosy nest somewhere down at the " Base " making barbed wire and having an easy time generally. That is not so. The Pioneer is a peculiar person who can be an infantryman one day, a trench digger in " No Man's Land " at night, an expert in barbed wire, a bridge-builder, a layer of railway tracks, a sapper, and suchlike. In fact, he is an infantryman and an engineer combined (but *without* the pay of the latter). All through he is a valuable reserve to the front line, and many is the time he is called upon; he is often " loaned " to another Division or Army Corps. When his friend the infantryman goes " back " for a rest the Pioneer still carries on in the vicinity of the batteries. Such is the Pioneer, who has a " soft job."

Our training now became more interesting. Lord Armstrong kindly made us free of the moorland above the town, a position on which was selected and each company was given a length of front to prepare for defence. We took to trench-making very kindly. Many of us were miners, and those who were not did their best to master the art of handling the pick and shovel. Battalion drill succeeded company drill, and soon we were practising attack and defence over the rough slopes of Simonside. Then we went farther afield and fought sanguinary battles on Corbie Crags. Our officers were initiated by Captain Dyer, Brigade-Major, and Captain Buckle[1] into the mysteries of appreciating a situation, which, on a snowy day with an east wind blowing over an exposed position on Garley Moor, is not very easy, we are told. Then followed night operations, in which many wonderful things happened. One company being ordered to extend till it connected with the company on its left,

---

[1] Captain G. S. Buckle, 1st Northamptonshire Regiment, afterwards killed at Chemin des Dames.

missed its connection and we will draw a veil over the end of the manœuvre. There is no need either to inquire too closely as to what happened after a patrol which was directed to take the C.O. to the right picket landed him at the left one. " Nearly two miles out," quoth the C.O. " No, sir, only one," expostulated the patrol leader.

One night a company commander sat and shivered on a bleak hill-side awaiting the arrival of an officers' patrol. There is no need to place on record what happened when the long-expected officer was found eating a hearty supper in the Mess, and explained that having lost his way to his commander he had found the Mess and thought he had better stay there till his commander found him. Then we played outposts, staying out all night and looking out for patrols of the enemy, represented by the Scouts or machine-gun men. We were rather jealous of the Scouts and envied them, they disappeared daily over the moor and we were sceptical as to whether they worked as hard as we did, so when we caught them trying to sneak through our line we chortled.

" E " Company all this time was being put through the early stage of soldiering, which we had traversed while in Newcastle. New officers as they arrived were posted to " E " and joined the little Mess in Mrs. Tully's best parlour, where they lived like fighting cocks, in fact so well did their kind landlady feed them that invitations to dine there were much in request. Mrs. Hawthorne also had a cheery welcome for all visitors, and had a curious and attractive liqueur called Angels' Tears, which made such of us as were privileged to taste it smile and Oliver Twist-like ask for more ; the Rev. Gibson Smith, Presbyterian minister of the little village, was also very popular with all ranks, though for other reasons, so that altogether " E " was very happy.

We, in Rothbury, also had our relaxations, company suppers and sing-songs, and other entertainments provided by kind friends, football matches and cross-country runs, a dance or two and a wedding followed by an informal " rugger match " among the officers in uniform " with swords," as they say of certain continental decorations, forming some of them. Near the end of our stay we held sports on the Haugh, and being blessed with a fine afternoon we all, and our guests, enjoyed ourselves. There were some original events, chief of which was the relay race in which platoon commanders in turn carried their company commanders, and the C.O. was similarly conveyed by a team consisting of the second in command, the Doctor, Adjutant and Quartermaster.

Most of us raised no objection to being inoculated against typhoid, but one hero refused on the ground that his brother had been inoculated before he went to France and had just been killed, another gave as a reason that his mother had told him to object, but added, " Of course, if I get the order I won't refuse to obey." He got the order.

On 24th March we marched over to Felton and were inspected by Major-General H. M. Lawson, C.B., G.O.C. Northern Command. This was the first of a long series of inspections which we went through in the course of our career. The G.O.C. expressed himself pleased with our looks, and remarked that as we looked so healthy he concluded that we were not at all crowded in our billets. On hearing the number of square feet per man we enjoyed, he issued stringent orders that more billets were to be taken up. This necessitated " E " leaving its happy home in Thropton and moving to Framlington, where the inhabitants, headed by Dr. Fenwick, did everything to make them comfortable. Their place was taken by two platoons of " C " Company, and other arrangements were made to provide us with more space, Lord Armstrong kindly housing a platoon in some outbuildings of Cragside.

On the 21st April the even tenor of our way was rudely disturbed by an order received about 1 p.m. directing us to proceed that evening by special train to Cramlington. We were to leave behind all men over war establishment and to take with us the ammunition which had recently been received. Naturally we thought the Hun was on the seas, and our bosoms swelled with martial ardour. We felt so sorry for those who stayed behind, but about 2 a.m. the next morning as we lay in rows, company by company, in the field near Cramlington and tried to sleep, we thought of those unfortunates left behind, and were not so certain that ours was the better part. We found our 16th Battalion in the field alongside of us, and were welcomed by a detachment of the Scottish Horse, with hot coffee, a most considerate thought, for which we were very grateful.

Tents arrived and under the energetic supervision of the Brigade-Major, Captain Dyer,[1] we learnt how difficult it is to pitch a camp correctly, but by the evening the camp looked fairly shipshape, and even if a bit more crowded than we had ever been at Rothbury, we were all squeezed in and slept the sleep of the weary.

We had at this period four hundred rather ancient rifles among our thousand men, hardly any of us had fired a rifle, except on the miniature range, so that perhaps it was as well for us and the neighbourhood that the threatened Boche raid was never carried out. Rifles poured in during the next few days, and for a brief period we actually had more rifles than men.

Our Tail which we had left behind in Rothbury soon joined us, and we settled down to work under new circumstances.

[1] Captain G. N. Dyer, R. West Surrey Regt.

CHAPTER III

CRAMLINGTON

WE may now be said to have passed out of our childhood and to have reached the public school stage of our existence. The whole Brigade was soon assembled, and we rubbed shoulders and compared notes with other Battalions. Brigade drills, especially ceremonial, troubled us much, and we were far happier when busy over the construction of a line of trenches to defend Cramlington and forming part of the Newcastle Defence System. We were now part of the North-Eastern Coast Defence Force, and an integral portion of the defensive forces of the kingdom; our trenches were no longer mere practice diggings, but were constructed with a view to being actually held should the Germans ever succeed in landing a force and attempting a raid on Newcastle and the Tyne. What the probabilities of success in such a venture were we could not say, but it was evident to everyone that a comparatively small force could do an incalculable amount of damage in a very short time, if it could once reach Elswick and the Tyne shipyards. Of course, the raiders could not expect to get back again, but Germany might well think the destruction of so many important works well worth considerable losses. Therefore, we took our work very seriously. The line was divided into three equal portions, which were allotted to "A," "B" and "D" Companies, "C" Company being given the task of preparing accommodation for the reserve. The machine-gun squad was entrusted with the selection and construction of machine-gun positions. As the picks and shovels in our possession were not nearly sufficient, we indented on various collieries near by, and in no case were our demands met with a refusal, though in some cases we were asked sadly what had happened to the tools given to the last lot, a conundrum which we could not answer, but we promised to return any given to us, a promise we faithfully fulfilled. The days we worked on the trenches were looked forward to by everyone. We took our dinners down in our billycans and cooked and ate them on the spot. We thought a little experience in cooking might come in useful when we got to the front, but few of us had occasion to use the knowledge we gained, for, when we were separated from the field kitchens, it was generally a case of bully and biscuits. However, we all enjoyed our picnic meals.

While we were in this camp we had our first experience of Zeppelins. One passed right over the camp at a great height, then went towards the Tyne and dropped bombs, some of which did considerable damage. On another night we had warning that a Zeppelin would be over at 10 p.m., and one hundred men in each Battalion were ready to give it a warm reception, but after a long wait they were sent back to their beds. Perhaps the Boche had heard of our preparations. As few, if any, of the men had fired a rifle, and as the rifles had all been condemned as inaccurate, perhaps it was well for their companions and the neighbourhood that they were not called on to fire.

While at Cramlington, Lieut. R. O. Hall was taken from us and translated to the red-tabbed paradise at the far end of the camp, Brigade Head-quarters; we were all sorry to lose him, and have watched with pride his upward progress to G.S.O.2. of 2nd Corps.

On the 20th May, 1915, the Brigade was present on the Newcastle Town Moor, when the King reviewed a large force. We had a long, tiresome day, and those of us who had attended reviews in the happy irresponsibility of civilian life, felt that the looker on had the best of it. His Majesty was graciously pleased to express his satisfaction with our appearance and marching; Field-Marshal Lord Kitchener especially complimented our Brigadier on the steadiness of the men.

3rd June, 1915. We again marched to Newcastle, but this time without the rest of the Brigade. The object of our visit on this occasion was to pay our respects to the city and to attend an entertainment at the Hippodrome, kindly arranged for us by the manager, Mr. Bebby.

The route followed was past the War Memorial and viâ Percy Street, Central Station and up Pilgrim Street.

The Lord Mayor[1] took up his position at the Town Hall, and our Raisers were beside him. Before the performance began at the Hippodrome we were provided with refreshments, both solid and liquid, so that every man was in a condition to enjoy the excellent show which had been provided for us, which terminated, much to our astonishment, by the exhibition of a film showing our progress through the streets of the town only a short time previous. We all enjoyed our day out and felt grateful to our Raisers for the invitation, and for the opportunity of paying a farewell visit as a Battalion to the grand old city, for we were shortly to leave the neighbourhood for further training, after which we were to get

[1] Alderman J. Fitzgerald.

seriously to work in the job we had enlisted on, viz. fighting the Boche. After the entertainment came speeches, several references were made to the reception we should receive when we came marching through the city again, our work completed. Alas ! the method of demobilisation has prevented any such march, and perhaps it is as well, for of those who passed the Lord Mayor that day, less than one-third would have been able to take part in it.

Shortly after the pleasant day, the 122nd Brigade was broken up. The Brigadier and his staff went to take over the 105th Brigade, our 16th Battalion went to join the 32nd Division, our 19th Battalion became the Pioneer Battalion of the 35th Division, while the 18th Durham Light Infantry joined the 93rd Brigade, 31st Division. We were left for some time to complete the Cramlington position and to repair and improve " Fitton's line," another position nearer to the coast.

Captain Worthington, who had been commanding " B " Company for some time, was offered the second in command of the Cheshires, who were in the 105th Brigade. We were sorry to lose him, but we soon got accustomed to giving up officers for the benefit of other Battalions.

Major Worthington was killed on 18th May, 1917. He was going round the Battalion positions near St. Quentin one night, and found one of the advanced posts was not correctly placed. In looking for a more suitable position with the officer commanding this company, he got close to the German front line, when a heavy fire of rifle grenades was opened on the party and a fragment of a grenade penetrated his brain, causing instant death. Letters from the G.O.C. 35th Division and 105th Brigade, his own C.O. and other officers testify to the high regard in which he was held by all ranks.

Captain Needham of the Notts and Derby Regiment, who had been acting as Adjutant since our earliest days, having been reported as fully recovered from the effects of the wound he received at the Marne, was ordered to rejoin his own Regiment, and Captain T. Reay took up the duties of Adjutant.

We suffered a serious loss when Lieut. J. Graham, our much-loved " doc.," tiring of the monotony of home service, applied to be sent on active service, and was promptly ordered off to the Dardanelles.

Interlude.

Pte. T. Atkins : " I say, Bill, have you heard as Doctor Graham is coming back to us ? "

Pte. Bill Atkins : " No, why ? "

Pte. T. Atkins : " Because they can't get him through ' The Narrows ' ! "

18th (Service) Battalion Northumberland Fusiliers 15

While at Cramlington, we had further evidence of our Raisers' public spirit; besides providing us with various conveniences and comforts, they raised another company for each Battalion, so that when the time came for us to leave and join our Division we left behind two complete depot companies. As these depot companies had to be commanded by a Field Officer, Major Bell, who up till now had been commanding " D " Company, had to remain behind, but he rejoined us later on in France, much to our joy. We hoped that all of those left behind would in due course rejoin us as gaps were made in our ranks, but to our great regret we saw but few of them again, for our two companies and the two reserve companies of the 19th Battalion were formed into the 28th Reserve Battalion, and were drafted to whatever Battalion of the Regiment needed them most. This was no doubt necessary, but it was very unpopular. The Raisers felt disappointed that the men whom they had recruited with considerable trouble and expense as a reserve for their particular Battalions should be used for other purposes, and the officers and men all regretted having to leave the Battalion into which many of them had enlisted in order to serve with friends and relations.

Before we left Cramlington we were inspected by Major-General Benjamin Burton, C.B., commanding in Newcastle, after which the following Battalion order was published :—

"*GENERAL BURTON'S INSPECTION*. At Major-General Burton's request the Commanding Officer has the pleasure to publish in Battalion orders a précis of the remarks addressed by the General to the Battalion to-day :—

' Colonel Shakespear, Officers, Non-Commissioned Officers and men of the 18th Battalion Northumberland Fusiliers, I am very sorry that you are leaving my Command, but I am glad for your sakes that you are going to join your Division and qualify yourselves to move to the Front as soon as possible. You have earned a very good name here, and I am pleased to see in my inspection to-day that in all small matters of detail, such as polishing of boots and buttons, every man has taken care to turn out as smart as possible. Such matters may appear small but a Battalion which is smart in small matters can be trusted to be smart in greater matters also. I wish you all the best of luck, and feel sure that you will always be a credit to the county from which you come.' "

MEMORIES OF THE M.O.

It is a difficult task to write one's memories of the old Battalion. I joined it at Rothbury late in the afternoon of 24th December, 1914. The first person I met was V. B. Rogers, who invited me to tea. Later I met Majors G. Renwick and Liddle, and later still yourself. I remember your first words, "Well I only got word this morning that you had been posted, and I expected you to take Xmas leave first." I was new to the Army, for I had not thought of such a thing. My first billet was Major Stephenson's room opposite the County Hotel. It was my first night on a camp bed without a fire in the room and with a candle for light; and it was bitterly cold. I went to bed in pyjamas, but gradually donned more and more clothes during the night. By morning I was nearly fully dressed, and I was more than pleased to know that it was time to get up. I think I was first for breakfast that Xmas morning. On Xmas day I moved to Mrs. Snaith's of wonderful memory. Later on her house had Reay, Coombs, Drury and myself, and I spent some very pleasant times with them there. The first thing which engaged attention was the necessity for an Aid Post and a small hospital. That was amicably arranged through the help of Dr. Barrow, and in a day or two we opened up the hospital there, with Nurse Webber acting as Matron. She was, in the words of the song, "A perfectly Priceless Old Thing." She really mothered the sick of the Battalion, and considered nothing a bother if it was for the men of the Battalion. And there it was that I began to get to know all the men who had knee troubles, heart affections, varicose veins, flat feet, backaches, headaches, etc. etc. I used to think they were all genuine cases, even if they had little to show, and it was only when the C.O. sent for me one day, and pointed out that there were over seventy sick and that no one had been marked "Duty" in red ink, that I began to suspect. Then the screw was put on, and many went back to work inwardly cursing, doubtless not because they were not treated, but because they had been found out. We got rid at last of the real crocks, and eventually, I think, had about the fittest body of men that could possibly be imagined. Gradually, and almost unconsciously, one came to imbibe the Army point of view, and the sick list fell and kept at a minimum. I don't think there was much malingering in the Battalion—at least, not after the first two months that we were at Rothbury. Inoculation came and brought us the types of objector. Here all the persuasive eloquence one had had to be tried first. When that failed with a certain number, I think a good sound lecture succeeded, and we got practically everyone done at last. Vaccination gave no trouble. It says much for the men

18th (Service) Battalion Northumberland Fusiliers 17

that there were less than a dozen septic arms from both these operations.

The move to Cramlington was an experience, for it was our first taste of a hurried move to new scenes. I can recall very vividly lying there in that field looking up at the stars, and wondering why anyone should have chosen such a life of discomfort. However, it was interesting to build up there the whole of the appliances of a camp, and I venture to think that in the end it was one of the best camps in all the country. Recruiting at Cramlington was an experience not without its amusing side. Incidents of all kinds recur to one's memory, notably the one which involved the burning of the verminous clothing which had not even belonged to the recruit, but had been borrowed from a friend as being more respectable. Altogether the two months there under canvas were exceedingly happy, and one was able to get some interesting work done amongst the men. I left the Battalion there in July, 1915, and saw nothing more of anyone till on 14th June, 1916, I became your M.O. again at Albert. From that date until 25th May, 1918, I remained as your M.O. No one ever had a happier time in the Army than I had during these twenty-three months. I tried to share as fully as possible in all the games of the men. I tried to get to know as far as possible all the idiosyncrasies of each man. I tried to help where I could, and where I could not I kept out of the way. And I have a suspicion somehow that the men believed that they got justice, and that they could rely upon having everything possible done for them so far as medical aid was concerned. I only know of one death from sickness in all these months, and I tried to deal promptly with all whose condition required it.

CHAPTER IV

SALISBURY PLAIN

Our Public School life finished, we enter on our University career.

We left Cramlington on 21st July by special troop trains, and detrained at Ripon, whence we marched to Kirkby Malzeard and pitched our camp in a large field; we were soon joined by gunners and sappers, and the 101st Brigade was in camp not far off. Thus the 34th Division took shape,[1] and Major-General E. C. Ingouville-Williams, late commander of the 16th Brigade, B.E.F., took command. He inspected us on the 24th and said he liked our looks, for we looked like soldiers. We certainly liked his looks. He looked every inch a soldier and a leader of soldiers. The acquaintance commenced that day ripened into a firm friendship. We all learned to trust him; we knew he was always thinking of his Division and its welfare; we loved him for his disregard of danger and cheerfulness under all circumstances, and we felt proud when we heard, after his death, that in his letters to his wife he had spoken of us as "my faithful Pioneers."

Our stay at Kirkby Malzeard was very short. It was here that we first hoisted our flag, presented to us by Mr. Richard Robson. We flew this in Staple, but after that we were generally too near to the Boche to make it advisable to advertise the position of our Head-quarters. The flag has now been handed over to the custody of Chamber of Commerce in Newcastle, and hangs on the Exchange alongside the flag of the 16th Northumberland Fusiliers.

One day we received our transport animals. Our Transport Officer, Lieut. Hunn (what's in a name!), a planter from Trinidad, who, in spite of being over fifty, had come over to see what he could do for the old country, had his work cut out. The animals were all raw and wild, most of them were mules and few if any of our transport lads had any knowledge of how to deal with these strange, fractious animals. "If you goes in front of them they bites you, and if you goes behind them they kicks you." However, in a very short time they made friends and we never had to complain of our transport. Lieut. Hunn unfortunately had to leave us before we left England on account of ill-health.

On the 10th August the bulk of us left for Totley, the transport

[1] For composition of 34th Division see page 102.

and small party remaining in camp at Kirkby Malzeard. Our visit to Totley was for the purpose of firing Parts 1 and 2 of our musketry course, which we did on the range of the Hallamshire Rifles.

We owed much to the kindness of Major Stuart Wortley, who allowed us the use of the Mess house and building on the range. We were considerably handicapped in our shooting by being pressed for time, and also by having only fifty rifles among one thousand odd men, and by the attractions of Sheffield which many of us long remember. Major Chambers, our second in command, was suddenly taken from us to command the 12th K.O.Y.L.I. We were very sorry to lose him and he was very sorry to go. While going through our musketry we made the acquaintance of Major C. P. Porch, who was Divisional Musketry Officer, whom later on we welcomed as second in command and learnt to love and rely on in fair and foul weather.

On 30th August the Battalion was reunited at Windmill Hill Camp, Salisbury Plain, where we found the rest of the Division encamped all around us. We soon found out that our 19th Battalion was not far off, in fact our officers would have fared badly on the first night had it not been for the hospitality offered them by the officers of the 19th.

We only stayed four weeks at this camp and then moved to No. 1 Camp, Sutton Veny. Before we left Windmill Hill we were inspected by the Rt. Honble. Sir A. H. Paget, G.C.B., K.C., V.O., who was satisfied with our appearance and turn-out. At Sutton Veny we were in very comfortable huts and quickly made friends with the 101st Brigade, the Battalions of which were all around us.

We were now entering the last lap, as it were, and many and false were the rumours as to our future. We were going to India. No! we were certainly going to Egypt and then to German East Africa. Not at all, Salonika is our destination. We once got as far as being equipped with sun helmets, in which, to us, strange headgear some of our officers insisted on being photographed, but we only kept the helmets a day or two and then returned them, and it became pretty certain that France was to be our destination. Equipment, tools, vehicles, etc., began to pour in on us. Company commanders signed for innumerable articles and were solemnly warned that they would have to pay for whatever they could not produce when called on. Our signallers and machine gunners got their long-expected equipment; our service rifles arrived and we returned into store the mixed lot of weapons we had carried hitherto. Musketry was resumed, and we took more interest in it, for each man knew that he now had the rifle with which he was expected to shoot Germans, and so he wanted to find out its ways.

Our technical training was now pushed on with vigour, such as trench work, bridging, sandbag work and barbed wire entanglements. Officers and N.C.O.'s wrestled with various problems, and lectures were many. Courses also were plentiful ; the subjects varied from machine-gun to cooking. Under Lieut. Holbrook's energetic instruction we charged successive lines of trenches held by stalwart dummies, who, unlike the men they were supposed to represent, never held up their hands and cried " Kamerad."

Then on 16th October we celebrated the completion of the first year of our existence. In the morning we were reviewed by Brigadier-General Malcolm, C.B., D.S.O., who was temporarily commanding the Division owing to Major-General Ingouville Williams having met with a motor accident. General Malcolm gave us high praise for our drill and turn-out, and we marched back to our lines very proud of ourselves. Before we were dismissed, Major Temperley and Mr. Renwick, on behalf of our Raisers, gave us a message of congratulation and encouragement. The afternoon was spent in sports and inter-company competitions of various kinds, and a dance in the Officers' Mess terminated a pleasant day.

General Williams having recovered from his accident, the Division began to understand what work is. Field days were numerous and lengthy, and the weather generally vile. Our task was generally to represent the enemy and to be annihilated by the unconquerable 34th. Sometimes we got a bit back as when, secreted behind a fold in the ground, we watched two Battalions of our foes shooting at each other, each firmly convinced he was decimating us. After the battle it was our duty to repair the damage done to fences, and from the hash they made of the barbed wire we felt sure our Brigades would laugh at any obstructions the Germans might erect.

In November Lieut. and Quartermaster A. R. O. Draper joined us. He was specially selected for us by General Ingouville Williams, who had known him for a long time, and we had often occasion to be thankful to the General for his choice.

On 4th November a "taking-over" Board was held, a preliminary to our leaving the kindly care of our Raisers and coming under the less sympathetic care of the War Office. This was finally effected on 20th November, 1915, one year and thirty-six days from the start of our career. We have referred several times to the assistance we received from our Raisers, but not nearly enough to show what the country and we owe to these patriotic individuals. That we were lucky to be raised by them is shown by a remark made of the Inspector-General of Infantry early in our Rothbury days, when the C.O. was explaining some deficiencies in our equipment. " Well, Colonel, you must not complain, you are much better off than many Battalions which have been raised much longer than yours." We have mentioned the flag which Mr. Richard Robson so kindly gave us, we were debtors to him also for much assistance in the matter of transport at Rothbury and Cramlington. At Rothbury we were indebted to Mr. Alfred Brewis for a small book which all value as a memento of the grand old Regiment, and we are now further in his debt for the time and labour he has expended to make this Record a volume we shall always treasure. To Mr. McBryde, as secretary to the Committee, we owe a heavy debt for his work on behalf of our dependents.

Just when we were getting ready for the last move, setting our house in order, eliminating all who seemed not up to standard, we were suddenly called on to surrender a number of men whose services were required for the manufacture of munitions. This was a rude blow, about ninety were taken. These men had been trained, fed, housed and equipped at the country's expense and just when the time had come for the country to benefit by this training they were suddenly taken away and sent back to the shops. No doubt they were badly wanted in the shops, but let us hope that this lesson will not have to be learnt again. Let us hope that when next it becomes necessary to raise armies, the needs of the munition works, collieries, etc., will be thought of earlier in the day than they were in our case. Here had we been training for over a year, and for the last three months going through special training to fit us for our job, when suddenly nearly 10 per cent of us were taken away and their places filled by others whose training was far less complete. This certainly was not conducive to our efficiency.

Embarkation leave now emphasised the nearness of our departure to the Front. We rehearsed for a great ceremonial parade before the King, which unfortunately never took place.

Christmas was made as jovial as possible. Thanks to Major Porch, our President of Regimental Institutions, we had a tiptop dinner, and we showed our appreciation by the loudness of our cheers when our Colonel called on us for three of the best for Major Porch.

On 28th December we were warned to prepare for embarkation. An elaborate table was issued giving what we were to do each day, but our indefatigable General kept us hard at work training all through these days of mobilisation. Then followed a few days of waiting. We were all ready, why did we not start ? The situation had changed, we were not to go yet, further training was contemplated. Thus we talked when suddenly one morning we got orders to embark the next day. So on a dull morning we paraded in full marching order for our final route-march to the station. We were to travel in three trains at considerable intervals, so each party paraded separately. To each party, before it marched off, the following kindly telegram of encouragement from our King was read and greeted with cheers.

O.C. 18th Northumberland Fusiliers.

The following message has been received from His Most Gracious Majesty the King :—

" Officers, Non-Commissioned Officers and Men of the 34th Division, on the eve of your departure for active service, I send you my heartfelt good wishes.

" It is a bitter disappointment to me that, owing to an unfortunate accident, I have been unable to see the Division on parade before it leaves England ; but I can assure you that my thoughts are with you all.

" Your period of training has been long and arduous, but the time has now come for you to prove on the field of battle the results of your instruction.

" From the good accounts that I have received of the Division, I am confident that the high tradition of the British Army is safe in your hands, and that with your comrades now in the Field you will maintain the unceasing efforts necessary to bring this War to a victorious ending.

" Good-bye and God-speed. GEORGE, R. I."

R. F. LOCK, Major,

Sutton Veny, D.A.A. & Q.M.G. 34th Division.
6.1.16.

Then we marched off and quietly got into our trains and departed. Our homes being far away few of us had anyone to see us off, and the good people of Warminster had seen far too many battalions entrain for embarkation to take much interest in us.

We left behind Lieut. McQuillen and twenty-two men of No. 5 Platoon, who were to rejoin us later on, travelling to France with a Battalion of the Tyneside Irish Brigade which was under strength. The adventures of this detachment will be described later on.

We embarked at Southampton, under the supervision of an old school friend of our Colonel, who, though a Post Captain in the Navy, assumed the disguise of a Lieut.-Col. to act as Embarkation Officer till he was again required on the water. We left Southampton that night in two steamers, and after a somewhat rough passage, which made many of us very uncomfortable, we landed at Havre early on the 8th January, 1916. Oh ! that nine hours crossing ! Who will forget it ! certainly not the man who, when about to receive his rations from the quartermaster-sergeant, was heard to exclaim he dashed on deck, " Wait a minute, Quarter ! "

OFFICERS OF BATTALION: December, 1915.

Key.

Top Row: Lieuts. Wood, McQuillen, Parkinson; 2nd Lieuts. Nicholson, Parry; Lieut. Holbrook; 2nd Lieuts. Cook, Flinders; Lieut. Shegog, R.A.M.C.; 2nd Lieut. Jellicoe; Lieut. Hall.

Middle Row: 2nd Lieuts. Rankin, Bowler, Reid. Lieut. Bean, Coombs, Armstrong. Vasey, Robson, Nixon; 2nd Lieut. Fletcher; Lieut. and Q.Mr. Draper; Lieut. Smith.

Front Row: Captains Smith, Fortune; Majors Francis, Stephenson, Porch; Lieut.-Col. Shakespear, C.I.E., D.S.O., Captain and Adj. Reay, Captains Sweet, Wilson, Drury, Dodsworth.

Photo

OFFICERS OF BATTALION: DECEMBER, 1915.

Elliott & Fry, Ltd.

CHAPTER V

FRANCE : SHAKING DOWN

WE spent most of the 8th January in a rest camp, where we first became acquainted with Y.M.C.A. canteen, an institution to which we owed much while in France. We stared considerably at certain German prisoners, who, under charge of some French soldiers, were working on the roads ; they seemed to be taking it very easy and looked mild, inoffensive beggars ; we thought we could manage to down them all right. Then came the entraining, a long job, for our transport ran to twenty-five vehicles and some hundred horses and mules, and neither they nor we were accustomed to the job. However, eventually we got off, thirty or so of us in each horse-box,[1] and our officers eight in a compartment. We travelled about twenty-four hours thus. During the day as many of us as could, sat in the doorways, our legs dangling outside, a practice which led to our first casualty, for Private T. Cowie, while sitting thus, was jerked out and lost a leg from the effects of the fall.

At last we reached Blendecques, where we detrained, and after some food, set off to march to our first billets. We were stiff from our journey, our packs were heavy, and we had many odds and ends attached to us ; the road seemed interminable. We missed our way in the dark and had to turn back. It seemed as if we would never arrive. Eventually we heard Captain Reay's cheery voice ; he had gone on to arrange billets and came back to meet us. Having arrived at Staple we had to be drafted off to our billets in various farms in the outskirts of the village, and in houses in the village itself. All this in a pitch-black night and we new to the game. None of us got to our billets before 4 a.m. and some slept under the hedge. Some lucky ones, while waiting to be told off to their billets, found an estaminet open even at that hour, and quickly learned the excellence of French coffee. We spent a fortnight in Staple. The people were very good to us and we made friends fast. We found barns with lots of straw were not half bad places to sleep in. Our time was spent chiefly in route-marching. We could hear the guns when the wind was favourable, and some of our officers rode up to Cassel to see the Very lights going up from the line. Very lights !

[1] See page 182: " Lines written on Arrival in France."

we soon saw enough of them without having to ride to Cassel. We were gradually initiated into the mysteries of the gas helmet, a flannel bag with windows to look out of. Very different from the respirators we got later on. Our platoon commanders were installed as censors of our correspondence. Extract from a letter : " P.S.—I am told my letter has to be censored, so I am not enclosing the 10/- note as I said I was."

The quality of the beer was a disappointment to us, but we found that everywhere in France, and in other respects we had no complaints to make ; in fact, we often looked back with regret on that fortnight among the kindly folk of Staple.

Whilst there we heard with sorrow of the death of Brigadier-General Fitton, commanding the 101st Brigade. He was shot by a sniper while paying a visit to the lines of the 16th Brigade near Wipers, and died of gas gangrene. It was cruel rough luck to be killed before his Brigade, which he had trained so well, had even entered the line.

Diary of party left behind when we embarked :—

On January 7th, 1916, the 18th (S.) Battalion North/d. Fusiliers proceeded overseas to France, leaving behind a small party of 22 men with Lieut. Wm. T. McQuillen in command. The reason of our being left behind was that the band of the 18th N.F. became Divisional Band with orders to proceed oversea with their unit. This meant that the Battalion was 22 men overstrong, so to right matters 22 men of No. 5 Platoon were left behind to proceed a few days later with the Tyneside Irish Brigade, and to rejoin the 18th N.F. in France. I was one of the party, being batman and orderly to Lieut. Wm. T. McQuillen, and herewith give some of the doings of that party taken from notes kept during the time of the Battalion leaving England to the time we rejoined them at Staple, France.

Jan. 7th, 1916.—The 18th (S.) Batt. Nd. Fusiliers proceeded from Camp at Sutton Veny, Warminster to Southampton for France. We cheered them off with regrets that we were not with them. During the next four days we had grand sport, in fact, the time of our lives. Mule-riding round the district was one of our favourite diversions. In this sport L/Cpl. Briggs (since killed in action) came to grief, being thrown on to his head. We were well provided with food and refreshments, and all agreed we had a splendid time !

Jan. 11th, 1916.—Our fun and freedom came to an end. We rose early to join a Battalion of Tyneside Irish, and together entrained at Warminster for Southampton, where we arrived at 11 a.m. We were not allowed to leave the docks, from which we sailed on a paddle steamer for France. During the passage many of the boys were very sick.

Jan. 12th, 1916.—We landed at Le Havre at 7.30 a.m., where we remained on the quay for what seemed hours, and then moved off to No. 2 Camp, which lay at the top of a very big hill. Through the streets and over canal bridges we went, and we shall never forget the time we put in, as each of us carried extra weight and took turns in carrying the drum of Teddy Simms—the " B " Coy. drummer. We at last reached the Camp, footsore and weary, but not downhearted, although chafing at the Irish Officers for making the pace so hot. Then we went out scouting for grub, and were fortunate enough to find four tins of bully beef, a bag of potatoes, some tea, sugar and milk, in a shed. We forthwith made a hash and some tea, and then thoroughly enjoyed a good feed. About 3.30 p.m. we received orders from the Camp Commandant to evacuate Camp according to plan, and to set out to rejoin our Battalion. We said good-bye to Le Havre at 11.30 p.m., leaving our officer behind to travel later on.

Jan. 13th, 1916.—Rouen was reached at 7 o'clock, and we were taken in charge by an officer whom none of us knew at the time, but learned later that he was Captain Rothschild of 60th Rifles, who was accompanied by an R.S.M. of the Royal Scots. Capt. Rothschild was, I believe, Adjutant of the 34th Division Details. He mistook us for the band because Teddy Simms still had his big drum. There was only one musician in our party, and he could only play a mouth organ. " Some band ! " you will say. We were dumped into a large hall, more like a warehouse, with canteen and writing materials provided. We were with British and Indian Troops. At 8.30 p.m. we entrained again for Etaples, after having had a rifle inspection. We had had no food all day.

Jan. 14th, 1916.—At Etaples we went under canvas and were served with some stew, which was more like water with fat meat in. There was another rifle inspection, but otherwise we did nothing special all day but clean up our tents and equipment.

Jan. 15th, 1916.—What a place Etaples was ! We had fatigues all morning, and were occupied in carrying material down to the Officers' Quarters. On our way back we had rather an adventure, in which we saved life. It came about in this way. While going back to the Officers' Quarters we noticed two soldiers in possession of a dug-out (Regiment unknown, but probably Manchester Regiment). The covering of the dug-out consisted of a couple of tree trunks, about 8 feet long and 6 inches diameter, laid on the top of the earth, which was sandy, soft and very heavy. Across the trees were the branches and twigs, and over these was piled all the excavated earth. The entrance was down a few steps, 6 or 7 feet down. In our party there were six of us, and we found that the roof of the dug-out had fallen in, so we set to work to dig out the occupants. The first man we got out quite readily, but the second was almost suffocated before we could effect a rescue. We of the 18th North'd. Fusiliers felt proud of the achievement. After this followed a rifle inspection, a foot inspection and then a survey of our boots. At night we had a splendid time at a Y.M.C.A. Hut, where Lena Ashwell's Concert Party gave a capital performance.

Jan. 16th, 1916.—This was our first Sunday in France, and we were compelled to spend the day in camp, as no leave was given to visit the town. Rumour had it that our Battalion was in the neighbourhood, and although it was raining heavily we set off over the fields and hills to find our old mates, but we had no luck. We returned a little depressed and quite fed up with Etaples.

Jan. 17th, 1916.—It was still raining, and after rifle inspection and fatigues until midday we received orders to proceed to the central training ground, commonly known as the "Bull Ring." Here we were informed that the sooner we passed through the tests the sooner we would get up the line. This made us work very hard, as we were very anxious to join the Battalion. We had squad drill, bayonet fighting, rapid loading, a lecture on the care of arms, and we finished up with a miniature attack, and when we got back to camp it took us hours to get the sand out of the rifles.

Jan. 18th, 1916.—We were paraded at 8.30 a.m. and were marched to the "Bull Ring" once again, where we were lectured on the care of arms, on gas and bombs, and then were given a lesson on march discipline, which mainly consisted of parading a broad road back and forward for an hour or more. Then came a telephone message for the 34th Division Details to hurry up and clear out, as we had no right to be there at all. We left "Bull Ring" at 12 midday to go up the line, where we met our second in command, Major Porch, now Lieut.-Col. Needless to say we all danced with joy to see him, because he was a man whom we all loved so well. We said good-bye to Etaples at 3.30 p.m. and our first call was St. Omer, where Major Porch invited us all to have coffee in a large hotel. We arrived at Staple, the Battalion Head-quarters, at 11 p.m., and jolly well pleased to be back with the old Battalion once more!

From Staple we moved a few miles to Les Ciseaux (the scissors, so named because the village was built round cross roads, resembling on the map a pair of scissors partially open).

The morning after we got into our new billets we were inspected by Lieut.-General Pulteney, commanding the 3rd Corps. General

Joffre also inspected the whole division drawn up along one of the interminable straight roads which are so common in France.

We now began to get busy. " D " Company moved off into the Forest of Nieppe and was billeted in a large farm some 10 miles from the rest of us. They worked in the forest making fascines and hurdles. They took kindly to the job and established a record for the number of fascines turned out in a day. The other companies were employed in road-making, levelling and draining camps, loading barges, and making fascines and hurdles.

The Battalions of the Brigades were being initiated into their new duties, going up in turn and being attached to the Battalions of the Divisions holding the line. We supposed some such training would come our way, but we were destined to be rudely undeceived, for on 9th February we moved up, " A " and " C " Companies marched viâ Vieux Berquin to Armentières (which we always called Armen-teers), and " B " Company relieved " D " in the Nieppe Forest, beating its record for fascines and hurdles, while " D " moved up to Rue de Bruges, where it was attached to the 8th Division which had no Pioneer Battalion. " C " Company was billeted very comfortably in a farm a little way down the Rue des Acquis, between Erquinghem and Armentières, and was able to march straight there, though in order not to advertise their arrival too much the last part of the journey was made by sections, for over against us on the Aubers Ridge sat the Boche, and from that commanding position he could see all that we did. " A " Company was not so fortunate ; it was destined to occupy a portion of what was known as the B.G. line, a line of breast-work running some 1000 yards behind and parallel to the front line. Not wishing to put too great a strain on the forbearance of the Boche by offering them a tempting target, " A " Company had to wait in the outskirts of Armentières till dark and then march down in small groups. Major Stephenson, commanding the company, had gone down early in the afternoon and made necessary arrangements with his opposite number, viz. the officer commanding the company of the 9th South Staffords which he was to relieve. He took advantage of this opportunity to pay a visit to the front line, and was the first of us to reach that much-talked-of goal, which, much as we had wished to reach it, most of us were always glad to quit. As each party came along it was quickly directed to its portion of the breast-work, and each man was allotted his spot in a dug-out. The relief was quickly completed, and " A " Company found itself established in the reserve line of the front-line system.

" D " Company was in comfortable billets some way behind the line, and " B " Company was behind in the Nieppe Forest. The

Head-quarters were still at Les Ciseaux, as "A" and "C" Companies were attached to the 9th South Staffords, the Pioneers of the 23rd Division, which was to be shortly relieved by our Division.

This detached state of existence became very common with us, in fact, it was quite unusual for the whole Battalion to be together. Though we were always conscious of the kindly yet firm control of Battalion Head-quarters, each company learnt to look after itself and each evolved little distinctive customs, which fostered *esprit de corps* in the company without destroying our pride in the Battalion. Our companies had varied experiences, and in this history we shall do our best to give justice to everyone, and we can assure our readers that nothing of importance has been knowingly omitted and that every effort has been made to collect material from all sources. If anyone thinks he or his platoon has been insufficiently dealt with he has only himself to thank, for was he not invited to send in an account of his experiences?

Early on the day following their arrival at their front-line stations, "A," "C" and "D" Companies started on their work in the trenches. There was no preliminary canter for us. Certainly the 9th South Staffords had left one guide per platoon, to show us what they had been doing, but then you know what guides are!

"A" Company's picks and shovels had been dumped in the dusk in front of the dug-outs. Naturally the next morning they went by platoons to draw their tools before starting work. No one knew that the spot on which the tools had been dumped was visible from the Boche's observation posts on the Aubers Ridge. A section might not have tempted his gunners, but a platoon he could not resist, and quite a smart shower of whizbangs came along, and though the tool drawers escaped, there was one fatal casualty later in the day, No. 18/31 Private Travis being killed by a shell a short distance in front of his dug-out.

The rest of us had been rather jealous of "A" Company; we thought they had had too much of the band on the march, and that generally things came a bit too much their way, but certainly they had the worst of it this time in the matter of quarters, for their dug-outs were uncomfortable and their movements were restricted to a very small area behind the reserve line. This line was a breastwork, just a huge artificial bank of earth. It was impossible to get down and make snug dug-outs safe from shot and shell, for the soil was too wet. What we called "dug-outs" were really "built-ups" and were of several patterns, some known as "dog kennels," mere boxes let into the parapet or parados, in which from two to four men could sleep, if they lay close and lay still, others called "bird cages" were more elaborate. The sketch shows the style of thing. A was a plank bed, platform B was the fire-step on which the defenders were to stand when the Boche appeared, but as this was the reserve line and Boche had never appeared, whereas the rain was ever with

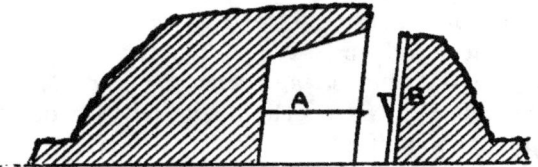

us and poured in from above, this opening was generally closed securely, so that no rain could get in and no one could look out to have a shot at the Boche. Few men knew for what the fire-step was intended. It was generally thought to be a shelf thoughtfully provided by the Engineers and very handy for one's shaving tackle and other odds and ends. The B.G. line ran from the Lille road to Bois Grenier, the cemetery of which village formed a gruesome post, and on to Crombalot, about 3 miles in all. It was like the curate's egg, parts—(very few)—were excellent.[1]

From this line started the communication trenches to the front line. These were mostly called avenues; Haystack, Wellington, Park Lane, Shaftesbury, Moatfarm and Greatwood were the principal ones. "A" Company's quarters were at the foot of Haystack and Wellington, and the Boche was rather too fond of shelling this area in hopes of catching parties either coming in or out of the avenues, to make the spot a very pleasant abode.

We got to know the old B.G. line pretty well, for its repairs and improvements were one of our main tasks during our first and second sojourns in Armentières. Bois Grenier itself was a good sized village, very much battered, but still quite recognisable as a village. Our G.O.C. had his Head-quarters in the village when he was commanding the 16th Brigade, in fact, this Brigade at one time occupied the summit of the Aubers Ridge, but had to retire to avoid being cut off, and the line we now occupied was the line his Brigade made in those early days. Poor Bois Grenier, then a prosperous village, now battered and only inhabited by the observers in the numerous observation posts which were established in the ruined houses. One evening, after a soaking wet day, plodding back to our billets, we looked back on the ruins of Bois Grenier; the jagged outline of the ruined church tower stood up sadly against the western sky where the sun was struggling to break through lowering clouds, the whole scene was sad and mournful, we could not help wondering whether better days would ever come again and whether the deserted streets would ever again echo to the sound of children's

[1] See map of Lys Sector—map 3 at end of volume.

feet and young folks' laughter, and while we looked and wondered we got our answer. The black bank of cloud to the west broke and five great beams of golden light shot forth, lighting up the ruined tower and housetops as if God's fingers touched them, bidding them be of good cheer for all should yet be well. The battered, ruined farms made us feel sad and savage, sad for the poor people who had been driven out and savage with the dirty beasts who had caused all this misery, and we thanked God that our folk at home were not called on to suffer thus.

Our Division soon took over from the 23rd, and the 9th South Staffords departed, and our own Head-quarters arrived. The poor band, which though part of us was the Divisional band, was marooned on a kind of island, but did not remain there long, for our General decided that the men would be more useful as Pioneers than as bandsmen and packed up the instruments and sent them to England, and the men rejoined us. We more than once tried to start a band again, but our efforts were not very successful. C.R.E.'s we found were unsympathetic and objected to our working strength being reduced to provide musicians.

We soon settled down to our work; at first the front line had an attraction for us, and enthusiasts used to find their way up during the "dinner easy" and have a pot at the Boche, at least at his front line. The Boche was very quiet when we first arrived. Of course he had his daily fits of hate, to which we got accustomed, but on the whole he was well-behaved. There were the usual gas scares, which heralded the arrival in the front line of most new Divisions. When it has been dinned into you that a delay of a few seconds in giving the alarm may mean the deaths of hundreds, and you find yourself for the first time all alone at night on the fire-step peering out across a narrow, sodden waste, on the opposite side of which is the unspeakable Boche, what wonder if a bank of mist driven by a gentle breeze, just such a breeze as you were told was the most dangerous, should make you give the alarm and set the whole show working. Easy enough to give the alarm and turn everyone out and get the guns going, but quite another business to quiet things down again.

Our machine-gunners, who in those far-off days were part of Battalion Head-quarters, were given two posts in the B.G. line, and Lieut. Smith, M.G.O. and the rest of the detachment lived in a little red villa known as "Grispot A," where they made themselves very comfortable.

"D" Company soon arrived and was located in La Vesee and Rue Fleurie. La Vesee was a large farm, and though the Boche used to treat the neighbourhood to a dose of shells almost daily, the farmer's wife stayed on and worked the farm. She also turned an honest penny by selling farm produce, etc., to our men. Her husband, who since the commencement of the war had been employed on transport work far back, came to spend his first leave in his home, but after a couple of days he went away, saying the place was too dangerous.

Our gunners apparently touched some sore spots on the Boche anatomy, for he began to show considerable aversion to them, shelling their positions pretty severely. Lieuts. Armstrong and Robson's two platoons of " D," which were billeted in Rue Fleurie, close to some guns, were rendered homeless, their billet being set on fire by a shell meant for their neighbours. They saved all their kit, rifles and ammunition, in spite of a pretty sharp shrapnel fire, and were complimented on their behaviour by the G.O.C. " C " Company also had to shift to make way for gunners whose farm had been set on fire by Boche shells.

Our work during this time was varied. " A " Company had parties working on communication trenches, etc., also on the B.G. line. They also put up an immense triangle of barbed wire in front of the B.G. line, using therein 80 miles of wire. " C " also was employed on trench work in the right Brigade area round Oxford Circus and White City. This trench work was wearisome. It was a matter of patching and mending and draining, but by degrees an improvement became visible; trenches which before were mere ditches knee-deep in mud, developed into quite respectable thoroughfares. " D " worked chiefly on the B.G. line. Parry's platoon had a nice piece of original work near to Moat Farm, which we called Fort Parry. " B " Company, after a short stay in the Nieppe Forest, went to Rue de Bruges and worked for the 8th Division till 22nd March. " C " Company joined " B " for a time and worked on London Wall, riding to and fro in G.S. wagons drawn by six mules. When " B " and " C " arrived from Rue de Bruges the whole Battalion was united for a few days. " B " Company relieved " A " in the B.G. line dug-outs. " A " was at once ordered off to Fleur-baix with the 101st Brigade, as the 8th Division was moved off to the Somme area, and the 34th had to stretch out and hold two Divisions' front till more troops arrived. The right Brigade area was very badly provided with communication trenches, and it was decided to reopen Greatwood Avenue and lay a tram line down it. The C.O. and the Adjutant arrayed in waders set off to explore the avenue, but they had not gone more than a few yards when the C.O., who was in front, found himself a fixture in the mud and the Adjutant had his work cut out to extricate him. However, there was a deep drain not far off, and " C " Company in a couple of weeks had the job completed, the avenue cleaned and drained, and the tram line laid.

Armentières at this time was distinctly a cushy billet. The town had been very little damaged and was fully inhabited. Estaminets were plentiful. Shops of all kinds abounded. The " Au Bœuf " and " Lucienne's " provided good square meals at not exorbitant prices. The " Pâtisserie " overflowed each afternoon at tea-time. There was a good canteen in Rue Marles with a large room in which entertainments of all sorts were given. Why the Boche bothered us so little we never knew, but we guessed that he had many interests in the place and hoped to reoccupy it intact. Be that as it may, it was a comfortable spot and we were sorry when we had to shift. Our sorrow, however, was lessened by hearing that we were going out for a month's rest. We were young in those days, and did not know what the word " Rest " meant in the B.E.F.

On 8th April the Battalion collected in Erquinghem, having been relieved by the Pioneers of the 1st Australian Division, and the next day we marched off for our rest. We had been just three months in France and two months in the line ; we had learnt a good deal of the Pioneers' trade and had got over the feeling that every shell must hit us ; we had picked up a bit of the lingo and generally we had shaken down.

CHAPTER VI

ALBERT

WE had four days of trekking from Erquinghem to Boisdinghem, which was to be our abode during our rest. We had got rather out of marching trim while in Armentières. Our packs seemed horridly heavy, and our feet soon got sore. Altogether we did not like this march much. We stayed the nights at Vieux Berquin, Sercus and Blendecque. Some of us, while at Sercus, had sufficient energy to pay a brief visit to old friends at Staple.

Boisdinghem was rather a wretched village. To get a drink or a wash you had to draw water from a well 300 feet deep. My! what a lot of winding up that bucket took.

We soon began to appreciate the humour of the B.E.F. vocabulary in which Rest=Hard training. A complete programme was drawn up, and we started with four days' squad and platoon drill. We felt a bit insulted, after all we had been through, to be put back to recruits' drill, but it smartened us up all the same. We suffered a severe loss here, our Adjutant, Captain Tom Reay, being carried off by the G.O.C., who was quick to spot a good man, and made Staff-Captain of the 103rd Brigade. We tried later to get him back again, and he did actually rejoin us for a few days, but was taken again and made second in command of our 25th Battalion. He was very severely wounded on 29th April, 1917, near the Sugar Factory at Roeux, while inspecting the front line of the 26th Battalion, to the temporary command of which he had been posted a few days before. A smart drill, keen, energetic and tactful, we were all sorry to lose him.

Lieut. W. Smith succeeded him and Lieut. W. H. Coombs took over the machine-gun detachment. Our "rest" was suddenly brought to an end and we were despatched to Albert to prepare the way for our Division. We soon got accustomed to these John the Baptist expeditions, but we never liked them. It was, of course, an honour to make the paths straight for the Division, but a Battalion attached to a strange Division does not have a very rosy time. It has to fight for everything it wants from baths to beer. We were lucky in having a Quartermaster like Draper, to whose persuasive smile and pleasant beguilings we owed many comforts. We entrained at St. Omer in the very early morning on the 18th April, Major Porch and "A" Company having preceded us on the previous day. We detrained at Heilly the same evening and marched to Bresle, where we found Major Porch had interviewed the C.R.E. of the 8th Division, under whom we were to work, and made all necessary arrangements. We were not very comfortable at Bresle. The billets were huge barns in which tiers of bunks had been built. If you get the top bunk of three, you have to be a bit of an acrobat to get there, and a bit of a saint not to swear when you drop your pipe over the edge, and if you are sleeping peacefully in the lowest bunk, it is not pleasant to be aroused by a kick in the back from the occupant of the 3rd floor as he struggles to reach that dizzy height. Our officers all dossed down on the schoolroom floor, except the Colonel, for whom a bed was found. The next day we were all split up again. "C" Company went off to Albert, "A" and "B" to Henencourt Wood and "D" stayed in Bresle.

"A" and "B" were employed on road-making in connection with the big Casualty Clearing Station, which was being prepared in anticipation of the approaching operations. "D" did some odd jobs. "C" went right into it. Lieut. Vasey and twenty men of his platoon, No. 12, on the night of St. George's Day were sent to try to reopen a piece of trench between two posts in the front line, just where it was nearest to the Boche in La Boisselle. They were silently creeping into the ruined trench when the Boche heaved over what was known as an "oil can," which exploded with fearful force and laid out half the party. Three of them were absolutely blown to pieces. These oil cans were new to us, in fact, there were many novelties. To begin with the country was very different; the flat green fields with deep ditches and thick hedges, which we lived among at Armentières, were replaced by rolling, open downs, reminding us of Sutton Veny, and when we got digging and struck chalk the resemblance was still greater. The villages, too, were different. They had an older look. The houses clustering round a fine château in spacious grounds. These châteaux made splendid Head-quarters for Divisions and Corps, but we missed the prosperous farms with large barns which made such comfortable billets for us further north.

We insert here a contribution from "A" Company.

"A" Company was sent as advance party, and arrived at Abbeville one dark and drizzly evening, only to find that no one knew anything about us, the result being that we had to make ourselves as comfortable as possible on the station platform for the night. Next day we started off for the Front once more, halting at one or two places of no interest on the way. We spent about a week at Henencourt Wood, and there celebrated our first St. George's Day by making roads and wearing red and white roses, which our kind friends " Our Raisers " had sent us from Newcastle.

The company was ordered to be attached to the 8th Division, being accommodated in a half-completed redoubt, known as " Ovillers Post," just behind the support line. Only half of the company went forward, as the remaining half were sent to an isolation hospital, owing to the elusive movements of a para-typhoid germ, which caused many sleepless nights amongst the M.O.'s of the Expeditionary Force. The little beggar travelled from one to another, and dodged all the expert efforts to bring him to book. Only one case was sent to Blighty, much to the dissatisfaction of some ardent warriors.

At " Ovillers Post " we constructed about eight super-safety dug-outs, of which we were very proud, for shell as he liked, the Boche could not have penetrated them. This is a pardonable conceit, although he never shelled them when *we* were there.

Sundays, in those days, were supposed to be holidays, the only work to be done being : kit inspection, physical drill and rifle inspections. By some mysterious ingenuity, " A " Company was ordered to do physical drill one Sunday morning in full view of the enemy. They would have enjoyed our graceful movements no doubt, but the Boche officers invited to witness the display fortunately could not avail themselves of so fine an opportunity of reducing the population of the British Isles, through an " oversight " of the officer in charge.

When the 34th Division arrived " A " Company was brought back to billets, after about a fortnight in dear old " Ovillers," to the palatial townlet of Albert, far famed for its drooping Madonna on the cathedral tower.

The rest of us were soon collected in Albert, where we worked at various odd jobs, " B " laid a tramway, " D " made deep dug-outs, " A " worked on their post and communication trenches, " C " worked mostly in the forward trenches. When they discovered that we had many expert miners among us the gunners pestered the C.O. for the loan of small parties to make observation posts. There were no semi-ruined houses here which could be made use of for observation purposes, so the best way to provide the gunners with eyes was to burrow a tunnel out from a communication trench, ending in a chamber provided with a small loophole commanding a view of the Boche lines. For this work skilled labour was necessary, and, of course, we were very glad to oblige.

Albert when we first knew it was a nice enough place ; rather battered about, but with many habitable houses, and there were a good many French folk there clinging to their much loved homes; some shops were open and the cathedral's shattered tower was still surmounted by the figure of the Virgin holding up her child, though the Huns' shells had displaced her from her original position, and she hung perilously, as if about to dive down into the square. We heard many tales about this figure. If it fell of itself we should lose the war, if the Hun knocked it down he would lose the war, etc.

The River Ancre, which flowed through the town, was patronised by fishermen, and as the weather grew warm by bathers.

Our Quartermaster's stores and transport lines were at Dernancourt, about a couple of miles away. Their work was easier here, for all the Company Head-quarters and the forward dumps for R.E. material were in fairly safe localities, whereas there were one or two nasty corners at Armentières over which the Boche used to play with a machine-gun about ration distribution time, and when you are sitting up on your mule in the dusk under those circumstances you feel mighty big.

It may aid the reader to understand what follows if we give a brief description of the trench system which the 34th Division was to occupy, and whence it was to attack on the 1st July.[1] The town of Albert lies in a hollow; to the east the ground rises gently for about a mile. A good part of this slope was dead ground to the Boche, but as its summit was not a level ridge, parts of it came under observation from high points in the Boche lines, such as Ovillers. There were two roads leading out of the town towards the trenches, one the main road to Bapaume and the other to Becourt Château. The former was hidden from Boche view as far as the Barrier; the latter ran up the side of a spur and was visible from Ovillers, so that it could only be used at night, and parallel to it ran the communication trench known as Becourt Avenue. From either side of the road at the Barrier started a communication trench, that on the southern side being Perth and that on the north St. Andrew's Avenue. Between Perth and Becourt Avenues ran Berkshire Avenue. Near the top of the slope there was a line of redoubts, Maxse, Tara, Usna and Ovillers Post, already mentioned, but the last fell in 8th Division area. Becourt Château was a fine old mansion with extensive outbuildings and surrounded by a beautiful wood, which, having suffered but little, was still full of birds, and as spring changed into summer it was pleasant to get away from the road and eat one's haversack ration under the trees and try to imagine oneself in England again. Just before you get to the château, on the right of the road, is a cemetery in a

---

[1] See Somme map at end of volume.

grassy glade at the foot of a wooded slope, a beautiful, peaceful spot, where lie several of our brave fellows.

The château was on a knoll running out from the main ridge towards the Boche lines, and from the edge of the wood a good view of their lines could be obtained. Our trench system lay on the face of the slope facing the Boche and along the valleys at the bottom. The Bapaume road runs through a dip in the main ridge and across a saddle to the village of La Boisselle, which is on a spur of the next ridge. To the north of it was the Mash and the south of it the Sausage Valley. North of the Mash Valley lies Ovillers and south of the Sausage at some distance lies Fricourt. Our line was fairly straight, but the Boche line made a tremendous salient to include La Boisselle, a V-shaped village, with the point of the V at the lowest part of the spur. Here was the crater area, a waste of chalk pitted with mine craters. The opposing lines here were not more than 15 to 20 yards apart, and were constantly varying. On our side there was a fairly good trench, along which, if it had not been blown in by a recent " Minnie " or oil can, you could get along with comparative safety. From this trench saps led out to the front to various bombing and listening posts, which could only be approached at night, a disagreeable area known as the Glory Hole, with which " C " Company was to become well acquainted later on. La Boisselle was, of course, a mere mass of debris, not a house remained, but nearly every house had had a cellar, and the Boche had improved on this excellent cover by mining operations. To the north they had made some trenches which we called the Y sap ; in this, and among the ruins, deep dug-outs and emplacements for their " Minnie " and " oil can " throwers had been made, whence they troubled us sorely. Occasionally our heavies would indulge in a bombardment to exterminate these troublesome gentry. During the performance not a sign of a reply from La Boisselle, but within a quarter of an hour of the last round being fired a " Minnie " was sure to drop over into our line, to show that we had not quite done with them. To the north the Boche line drew away from ours and crossed the Mash Valley, No Man's Land, some 600 yards wide. To the south, too, across the Sausage Valley the lines drew apart, but not to so great an extent. The trenches were mostly in chalk, which stood fairly well without being revetted, and dried more quickly than those round Armentières, but in wet weather the sides fell in and the chalk churned up into a heavy, glutinous mass, through which progress was slow and laborious.

Shortly after we reached Albert, to our great joy, our old "Doc.," Captain Joseph Graham, rejoined us.

Our own Division arrived on 10th of May, and then we really

got to our jobs, and from then till the fateful 1st July we were all at it. Communication trenches to be cleaned out, deepened and improved, tramways to be laid, deep dug-outs to be mined out, emplacements made for the medium and heavy trench mortars and Russian saps to be dug. These last were a series of tunnels running out from the front line, just below the surface, the idea being that their ends would afterwards be connected and form a new front line or a " jumping off " line for the assault. They were, however, never used, and in September, when we were back in these parts and " No Man's Land " had moved far to the east, the C.O., going round revisiting old scenes, nearly came to grief through putting his foot through the roof of one of them. " A " and " D " worked on the deep dug-outs on the slope to the south of the Bapaume road. These consisted of a number of chambers about 20 feet below the ground, connected with one another and extending in all 240 yards. They were used for reserve troops before and after the assault, and for Advance Brigade Head-quarters till they could move further forward. " C " Company also made deep dug-outs in Panmure Street, and, wonderful to relate, they actually inhabited them during the attack. We say, wonderful to relate, for it usually was the Pioneer's fate to make cover for other folk. " C " also made emplacements for medium trench mortars. The sites were selected by that fire-eater Captain James, who from instructor in bombing to the Division had been promoted to the command of the trench mortars, and consequently they were selected entirely with a view to their suitability for " strafing " the Boche, and some were in very exposed situations, and came in for a lot of unwelcome attention. In all this work on the eastern face of the slope facing La Boisselle, the difficulty was to dispose of the spoil so as not to attract the Boche's attention, for down here we found him far more touchy than round Armentières. In fact, complaints were heard of Staff Officers being sniped by whizbangs when looking over a parapet in the second line.

Any noticeable accumulation of new earth on a parapet or parados attracted fire, so it was necessary to put the spoil from our excavations into sandbags, which at night time were carried to some distance and their contents emptied carefully along the parapet or parados in such a manner as not to attract attention. This disposal of spoil became a very serious matter in the case of the heavy trench mortar emplacements, which Lieut. Nixon constructed with a picked party of men of " B " Company. These heavy trench mortars were new weapons in those days. Two were allotted to the Division. They had a range of about 1000 yards, and fired a shell weighing 200 lb. which was reputed to make a hole 25 feet deep.

La Boisselle was to be their target. It was perfectly certain that after a round or two had been fired the Boche would search for the guns very thoroughly with his heaviest metal; it was therefore necessary to hide them very safely, especially as we had so many scores to settle with La Boisselle, from the subterranean chambers of which the Boche hurled his " oil cans " and " Minnies." Captain James selected two spots on the reverse slope of a tiny undulation, just high enough to hide the actual surface of the ground from direct observation. The spots were on either side of Athol Street, a most unhealthy thoroughfare. Partly to hide the flash and partly for security's sake it was decided to put the guns 25 feet below the surface. After much discussion with Captain James, plans were drawn out, and in due course approved, and we went ahead. Each emplacement was reached by a long gallery running parallel to Athol Street. This gallery was entered by four different flights of steps. Off these galleries were chambers for ammunition and for the gun crew. In all there were 200 yards of tunnelling, and 300 tons of chalk had to be shifted in sandbags and stacked along the sides of adjacent trenches during the day time, and at night carried away and disposed of cunningly.

The tunnelling party was divided into three shifts and work went on day and night. Lieut. Nixon, as soon as excavation was advanced enough to admit of his doing so, took up his abode there and lived the life of a mole, only paying occasional visits to his billet.

We had the assistance of forty men of the heavy mortar detachment who worked as hard as any of us. The removal of our sandbags was to be carried out by working parties supplied by the C.R.E., but with the best of intentions that officer could not find the necessary number of men, and in consequence the trenches became blocked with the fruits of " B " Company's toil, and the C.O. received daily threatening letters from the G.O.C. the Brigade in the line, ordering him immediately to clear the trenches. Finally two companies of the Warwicks were told off to assist us, and under Major Porch's and 2nd Lieut. Webb's supervision the trenches were cleared and kept clear, and the Brigadier's wrath was assuaged. In order to avoid giving away the show, the emplacements were mined out from below. The chalk being very rotten this was a difficult and somewhat dangerous job, but it was safely accomplished. The break through was made in the night and the hole carefully covered over. We may as well finish the story here. The work was finished just in time, and the two mortars fired throughout the bombardment and there was not a casualty among the detachments. Two of the eight entrances were blown in, and the craters all round were evidence of how hard the Boche had tried to knock out these invisible tormentors.

As time passed on more and more guns arrived; 18 pounders jostled each other in rows on the slope east of the town, 60 pounders and bigger guns further back, long naval guns here and there in the Ancre Valley. The Brigades in turn went out and practised the assault over a flagged course. The 19th Division came up somewhere behind us, and parties of their officers were to be met daily making Cook's tours of our trenches. We had early made the acquaintance of the Pioneers of this Division, the 5th South Wales Borderers, under their wonderful C.O., Colonel Trower, who in spite of his sixty years was the liveliest of the lot of them. Then came a feverish period of final preparation. The trenches were crowded day and night with carrying parties taking up materials to the forward dumps. Each Brigade had its own dump or dumps situated somewhere fairly near the front line; in these with infinite labour were collected immense supplies of tools, bombs, small arm ammunition, bully beef, biscuits, water, etc. Further back in Becourt Wood and north of the Bapaume road two big divisional dumps were made, and away back in the outskirts of Albert was the main bomb store.

The Boche certainly lost a chance here, for had he bombarded our lines heavily during this week our losses must have been very heavy, and our attack would probably have been delayed. Fortunately for us the Boche behaved himself and the weather also was fine.

The last piece of work we were called on to carry out was emplacements for twelve French 75's which had been placed at the disposal of our G.O.C. at the last moment.

At last all was ready, not only on our front, but all the line from Gommecourt southwards to Maricourt in the French area, and operation orders accompanied by large scale maps informed us of what we had to do.

Leave had been opened for us soon after we arrived in Albert, but as we were then attached to the 8th Division, which had been far longer in France than we had, we did not get much of it till our own Division came up, even then the allotment was not large and but few of us got away.

On the 23rd June we moved out of our billets, the Battalion, less " C " Company, going into a bivouac in a ditch alongside the railway embankment just outside the town on the Dernancourt side. We were supplied with tarpaulins of various sizes and made ourselves fairly comfortable. " C " Company moved up into the front line opposite La Boisselle. In the plan of attack the 101st Brigade and two Battalions of 102nd Brigade[1] were to assault to the south

[1] The Tyneside Scottish Brigade.

and two Battalions of the 102nd to the north of La Boisselle. In order to avoid all chance of confusion and to prevent the attacking waves becoming involved in the village, " C " Company was employed to hold the front line opposite the village. It was a very severe test for a company which had never held any part of the line before, for this particular piece of line, all among the craters and within a few yards of the Boche front line, was very unhealthy. The company fell in outside its billets on the evening of the 22nd, and the C.O. came along to see it off and speak a few words to the men, telling them that he was perfectly sure that they would uphold the good name of the 18th and the county they came from. As they marched along in the mud, for the weather had broken and it was raining hard, they had to pass " D " Company's lines, whence in a very good imitation of the well-known tones of Mr. George Renwick, a voice proclaimed, " *You* came of your own accord, *you* did not have to be fetched, you —— fools." This set them all laughing and they felt all the better for it.

The company held this portion of the line till the night of the 1st July. The casualties were less than might have been expected, and the G.O.C. who visited the line during the bombardment complimented Captain Francis on the disposition of his company, to which he attributed the small losses. The company earned five military medals during this tour of duty in " the Glory Hole." Two of them were given to men who volunteered to carry food and water, etc., to the advanced posts throughout the bombardment.

The cause of our having to vacate the town was that a heavy bombardment was expected in reply to ours, but as a matter of fact, the Boche did not spend much metal on the town, and an officer who passed through during our residence in the ditch said he was astonished to see quite a considerable number of French people, who evidently had no intention of leaving, and seemed quite pleased to have their town to themselves. One big shell dropped just in the gateway of the Battalion Head-quarters, a position usually occupied by the stout form of Private Mather, regimental policeman, otherwise the place was untouched. Our bombardment began at 4 a.m. on the 24th June and lasted with very little intermission till 7.30 a.m. on 1st July, when the assault was delivered. Originally it was to have taken place on the 29th June, but it was postponed forty-eight hours, whether on account of the weather or for other reasons we never knew, but if the bad weather was the cause, the weather prophet certainly deserved a " mention," for the 1st July was a perfect day.

Before giving an account of our experience in the attack, we must give some idea of the duties thrown on us. As already stated each Brigade stocked a forward dump in the front-trench system. The 103rd Brigade dump was almost in the front line, the 102nd in St. Andrew's Avenue and the 101st below Becourt. As soon as these dumps were complete they were handed over to officers or N.C.O.'s of the 18th Northumberland Fusiliers. " A " Company was responsible for the 101st dump, " B " for the 103rd and " D " for the 102nd. Three columns were told off from these companies and other parties attached to us to carry from these dumps to positions in the Boche lines, selected as the sites of the advanced dumps, which were to be formed as soon as the advance had progressed far enough. The large maps supplied us showed every detail of the Boche trench system, and each Brigade's movements were clearly laid down in accordance with those of the units on the right and left of the Division and also of the artillery barrage. The 101st and 102nd Brigades were to advance south and north of La Boisselle ; when the eastern end of the village had been reached, two companies of bombers were to return through the village, taking the defenders in rear and clearing the village till they joined hands with our " C " Company waiting at the western end like a terrier outside a rat-hole waiting for the rats to be driven out by the ferret. The 101st and 102nd Brigades, having reached the positions assigned them, were to dig themselves in, and the 103rd Brigade was to push on through them, capture Contalmaison and dig themselves in on the far side. Such was the plan, but alas !

There were two big divisional dumps which were also in our charge, one in Becourt Wood and one near the Bapaume road. The main dump for bombs was in a suburb of the town, and here Captain Dodsworth, and all the halt and the maimed, detonated bombs, loaded wagons and otherwise, made themselves very useful. During the first five days of the attack one hundred thousand Mills bombs and about eighty thousand Stokes shells, Very lights, rockets, etc., were sent up. Though the Boche never actually " found " this dump, he got very near it once or twice, and when he set fire to a G.S. wagon loaded with Mills bombs there was a grand pyrotechnic display.

To give some idea of the amount of stores handled by the Battalion and the detachments attached to it during the first five strenuous days of the Somme battle, we give the following list of stores issued :—

Mills No. 5	64,946
S.A.A.	309,733
Stokes	486
Rations complete	14,514
Rifle grenades	2,160

Photo *Lieut. Webb, M.C.*

LA BOISSELLE: LOOKING EAST FROM OUR LINES ALONG BAPAUME ROAD SHOWING CRATER OF "Y" SAP.

CHAPTER VII

1ST JULY, 1916

ON the 30th June at 10 p.m. we moved off from our bivouac, and after a detour to avoid other troops we entered Becourt Avenue, and very slowly, with many halts, we found our way to some dugouts and shelters in Becourt Wood, and by 1 a.m. were all settled in for the night, except two parties ; Lieut. Parkinson and a picked lot of diggers of " A " Company were busy digging emplacements for the Stokes mortars of the 101st Brigade out in No Man's Land, close to the Boche, to enable those useful weapons to deal effectively with a strong point. They did the job satisfactorily and got back in time to take their share in the next day's work.

Lieut. Nixon and his platoon, No. 6, were entrusted with a very disagreeable job. The 179th Tunnelling Company had made a tunnel from our lines toward the Boche lines. This tunnel was said, at its far end, to be within 2 or 3 feet of the surface, and not more than 30 yards from the Boche's line. No. 6's job was to break through and carry a trench into the Boche line as soon after the attackers had crossed as possible. It was not considered safe for the party to be in the tunnel when the two big mines went off as the tunnel was not timbered, and the O.C. 179th thought the shake of the explosions might bring down a deal of stuff from the sides and roof. When Nixon got down on the night of the 30th he was told that the tunnel at the far end was 12 not 2 feet below the surface, and it was therefore quite evident to him that if he waited till after the explosions to commence work he could not get the job done in time to be of any use ; so he determined to risk being entombed by the mine explosions and set to work at midnight, and even then it was 10 a.m. before they had got a practicable exit into the Boche line, but that evening a whole Battalion passed safely through the tunnel.

These two mines, one under the above-mentioned and much-hated Y sap, and the other under the front line to the south of La Boisselle, were exploded at 7.28 on the morning of the 1st July. Each made a crater of about 100 yards in diameter. They were some 50 feet below the surface, and yet in one of them the tunnellers heard the Boches talking in their dug-outs below them. The last 150 yards of each tunnel were excavated entirely with bayonets, as the use of picks would have made too much noise; as it was the Boche got suspicious and began digging down, but on the tunnellers stopping work the Boche also stopped, and after a day or so the tunnellers resumed work more carefully.

At 7 a.m. on the 1st July we were drawn up in four columns in the hollow west of Becourt Wood, there were three columns of carriers of the strength of three platoons each, and one of two and a half platoons of "B" Company, noted diggers, all of them Northumberland and Durham colliery men, detailed to dig a communication trench across No Man's Land to the Boche lines as soon as the attacking force had all passed over. It was a lovely morning, bright sun and very little wind. The guns kept up an incessant roar, but above us hovered a lark quite undisturbed.

The mines went off and a few minutes later the 103rd Brigade began coming over the hill in beautifully regular lines, dressing and intervals maintained as well as on a ceremonial parade. Everyone felt proud of that lot of Tynesiders.[1] Bullets began whistling over and we were moved closer in under the hill, and sat down among the trees.

A stretcher bearer of "B" was the first man hit, but he got off easily and went off to the dressing station in the château, saying if he could not carry he could help with the dressings. 2nd Lieut. Nicholson, who was in charge of the Divisional dump, was the next to get hit, but he stayed at duty till the 5th, when an officer of the relieving Division took over charge of the dump and he was ordered to hospital to get the bullet taken out. At 8.30 the last of the attacking force having passed on our columns were despatched. The carriers had to get to the three Brigade dumps, and "B" Company's diggers had to get down to the front line. This sounded very simple, but we experienced many difficulties, the trenches were already getting crowded with returning wounded, the Boche fire was heavy enough to make progress over the top inadvisable, the trenches had suffered a good deal from his shell fire and progress was difficult and slow. It was difficult to keep touch and there was much delay in the columns getting to their destinations. The digging column, under 2nd Lieut. Cook, especially, was hung up, and Cook was knocked over, having got out of the trench to see if he could get his party to its destination above ground. This party eventually rejoined "B" Company at the 102nd Brigade dump. The digging of the trench was abandoned, as the Boche still held La Boisselle and a good part of the line opposite. Lieut. Coombs, who had rejoined his old Platoon No 3 for the offensive, was wounded just as he had brought it to its destination. He died just as he was being taken out of the ambulance into the Casualty Clearing Station at Corbie.

[1] The Tyneside Irish Brigade.

18th (Service) Battalion Northumberland Fusiliers

A good officer, a cheery companion, and a gentleman to his finger tips. When our C.O. got command he wrote to the C.O. of his old school's (Wellington College) O.T.C., to know if there were any candidates for commissions, but he was told he was too late, all had joined long before December, 1914, but Mr. Coombs, who was a master in the college, would be glad of a commission, and so he joined us.

Our Head-quarters were in some dug-outs on what was known as Chape's Spur, an old Battalion Head-quarters whence there was telephone communication to Division and Brigade Head-quarters.

Our Doc. got everything ready in a dug-out close by, but few wounded came up that way and he soon adjourned to the big dressing station in the château, where there was a great demand for surgeons day and night. One day, while he was busy with a poor chap, he suddenly heard from behind him a voice which he knew, exclaiming indignantly, " Here, don't you touch me. Yon beggar's my doctor ! I'll wait till he's finished with yon fellow," and so he did.

After we had all reached our posts there was an anxious wait. Until the first objective, i.e. the Boche second line, had been seized, it was useless for our columns to move ; time went on and we got no news. Those at the dumps saw wounded crawling back, but they could tell little. At last at 1 p.m. an order came to the C.O. to organise a bombing attack in conjunction with a party of the Lincolns on a portion of the German front line where the Boche were still troublesome. " A " Company's Platoons, which were waiting at the 101st Brigade's dump, were despatched on this mission under Major Porch's guidance. They reached the rendezvous, but the attack was countermanded by the Brigade. Unfortunately they were caught in heavy bombardment and had a good many casualties. Lieut. Wood was so severely wounded that he has never been able to rejoin us.

Lieut. Nixon and his men had been working continuously since midnight, and by the afternoon communication was possible with parties of the 102nd Brigade which had established themselves in the big crater south of La Boisselle and the trenches near to it. Their work was much interfered with by the poor wounded who kept on crawling into the tunnel to get out of the machine-gun fire.

" C " Company, which had been waiting for the " Ferret " Companies of the 102nd Brigade to drive the Boche out into their arms, was suddenly ordered to attack La Boisselle. The company does not deny that it was not very sorry when, just as all was prepared, a counter-order came saying that the attack would be made that night by *two Brigades*,[1] and the company might withdraw to the

---

[1] The reduction of La Boisselle was completed after hard fighting 5th July, 1916. *Vide* Lord Haig's Somme Dispatch.

dug-outs in Panmure Street, which it did and got its first decent night's rest since 21st. The rest of us spent the night as best we could near our stations. During the night news arrived that a party of the 101st and 103rd Brigade was holding out in a portion of the Boche line marked as Scots redoubt on our maps. Early on the 2nd four parties of carriers set out to find this party, which was under command of Sir George McCrea, of the 16th Royal Scots, whose cheery optimism made everyone feel that to be cut off in the German lines without food or water and with bombs running short was really rather an enviable position. With him was that fine soldier Major Temple[1] of the 27th Northumberland Fusiliers, and between them they were making things hot for the Boche, but supplies were getting low and water was especially needed, and Sir George, when he met our C.O. in Henencourt Wood later on, said, "I nearly cried for sheer joy when I saw your fellows struggling on with their loads of water and bombs."

These parties did not get back till about 6 p.m., and no sooner had they arrived than came a request for guides to take out a big party of carriers made up of men from several units. Major Porch, though he had only just got back from Scots redoubt, at once volunteered to go, and with him went Lieuts. Bean and Nixon. They got through all right and returned about 6 a.m. on 3rd. "D" Company on 1st, 2nd and 3rd were busy supplying the wants of the fragments of the 102nd Brigade, which, under Major Acklom, were holding on in a big crater and the Boche front line, and of the 19th Division which had come into action in that part of the battlefield. On the 3rd large parties again went out to Scots redoubt. Towards evening the battle seemed to die down and it was possible, without incurring undue risks, to walk about in the open round our old front line and in the crater area. The Boche still clung on to the top of La Boisselle, but we were firmly established in the lower half. There was a holiday spirit abroad. Men of many Battalions were returning from the battered village with trophies and wonderful tales of the Boche's luxurious deep dug-outs, with painted walls and vases of flowers on the table, of Quartermaster's stores replete with every necessity, sure evidence that they never expected to be evicted. It was a lovely evening and everyone seemed cheerful and inclined to look on life with smiling eyes in spite of the poor dead lying thick around. The mere fact that we were able to walk about at our ease where three days ago it was almost certain death to show oneself for a moment gave us an impression that at last things were coming our way a bit.

On the 4th orders came for two companies to march back to a

[1] Col. R. D. Temple, D.S.O., 5th Worcestershire Regt.

camp west of Albert, and " A " and " C " were told off for this, but the enemy showed signs of counter-attacking and the two companies were ordered to stand fast. Captain Sweet and two platoons of "B" went into La Boisselle on the call of an officer of the 19th Division, but the Boche attack was beaten off and they returned. Just while " A " and " C " were getting ready to march back, in the afternoon, the C.O., with his ear to the telephone in his underground abode, overheard a Yorkshire Battalion from the neighbourhood of Scots redoubt calling urgently on its Brigade for bombs. Knowing that we were the nearest source of supply, with the sanction of our General, half of " A " and half of " C," under the leadership of Major Porch, made one more journey over the now well-known route and then rejoined their Head-quarters. " B " and " D " were employed on the 4th and 5th on the gruesome task of burying the dead. " B," which since the 1st had been existing somehow in mine shafts in the front line, moved up to Becourt Wood. Early on the 6th came orders for us to march back, as we had been transferred to the 37th Division. This was a sad blow, none of us exactly regretted leaving the La Boisselle area, but we all felt disgusted at leaving the 34th Division, and our disgust increased when we learnt that it was all a mistake. The 102nd and 103rd Brigades, all Northumberland Fusiliers, had lost so severely that unless they were relieved the Division could not remain in action, and by a mistake we, being also Northumberland Fusiliers, were included in the order, although our losses had been small. When our General got the orders he did his best to get it cancelled, but it was too late. "Wait and see" found no place in G.H.Q.'s vocabulary, and before we reached Henencourt Wood the Pioneer Battalion of the 37th Division had arrived to relieve us. Our sorrow at leaving was somewhat lessened by the receipt of letters from our General and from General Gore commanding the 101st Brigade, which showed that our small share in the battle had been appreciated. Considering how we had been wandering about the battle-field for five days under fire more or less all the time, our losses were ridiculously small. We had fourteen killed and eighty-seven wounded, of whom ten were still at duty. As we had gone in nearly one hundred over strength we came out only a few under our full establishment, which made our transfer to the 37th all the more vexatious. We " embussed " about 8 p.m. on the 6th and travelled by various routes. One party passed through Albert, and when the well-known cathedral tower came in sight a voice exclaimed, "Look, Bill, here we are back again. They want more bombs and they've sent for us." At 8 a.m. we all found ourselves at Pas.[1]

[1] Pas is 12 miles N.N.E, of Albert.

The day we arrived here Major Porch was taken from us to command the 25th Northumberland Fusiliers. He was an officer of great experience, devoted to his duty, always working to increase the efficiency of the Battalion and the comfort of the men. He never spared himself. We all rejoiced when later on he received the D.S.O., and still more when a bar was added to it. Major Robert Stephenson succeeded him as second in command and Captain Dodsworth took command of " A " Company, with Lieut. Vasey as his second in command.

Extract from Diary of the late Private T. Wilson, "B" Company:—

We went back out of Albert about 2 miles for a rest the time the bombardment was going on till June 28. Then we got all ready for the big advance, and the night before it had to come off then we got word it was put off for forty-eight hours, so after forty-eight hours were up we went into Becourt Wood on Friday night, June 30th. Stayed in the Wood till next morning, July 1st, which I will never forget as long as I live and I think Tyneside will never forget too. We were in the attack from the 1st July till the 6th July, working both day and night without any sleep and just a hard biscuit every day to eat ánd bully beef, and the sights we saw was heartbreaking to see and the smell of the dead was awful to stand. Every man worked like a lion every day till we got relieved on 6th July, and mind it was a relieve to us all as we never had a wash nor a shave for six days, and we were up to the knees in mud and our feet was very wet. We had to cut our socks off our feet with them being wet and muddy mixed, so we were good as new men after we got a wash and shave. Then we left the trenches and arrived at a place called Pas after about seven hours' ride on buses. When we were in the attack at Albert we lost a good few men, but nothing near as many as the Tyneside Irish and Scottish. The 27th Irish Battalion got all wiped out but about twenty of them. Just two days before we left the trenches we had to go all over the battle-field to gather the dead up and carry them to a certain place, lay them all side by side till we got a lot together before they buried them. I may tell you that both the smell and the sight was cruel to stand and see all the dead bodies all over.

From: MAJOR-GENERAL E. C. INGOUVILLE WILLIAMS, C.B., D.S.O.
To: O.C. 18th Northumberland Fusiliers.

MY DEAR COLONEL SHAKESPEAR,

It is with deep regret that you have to leave me for a time to refit and rest, but I sincerely trust that you will soon be back again with the 34th Division. I can confidently say that no better

Pioneer Battalion exists in the Army, and their gallant and faithful service will ever be remembered by their Divisional Commander. It will be a satisfaction to all to know that they have earned a great reputation for hard work and devotion to duty.

In addition I wish specially to express my great satisfaction for the way they have been commanded.

Yours very sincerely,
E. C. INGOUVILLE WILLIAMS.

5th *July*, 1916.

DEAR COLONEL SHAKESPEAR,

Will you please express to all ranks of your magnificent Battalion my admiration for their gallant conduct and the grand work they did for my Brigade during the battle of July 1st–4th ? Without their assistance the troops in the forward line would not have been supplied with water, rations or ammunition, which would probably have entailed the loss of the position gained.

The zeal and goodwill with which they took on any arduous job was beyond all praise.

Yours sincerely,
R. C. GORE, Brigadier-General,
Commanding 101st Brigade.

6th *July*, 1916.

CHAPTER VIII

WANDERERS

ON the day of our arrival at Pas, Major-General Count Gleichen, commanding the 37th Division, assembled the commanding officers of the nine Battalions which had been transferred from the 34th Division. It was a sad gathering. Our C.O. was the only one remaining of the nine who led their Battalion into action on the first, and very few of the seconds in command remained. When the G.O.C. asked for the strength of each Battalion it appeared that our Battalion was stronger than one and not much weaker than the other Brigade. The 103rd Brigade had lost their commander, General Cameron, but fortunately he was not severely wounded and we met him again later.

We spent four days at Pas, and enjoyed the rest. Most of all we enjoyed the baths and the clean clothes. Our transport, under Mr. Draper, arrived on the 7th. They had had a busy time during the five days of the attack, doing various odd jobs for the Division.

On the 11th July we moved up to Bienvillers, and " B " and " D " Companies went into the line. They had a very uncomfortable time, as gas cylinders were installed in the front line ready to be discharged as soon as the wind became favourable. These horrid contrivances leaked and a sickly smell of rotten eggs pervaded all the trenches. The wind became favourable on the night of the 14th and 15th, and the gas was discharged, accompanied by a heavy bombardment of the Boche lines, to which he replied vigorously, and " B " and " D " had several casualties; whether we did the Boche any harm seems problematical. Their line opposite seemed very thinly held, in fact some said it was only occupied by a caretaker, who patrolled the line at night and let off a Very light every now and then.

On the day after the gas attack we were suddenly ordered back out of the line, and set off on a pleasant walking tour through France, which ended on the 18th at Verdrel. *En route* we stopped at Magnicourt and Ostreville. We enjoyed this little tour. The weather was good, the country pretty and well wooded, and while not hilly enough to make marching fatiguing, it was sufficiently broken to make it lovely and interesting. It was very pleasant to be in country which was free from the mark of the beast, to pass through villages in which the houses were whole and the inhabitants living normal lives.

After a few days in Verdrel[1] we were lent to the 63rd Division, and the companies moved into huts in the Bois de Bouvigny, and were engaged on reopening certain old trenches, as all this area had been fought over earlier in the war. The work was unpleasant, although "cushy" as regards shell fire, etc., for we unearthed many ghastly relics which necessitated a liberal use of chloride of lime. The way in which some experts among us could distinguish a dead Boche from a Frenchman by his smell was truly remarkable.

While here we heard the sad news of the death of our late commander, Major-General Ingouville Williams, who was killed while reconnoitring near Mametz Wood. It was a blow to us all, for we had learnt to admire and trust him. There was no braver man nor one who looked after his troops better.

Suddenly on 26th July we moved at an hour's notice from our quarters in the wood to the trench system south of Souchez. Our Head-quarters and "B" and "D" Companies were in Villers au Bois. "A" was in the Zouave Valley, and "C" was in Ablain Nazaire.

Villers au Bois is a small village and had been pretty well knocked about, but still contained some good billets. The companies living there had a long trek to and from their work across a broad, level plateau to Cabaret Rouge road and then up interminable communication trenches leading down into the Zouave Valley. The country now was a blaze of colour, masses of scarlet poppies, yellow mustard, blue cornflowers fringed the trenches and some white flowering creeper hung down in festoons. Most of their work was at night, as the Boche, from certain commanding points on the Vimy Ridge beyond the Zouave Valley, could see all we did on our slope, and, indeed, a good deal that went on in the valley itself. The communication trenches, running down into and across the valley, had to be very deep, and so great was the risk of their being closed by a barrage that a reserve of two or three days' rations were held in the valley for its garrison. The valley itself was a curious place. Our front line ran along the top of the eastern edge. It was most important to maintain our hold on this edge, for by so doing we denied the Boche direct observation over the plateau to the west, and also secured a good jumping-off place for an assault. The slope behind our front line was screened from Boche observation and was honeycombed with dug-outs. The soil was chalk and lent itself to mining and the construction of deep dug-outs. In ordinary

[1] Verdrel is 10 miles due west of Lens.

times the garrison could safely disport itself in the open on its own side of the valley, but occasionally the Boche took it into his head to shell the valley, and then there was a scuttle to cover, which reminded one of the scene in a rabbit warren of a summer's evening if the innocent bunnies' frolics were interrupted by the appearance of a sportsman and his dog.

"A" Company and two platoons of "C" occupied dug-outs in the valley and worked on a support line and improved dug-outs. "C" Company's Head-quarters and two platoons lived in cellars in Ablain Nazaire. They lived in the cellars because there was nowhere else to live. The houses had been absolutely blown to bits. The cellars, however, were very good and the head-quarters had excellent accommodation in what had been the Boche Commandant's abode before the French ejected the unclean crowd. The village was very much under Boche observation, and movement during the day was discouraged, so that life there was rather boring. The two platoons worked the front line during the night. It was a long weary tramp through the ruins of Souchez across the Zouave Valley and up the opposite side. The front line in this part when we arrived consisted of isolated posts, known as grouse butts, which could only be approached at night, and the Boche was very close in front. The two platoons of "C" had to connect up these isolated posts with each other and with the rest of the front line. It was by no means a pleasant job, as the Boche was above them and very near. The 37th Division was relieved by the 9th, but, of course, there was no relief for the Pioneers, who require no rest, so we remained behind. While we were here, Major Robert Stephenson, one of the best loved officers, was suddenly summoned to take command of the 9th South Staffords, the very Battalion to which he had been attached in February to learn his job. He was a great loss to us, and we flatter ourselves he was sorry to go. He got command of a good Battalion, and its record of honours gained since he took it over shows that it has improved under his control. All the company commanders were summoned to Head-quarters for a farewell banquet in his honour, and "A" Company's commander states that on receipt of a message from the Adjutant, "Come at once, be prepared for a shock," he nearly fainted, and all his past life flashed through his mind. After a time "A" and "B" changed places and "D" Company lost its commander shortly after it reached Villers au Bois, not from any action of the enemy, but from a fall from his horse, which dislocated his collar-bone. Captain Norman Smith, second in command of "C," took over "D." Captain Drury, who came out as second in command of "D," had gone home sick early in February and died there after a long illness.

He was a most amusing and witty companion as well as a good officer, who would probably have gained distinction had he lived.

On the 22nd August " D " Company relieved " C," and that night at 10 p.m. a telegram arrived saying that the Battalion would entrain at Calonne Ricouart some time the next day. Practically the whole working strength of the Battalion was busy up in the trenches some 5 miles away. " B " and " D " had all their tools and kits, etc., the former in Zouave Valley and the latter in Ablain Nazaire. " D " had marched out 5 miles to Ablain Nazaire that morning and another two at least to the trenches for work. The transport was just returning from taking up rations and materials. It was caught as it passed through Villers and sent back. Wires flew about and the Battalion assembled at Villers in the early morning. The tools, etc., of " B," which had to be humped from the Zouave Valley to the Cabaret Rouge, where the transport was waiting for them, did not arrive till just on daybreak, and the transport had a very risky journey back. However, by 10 a.m. on the 23rd we had all breakfasted, had what sleep we could get and were off on our 12-mile trek to the railway. We arrived there very weary, some of us having been going pretty continuously for twenty-four hours. However, we left no stragglers behind. That night we arrived at La Gorgue and found that we were expected to march on to our billets in Erquinghem, another 10 or 12 miles. However, the C.O. did not think this possible and got sanction for us to stay where we were, so we lay down in the station yard till morning, and many of us thought of the night of 22nd April, 1915, when we rushed to save Newcastle and slept in the field near Cramlington.

That our Vimy Ridge work during this period was appreciated is shown by the following two letters :—

HEAD-QUARTERS,
37TH DIVISION,
B.E.F.,
3.9.16.

MY DEAR SHAKESPEAR,

Only one line—on my return from leave—to wish you and your Battalion good-bye, and to thank you for the *excellent* work you have accomplished whilst attached to the 37th (and 9th) Divisions.

I am very sorry to lose the Battalion, though I own to being somewhat consoled at getting my own one back !

Wishing you the best of luck, believe me,

Yours sincerely,
GLEICHEN.

25.8.16.

Dear Colonel Shakespear,

I was very sorry not to have the chance of meeting you and thanking you for the excellent work your Battalion did for us here.

You were hustled off again at a moment's notice, which no doubt could not be helped.

I was particularly struck by the capital work that was done by your good fellows, and I hope you will tell them so.

All good luck to the Battalion.

Yours sincerely,

W. T. Furse

(M.G. Commanding 9th Division).

We reached our billets in Erquinghem next day and were rejoiced to find ourselves back with the 34th Division. Major-General Nicholson, commanding the Division, came over to see us and promised us a day or two's rest, but the next day came orders for us to journey back to the Somme. The 15th Division, which had been in the line some time, and was destined to take part in the coming attack on Courcelles, Martinpuich, etc., had to be brought out for a short time before the attack. To hold their line during this period the 34th Division was called on to supply a Brigade, and as the Brigades were very weak and were largely composed of new drafts, we were sent along with the 103rd Brigade to make up its strength. We travelled by bus to Merville on 25th August, where we entrained, and in due course found ourselves back in the vicinity of Albert. In order to strengthen the Battalions of the Brigade equally, one of our companies was attached to each. " A " Company to the 24th, " B " to 25th, " C " to 26th and " D " to 27th. The Brigade took over the line on 28th August. The Brigade Head-quarters were in Contalmaison. The four Battalions were disposed in four lines, one in front of the other, the front line being about 800 yards west of Martinpuich. Each Battalion held the front line for forty-eight hours, and from the following extract from the diary of Private Wilson you may gather that forty-eight hours was quite long enough :—

August 28th.—Marched through Albert up to Becourt Wood, rested just outside the wood all night till morning. This is the time we were attached to the Irish Battalion as infantry. We went into the trenches on the 30th August about 5 o'clock in the morning, and it was like hell on earth all the time we were in the trenches, we were in 48 hours, and mind the 48 hours was like 48 days in going over. Then we got relieved, and mind it was a relieve, too, as we were under heavy shell fire all the time and there was no place to shelter, we just had to stand up against the trench side trusting that he may not hit the trench with a shell, or if he did it would mean death for us all. It was here when I was on the machine-gun section (Lewis gun) and there was 6 of us in a team, but before we got relieved there was just 2 of us left, because there was a shell bursted on the trench top, and it killed one and wounded 2 and the other one was shell shocked. So we got relieved on 1st Sept., went about 3 miles back out of the trenches, just past Contalmaison, rested for 2 days, then went into the 3rd line of trenches for 2 days, then into the 1st line for 2 days, then back into the Front line for 2 days, then back into the 3rd for 2 days and once again into the 2nd line. We lost a lot of our men the time we were in the trenches these few days, but no one expected any other as it was all heavy artillery fire that the Germans were killing and wounding all our men with. But I can say that no one knows what war is like but just those who has been in amongst it.

In Contalmaison we saw some graves of men of the 103rd Brigade who had been killed on 1st July. So some of the brave lads did reach their objective on that dreadful day. Contalmaison, you will remember, was to have been taken by the 103rd Brigade on 1st July, and here was the 103rd Brigade with its Head-quarters there at the end of August and the Boche lines not very far away. The Head-quarters of the Battalion holding the front line was an old German line, where there were some good dug-outs, but in front of that there was no effective cover, the trenches were unrevetted and the soil loose and crumbly, the whole surface a mass of shell craters, level and bare. Our stay in these parts was not pleasant, there was a monotony about it that was unpleasing. To go up for forty-eight hours into unsavoury trenches and be shelled continuously, come back in other trenches nearly as unsavoury but less shelled, that was the only variety. Towards the end of our stay " D " Company had a rather more exciting experience, connecting up our line with a new line which the Canadians on our left had seized. We came back on the 12th to Albert, and the next day we moved to Laviéville. There we stayed till the 15th, when we returned to the Front to help consolidate the position taken by the 15th Division. It was in this offensive of the 15th September, 1916, that Tanks were first used, and we heard marvellous tales of them, though we did not see many.

The 50th Division was in action close by on our left, and Brigadier-General Cameron, who had been wounded on the 1st July while commanding the 103rd Brigade, arrived to take command of a Brigade of the 50th. We found him one day looking back from the old German line down on to the lines we had held up till the 1st July, and we agreed with him that it was marvellous that we had been able to exist there, so completely did the Boche line command ours.

We lost during this period just about as many as we did in the five days of the 1st July offensive. No officer was killed, but Lieut. Dodds was hit by a sniper while he was trying to find some remains of one of his men who had been blown up by a shell. The bullet pierced his steel helmet, glanced off his skull and went out again through the steel helmet, and he never went off duty. Lieut. Dodds soon got promoted into the 25th Battalion; he was twice wounded, and finally died a prisoner in German hands. He was a grand fighter.

We left Albert on the 18th September and the 22nd found us back in Armentières with our own Division, and very glad to be there. At first we had two companies in the B.G. line, one in each Brigade area. Lieut. Parry and his platoon occupied the portion of the line they had made earlier in the year, which we had named Fort Parry. Later on we kept only half a company in each Brigade area, the rest of the Battalion being in Half-way House, Pig Farm, and some houses near by. Pig Farm was so named because the Battalion pigs destined to form our Christmas dinner were kept there. We watched the growth of these pets with great anxiety. There were four of them, and it was popularly supposed that each one had been allotted to a particular company which would lose its Christmas dinner if its particular porker died. Men would come and stare at them, and it is said that a representative of "B" Company, having been pointed one of the animals as "B" Company's, turned away, remarking sadly, "Poor beggar, he's sure to die." However, they all lived and throve on the refuse from the Battalion cook-houses, which would otherwise have been buried, and we ate them with much gusto at Christmas.

We made ourselves very comfortable at Half-way House, and had a reading-room and big barn for drill purposes, also used on Sunday as a church. Captains Duncan and Hinchcliffe, chaplains attached to the 103rd Brigade, used to come and give us services of our own of a Sunday evening, which were much appreciated. Duncan won the M.C. during this period for his bravery in rescuing a wounded man from No Man's Land during a raid. Hinchcliffe we had got to know well down in Martinpuich, where he used to come up to bury the poor fellows who could not be carried back. We were all sorry to see his name in the list of wounded, and we hope he is all right and wish him the best of good luck wherever he is. Duncan died a soldier's death in Arras, running to see if he could help a man who had been knocked over by a shell. He was holding a service at the time, but ran out to help and was killed by the next shell.

Several old friends rejoined us about now, among them Major Percy Bell, " D " Company's first commander, who had remained with the Depot Company and now joined us as second in command, and Captain L. Rogers, who took command of " D " Company, Captain N. Smith having applied for transfer to the Royal Engineers. Just before Christmas we got a large draft (so large that an extra pig had to be bought in a hurry). Very few of these were Northumberland men, and many were only poor Southerners, but we welcomed them and soon they were as proud of the Battalion as any of us.

Our work during this time was as usual very varied. " B " and " D " were chiefly occupied in the trenches, " D " in the right Brigade area and " B " in the left. " B " found parties for concrete dug-outs and revetting and draining, while " D " first drained and then made support lines. Draining was all important in those low lands. To have the communication trenches well maintained and drained makes a lot of difference to the Battalion holding the line, and our humble efforts in this direction were appreciated. " A " and " C " Companies worked on hutting and screening. One platoon of " A " did nothing else for some time but repair huts, travelling to and from their jobs in motor lorries. Screening was the way we tried to overcome the advantage which the possession of the Aubers Ridge gave to the Boche. Long lines of canvas screens, some 10 feet high, were erected along roads, or in any position where they could conceal our doings from the Boche. For part of this period " C " Company was attached to a mixed force, known as Franks' Force, after its commander, which was formed to hold the Divisional front on our left till a Division was available. Since our first sojourn in Armentières the Boche had perfected and largely increased the number of his Minenwerfer and made himself a great nuisance with his " Minnies."

Christmas, 1916, came and went, we ate our pigs and other good things for which we were indebted to the Comforts Committee of our kind Raisers, but we did not get much of a holiday. The officers all dined together at Head-quarters, which was in a fine house, untouched except by a 5.9 through the third story. In the dining-rooms hung a magnificent cut-glass chandelier, holding twenty-four candles, all ablaze. Nineteen sat down to a good meal provided by the careful foresight of the " Doc.," whose health was drunk with musical (?) honours. The Divisional Theatre produced a very good pantomime, with two real French actresses in the cast.

After much persuasion the C.O. got sanction to send one company at a time out to train. We had been out close on a year and had only had four days in which to train and smarten up. Our N.C.O.'s were put through a course under the Adjutant, sergeant-major and other instructors, so that they might be ready when the promised training started. At last, on 7th January, 1917, a year and a day since we left for France, " B " Company marched out to Noote Boom for a fortnight's steady training. Unfortunately before their training was half over they were found to be indispensable, and were called back to prop up the front line, which was in danger of collapse.

Captain W. Smith left us about this period to join the Tanks and Lieut. Nixon became Adjutant. Captain Smith was by profession a mechanical engineer, and being also a first-rate machine-gunner, though we were sorry to lose him, we could not dispute the fact that he was just the man for the Tanks. We ran across him several times later when his Battalion of old "Creepum-Crawlums" were up Wipers way, and, strange to say, when having been wounded down Cambrai way the first folk he ran up against were his old Battalion, and Captain Graham soon had him fixed up.

CHAPTER IX

ARRAS
(See Map at end of volume)

On the 26th January at 1 p.m. we got another hurried order to move, and by 4 a.m. the next morning we were in billets north of Meteren. You may wonder why our moves were often at such short notice, well so did we. We only stayed a couple of days at these billets, but the Corps Commander, Lieut-General Sir A. J. Godley, found time to come and thank us and all units of the Division for the good work we had put into the lines we had just left in such a hurry.

On the 29th we had a pleasant bus ride to Robecq, whence we foot-slogged it via Fouguereuil, La Conte and Hermaville to Etrun and St. Catherine, arriving on 2nd February. This was a good march in good wintry weather, sunshine and blue skies above and snow below. We had only one uncomfortable night, that at Hermaville, where, owing to slippery roads and a misunderstanding about lorries, some of us did not get our blankets till 4 a.m., and we would not have got them then had it not been for our never-weary Quarter-master, who persuaded the lorry drivers that they enjoyed driving about on a wintry night over snowy roads.

"A" and "D" Companies went direct to St. Catherine, a suburb of Arras, where they were billeted in a huge "Brasserie." The officers, fifteen of them, lived in a large cellar, and the other ranks were up above in large, lofty and well-ventilated rooms. "B" and "C" and Battalion Head-quarters stayed at Etrun. We were here attached to the 9th Division and were engaged on another John the Baptist expedition.

Until now the trenches which were to be occupied by our Division had been based on Arras, and all the communication trenches ran from Arras or its neighbourhood to different points of the front, to which in many places they ran parallel. As our Division was to be based on St. Catherine and not on Arras, it was necessary to re-design communications, making use of the old trenches as much as possible. The ground was frozen, so that for 18 inches below the surface it was like rock, in fact, we used our "steel points" in making these trenches, the only time we ever did use them. This job kept " A " and " D " busy for a long time. " B " and " C " were employed under the Chief Engineer of the Corps, putting up Nissen huts. They joined us later on and were employed in constructing shelters on the slopes of the Roclincourt Valley.

We were working in chalk again here. " A " Company, in addition to the trench work, laid a light railway from St. Aubyn into Roclincourt. We had here an instance of how benevolent the Boche can be, for this little railway was laid in broad daylight in full view of his lines below Thelus, and yet the party was hardly ever interfered with. Our Battalion Head-quarters did not stay long at Etrun, which was too far back, and after a little search a suitable cellar was found at the entrance to St. Catherine, and converted into a very convenient residence. When our own Division arrived, which it soon did, our Battalion Head-quarters became a convenient assembly point for D.H.Q. officers coming up to the line on various errands, and was sometimes spoken of as the "Pig and Whistle."

As the time for the great assault came near multitudinous odd jobs turned up. A big bomb store, and approaches to the Dressing Station, both on the Lille road, were two of them. The latter was entrusted to the band, which had been revived in Armentières, and under Sergeant Yates they did excellent work, but were very unfortunate and suffered a good many casualties from shell fire, the Boche having taken a dislike to this spot.

Guns arrived and were located all round us, till it became almost impossible to get in or out of the place while they were firing. We constructed accommodation for ourselves to be occupied at the last moment before the assault. An urgent call came for a trench to be cut across the plateau above Roclincourt in one night, which was done to the C.R.E.'s satisfaction. Operation orders came out and we began to understand what was before us.

Just at this time, much to his disgust, our C.O. was sent to hospital suffering from a bad carbuncle, and did not get back to us till the 7th July. Major Percy Bell commanded in the interval, Major Francis acting as second in command.

At last all was ready, and the 4th April we moved back to X Hutments to have a few days' rest and preparation for the big assault which was fixed for the 9th April.

On the eve of the battle we marched up again to assembly places, these being corrugated iron shelters let in to embankments just east of the Arras-Lille road. As we passed the numerous batteries the noise of our heavy guns pounding away at the Boche trenches, batteries, etc., was colossal. At Zero hour on the 9th April, 1917, our hurricane barrage opened out, and a more perfect combination

Photo   *Alfred Brewis.*
ORDERLY ROOM, ST. CATHERINE, FEBRUARY–APRIL, 1917.
The doorway on left led to cellar which was the Head-quarters billet, alias the "Pig and Whistle."

Photo   *Alfred Brewis.*
ROCLINCOURT FROM ARRAS-LILLE ROAD, SEPTEMBER, 1919.

18th (Service) Battalion Northumberland Fusiliers 61

of field guns and heavies it would be almost impossible to imagine. The advance took place with comparatively little opposition, and we got orders the same afternoon to proceed to the captured objectives to consolidate and join up the positions by improving existing communications, etc. "A," "B" and "D" Companies went up, and work was commenced at dusk. During the actual work many gruesome sights were encountered, but the activity of "brother Boche" was practically nil, as he was completely disorganised. However, our own artillery activity caused us trouble, as some scared individual must have reported that we were Boche, and our "Heavies" kindly sent us over a considerable number of Death Warrants. The elements seemed to join in the battle with evident gusto, as blinding snowstorms added to the joy of all concerned.

On the morning of the 10th we were ordered to hold a line whilst a small attack took place, afterwards "A" and "B" Companies going forward to captured positions to reinforce the 103rd Brigade, who were expecting our "grey" "animal-friends" opposite to counter-attack at any moment. That afternoon they did attack during a snowstorm, and owing to this storm we had not the pleasure of seeing what happened to them, but none were polite enough to pay us a visit.

We stayed here all night and then were relieved by 51st Division, and proceeded back to our original assembly positions, only to be sent up to another sector to join their front line up with—well! we don't know yet! Still, we joined it up! Again there was a blinding snowstorm, and one had to keep two or three men employed walking up and down a track so as to keep a path visible as a direction mark "home," there being no stars and there having been no chance of taking a compass bearing.

There were more men affected by the elements in this "show" than by enemy fire. The programme of work which had been arranged for us had to be more or less cancelled, owing principally to the bad weather, which took such a big toll of the infantry that it was necessary to call on three of our companies to fill up the gaps. We were highly complimented by the Brigade commanders on the work done by these companies. It was on returning to billets after being relieved that the Battalion lost Captain L. N. Rogers, one of our most capable officers, whom everyone loved and respected. He was killed by a small fragment of a shell which struck him in the head soon after he had left the front line.

After this strenuous first week of the battle we did not, as was expected, go out of the line, but were attached to the 4th Division, when their work chiefly consisted of road repairing. During this period with the 4th Division, and until the 30th April, the billets were alternately in Boche dug-outs in their old front line, which were terribly knocked about and required a great deal of work before they could be entered ; in tents on Lille Road, and in bivouac in No Man's Land.

During the last two days in April we were again called upon to support the infantry ; Head-quarters and two companies being attached to 101st Brigade and two companies to 102nd Brigade. The position was immediately in front of Roeux and the Chemical Works, the Battalion Head-quarters being in the deep railway cutting in front of the Chemical Works.

At this famous spot the Boche could be seen creeping about in the open, and in some cases fully exposing himself to our fire in broad daylight, not knowing exactly what to do with himself. " A " Company constructed several T-head trenches in No Man's Land so that observation could be kept over what might have been very useful cover for the enemy. The cost of lives to take this portion of ground must have been very great indeed, both to ourselves and the enemy, judging by the truly abnormal number of dead on the battle-field. The enemy's retaliatory shelling in this sector reached hitherto unknown proportions, mostly being directed on reserve positions.

It was with feelings of joy that the news was received that we were to leave the line with the Division for rest, and on 1st May we embussed in Arras and proceeded to Beaudricourt. Whilst waiting in Arras we had the fascinating experience of seeing an enemy plane hit by the first shot fired by a neighbouring " Archie." We are sure our " Archie " friends will forgive us for saying that we nearly collapsed through shock, and suggested that all the "Archies " in France should "lay down tools " and celebrate the occasion by a banquet. Six days were spent in this most charming little village, and, with fine weather, in a few days everybody looked in splendid condition. We were inspected by the G.O.C. the Division on the fifth day out of the line, and were highly praised for our " splendid turn out."

On 5th May orders were received to proceed to the training area, which was to be Candas,[1] near Doullens, on the following day, viâ Boque Maison, where the night of the 6th May was spent. This was our first real spell " out of the line " since February, 1916.

On arriving at Candas a training programme was prepared, but this was greatly interfered with owing to so much work having to be done in preparing rifle ranges, bayonet assaulting courses, etc.

---

[1] Candas is 22 miles W.S.W. of Arras.

It was at about this time that the Boche began to harry our back areas by air raids, which gradually increased in intensity as time went on.

On 28th May we were sent forward, again to the Arras front. We went in motor lorries as far as St. Nicholas, where we camped for the night. We then took up our various positions near the well-known railway cutting at Laurent Blangy, "A" Company with "C" Company having shelters in the valley immediately east of the cutting. Our first job here was to repair the various C.T.'s in the captured Hindenburg System, known as the Fampoux-Gavrelle line. Later, after a small attack had been made on Greenland Hill by our Division, our task was consolidation and wiring in No Man's Land. This in itself proved to be less unpleasant than was expected, but the journeys to and from the scene of work were very strenuous and also rather precarious, as the Boche had all C.T.'s, etc., well "taped" and caught our men on several occasions. Yet, those who went forward each night had some consolation, for they missed the Gotha's bombs further back. We had a visit from Harry Lauder on June 8th. He sang a few songs, and it was a treat for us, but Fritz spoiled our concert because he started to shell the place where we were having it; but we still enjoyed the concert all the same. At this time we were very short of officers, "A" Company only having Captain Dodsworth and Lieut. Keenlyside, the others being either in hospital or on courses. Enemy gas shelling was also becoming troublesome, and aerial fights were very common, the enemy seemingly having somewhat of an advantage on this sector. The three weeks' stay at this last place was noticeable for a lot of sickness amongst the troops, high "temperatures" being very prevalent. Almost every unit was considerably reduced in numbers apart from enemy fire. For this reason, if for no other, we were glad when orders came to leave, and proceed once more to a back area to make rifle ranges, etc. This time the companies were scattered well apart, "A" Company going to Houvin-Houvigneul, whilst Battalion Head-quarters stayed at Hermaville, at which latter place we joined them, after about ten days' work. Hermaville was quite a nice little village, and several of us were quite sorry to leave.

MEMORIES OF THE M.O.

April 4th, 1917, *V. Day.*—Everything was packed up during the forenoon. The men living below Chalk Farm were withdrawn, and at 2.15 the Battalion began to move out of St. Catherine in half platoons. We marched back to X hutments at Ecoivres, and arrived there at 6.30 p.m. I recall that on the way down an old padre rode along on a horse, telling all the men that America had come into the war. The universal comment was B.F., but that is by the way. We settled down in Nissen huts and all were very crowded.

April 5th, W.—Chiefly remarkable to me on account of the huge number of sick. They took 2½ hours to dispose of. One felt, too, the delight of living above ground again after having been so long in that cellar at St. Catherine. Zero was put back 24 hours to-day.

April 6th, Q. Day.—Nothing much to report. Walter Smith came back to lunch and Major Bell and I went back with him to Maroeuil Wood and saw all over the Tanks.

April 7th, X. Day.—Very uneventful.

April 8th, Y. Day.—Forenoon spent packing up. General Nicholson visited the Battalion quite informally and thanked the officers and men very heartily for the great work they had done. Much H.V. shelling around the camp while we were at lunch. Left camp at 6.20 and marched to Louez, where we had dinner with Draper at his store. Off at 8.30 and marched to Battalion Head-quarters by overland route No. 2. The roads were absolutely packed with men of 9th, 34th and 51st Divisions and with transport of every kind, and offered a wonderful target had the Hun known. However, it was as peaceful as war could be, for the only noisy element was our own guns. Got to Battalion Head-quarters on Lille road at 9.45 and got to my R.A.P. at 10.50. Had to clear it of tools and water, and ultimately had it in shape about 3 a.m. on *Monday 9th, Z. Day.* About the movements of the Battalion on 9th and 10th I cannot say much. On the night of 10th L. N. Rogers was killed. The weather was absolutely vile and the numbers of sick became very great. On 12th April I saw probably 200, and nearly all were genuine cases of sheer exhaustion from work and weather. On 13th April we had orders to remain behind when Division was relieved. I saw A.D.M.S., etc., in an endeavour to prevent it, as the men were much used up. On the 14th we had one day's rest and then on the 15th we went up to help the 4th and 9th Divisions. On the night of the 15th the Battalion was living in old Hun dug-outs in Boche second line of trenches.

On 17th we were relieved by 1/8 Royal Scots, 51st Division. About 3 p.m. we got back to a camp in Lille road. There we all got cleaned up and we had a chance to get the men pulled together again. There we remained till the night of 25th April, when urgent orders came to move at once to Black Line. We did so and found no room at all for the men. Ultimately we were sent back to the old camp.

We went up again on the morning of 26th, and the men dug themselves in near the black line. On the 28th the 34th Division attacked—probably the Chemical Works—and our men went up at 3 p.m. to open communications. Very early next morning I had news from Major Bell that they had been retained to help infantry, that I was not to come up but was to send up supplies of all kinds. On the forenoon of the 30th April the 21st West Yorks took over our camp. Major Bell came back at 7 p.m. On the morning of 1st May we marched to Arras. There we embussed and proceeded to Beaudricourt—a very nice clean little village.

Here we remained till 6th May. The Battalion had a sports meeting and plenty of football, and I think everyone enjoyed himself thoroughly. The weather was very good. Marched to Boquemaison on 6th and got settled there for one night. Sent Renton to hospital with measles. On 7th marched to Candas and ultimately got settled down there. Here we remained and had a very good time till 28th May. That morning we embussed and proceeded to St. Nicholas. Camped there overnight. Moved up on afternoon of 29th by overland route to railway cutting near Athies. The railway cutting was rather an unhealthy spot, so company sick parades were instituted to minimise risks as far as possible. On the night of 2nd June the Battalion had its first experience of bombing. On the night of 3rd several men were wounded by a bomb. At 8 p.m. on night of 5th the 34th Division attacked. We had a good few casualties. Six platoons were out opening up communications, and they did the move exceptionally well. We remained in and around this railway cutting till 19th June. The Battalion was busily engaged through all that period digging trenches, mining, making bombing posts, etc. On the 19th we marched back to Arras and thence bussed to Hermaville. " D " Company were at Penin. We remained at Hermaville and had a good time till 30th June. All the Battalion was inoculated.

On the evening of 30th June we marched to Aubigny and entrained there at 11.45 for a place called Hopoutre. Arrived Hopoutre 7 a.m. on the 1st July and marched to Poperinghe, where we billeted. I had a visit to-day from Corporal Park, who was medical orderly at Rothbury.

On the 2nd we moved to the camp, where Colonel Shakespear rejoined us on the 6th July.

F

CHAPTER X

"WIPERS"

IN the first week of July we were torn away from the delights of Hermaville, much to the regret of some of us, and proceeded (in the army you never "go," you either "march" or "proceed") by train to Poperinghe, from which historic town we marched some six miles north to Crombeke Wood, and pitched our tents among the trees, so as to avoid attracting the unwelcome attention of the Boche's bomb droppers. Here we were associated with our 17th Battalion, the North-Eastern Railway Pioneers. This Battalion had been converted into a special railway construction Battalion, with special establishment and equipment. With a view to facilitating the rapid forwarding of heavy gun ammunition and other supplies during the approaching offensive, a number of columns were to be formed of railway troops and Pioneer Battalions. Each column was assembled in the "Back Area" and given about a month's training, so as to be able to push the lines along as fast as the troops could push the Boche back. Lieut.-Col. King, commanding the 17th, commanded our column, and under his supervision the Battalion was divided into two shifts, each to *work* eight hours, time for meals and going and coming was not included, and strikes were prohibited. Each shift consisted of a number of different gangs, each of which had some particular duty to perform. These gangs were made up of about equal numbers of 17th and 18th men.

We began work on a 60 c.m. track close to our camp. Later we went by shifts to a practice camp near Watou. We also had four companies of Pioneers attached to us, one from each of the Pioneer Battalions in the 18th Corps, viz. 6th East Yorks, 1/8th Royal Scots, Sussex and Gloucesters. Our Head-quarters took over all the Q side of the column's work.

The rations for the whole column, about three thousand men, were drawn in bulk and forwarded by the motor lorries of the 17th to the advanced camp, where they were taken over by Mr. Draper, our Quartermaster, and divided up ready for distribution to the different parties. This was no light job, as the parties were numerous and of constantly changing strength, but Mr. Draper, with his customary thoughtfulness had somehow managed to get a day ahead with his rations, so that he could distribute early in the day, irrespective of the hour at which the lorries arrived.

On the 27th July we set off from Crombeke Wood for P Camp, only to be turned back when we had done half the journey. On the 28th we made another start and reached P Camp, which was also in a wood, but there were a good many huts. There we waited for the day of the attack. The light and heavy railways had both been laid as far as the canal, and an embankment had been made across the canal.[1] The far bank came under the Boche's observation, so it was not thought expedient to push the rails further forward until the Boche's front line had changed hands. At last we got our orders to move forward on the 31st, as the assault was to be delivered at dawn. The attack was successful opposite our front, and the Boche was pushed back to St. Julien, the lower portion of which was occupied by our troops. The Battalion Head-quarters and Advanced Ration Dump moved up to Dawson's Corner, and the two shifts encamped not far off alongside the light railway. Most of our officers were detached and given special jobs, of various sorts, connected with construction or traffic on the line. For the first day or two our progress was not very satisfactory, as the embankment across the canal close by No. 4 bridge was not wide enough to carry both light and heavy tracks. The Boche lost a great chance here. He must have noted the embankment and the two lines of rails laid up to it, and he must have known that they would not stop there once we had pushed him out of his front line, and it was only natural to expect that he would tell off certain guns to keep the embankment and its approaches under heavy fire. What the result of this would have been was shown by the effect of one of the few shells he did land in the cutting close by the embankment, which caused forty casualties among the company of Gloucesters attached to us. As it was, he contented himself with sending over a shell now and again, and we got over the dangerous embankment more easily than we expected to do. Once the embankment had been widened, we went ahead and soon had the rails laid up to the Boche's old line beyond Burnt Farm. The weather was villainous, and we were awfully uncomfortable, especially during two nights when we were shifted across the canal to get us nearer to our work; but what with heavy rain, the Boche shells and the noise of our own guns just behind us, we could get no sleep, and were very glad when we were ordered to move back again to our old camps.

We made lines in all directions so as to reach the various battery positions, so we had good opportunities of studying this portion

[1] i.e. the Yser Canal running north from Ypres.

of the famous Ypres salient. The contrast between the wretched water-logged lines which our fellows had held since 1914 and the Boche lines, generally on high ground and plentifully supplied with concrete shelters for the garrison, was striking, and looking down from what was known as High Redoubt in the old German front line on to our line in the low ground by Burnt Farm one stood in silent admiration and wonder at the dogged bravery of the men who had been able to live in those wretched lines for three years and beat back every effort of the Boche to turn them out. Some of the Pioneers working with us belonged to Divisions that had held these lines, and they told us of their experiences when working in these water-logged trenches at night, for but little day work was possible.

When we first encamped near Dawson's Corner we were disturbed a good deal by long range shelling and suffered a good many casualties, and there was some thought of shifting; but the neighbourhood was very crowded, and there seemed no particular object to be gained by moving, as the whole area was equally liable to be shelled, so we decided to grin and bear it; and as the Boche got pushed back the shelling became less, but its place was more than filled by the bombing at night.

The 17th was ordered away, and we said good-bye with regret to Colonel King and all his officers and men, and we were pleased to hear that Colonel King said he had never had more loyal and whole-hearted assistance from any unit.

We now worked with the 7th Canadian Railway Battalion. The shift system was abolished, and we got back into our companies again and resumed our normal Battalion life. As the pressure of work eased off we got permission to send one company at a time back to P Camp for a few days' rest and smarten up. During our stay in these parts we enjoyed the company and friendship of Captain Chapman of the Army Chaplains' department, who ministered to us and various Labour companies in the vicinity. After thirty years' hard work as a missionary in Japan he was enjoying a well-earned furlough when the war broke out. Having no son old enough to serve, he joined up himself and, scorning all the easy billets offered him in England, he gave the Chaplain-General no peace till he got across to the B.E.F. Not content with attending to our spiritual wants in camp and of a Sunday, Captain Chapman was out every day visiting the working parties, especially those which seemed to be getting most shelled. When we left the Wipers area we left our brave old friend there, living in ramparts of Ypres looking after the souls of the 48th Heavy Artillery group. Good luck to him!

Although our line was primarily made for the benefit of the gunners, we were by no means popular with them; in fact, many

Photo] MISSION JUNCTION : YPRES SALIENT. [Lieut. Webb, M.C.

It was at this bridge that a shell caused some forty casualties among an unloading party of the Battalion.

of them were very rude to us, declaring that our wretched little railway attracted the Boche's shells to their positions. Our view was different, and we did not take our line any nearer their guns than we could help, feeling certain that it was them, not us, whom the Boche honoured with his attentions. The gunners certainly had a thin time of it, for they had but little cover and their positions were easily spotted by the Boche, who, having occupied the ground for three years, naturally knew every inch of it and made the most of his advantage. There was a long pause in the operations, and some weeks of glorious weather passed by without any forward move. Of course, we heard many rumours as to the cause of this, but we were away from our Division, and it did not seem to be any one's special job to supply us with even the meagre details and vague generalities that were dealt out to battalions through Divisional and Brigade Head-quarters.

Our work, however, did not cease, and the Boche did not stop his nightly trips by air to bomb our lines. As he had dropped several bombs close to the Head-quarters camp, the C.O. sent back to the transport lines all the horses which could be spared. Sad to say, the very night after they had arrived the Boche dropped a bomb in the middle of the lines and killed forty of our poor beasties. Fortunately only one man was killed, though several were wounded. We were quickly supplied with fresh animals, but they were not as good as our old friends.

While in this neighbourhood we met many strange folk, Chinese and others; but we had most to do with a cheery crew of West Indian negroes who used to load and unload the ammunition that formed the chief load of our little line. These swarthy gentry seemed always smiling even when travelling through a shelled area on a train loaded up with high explosive shells. One of them, however, remarked, "This country no bon. We should bomb the whole of Germany." One morning a sergeant of this corps came to Mr. Draper and asked for something to eat, as the rations of his party had miscarried. On being offered bully beef, he objected that he never ate bully. "You are very particular," said Mr. Draper; but the son of Ham replied, "No, Sar, I'm not 'tikler, but my stomach mighty 'tikler."

The Boche was often very successful in his efforts to destroy our line, and a strong repairing party had to be always ready to go out to whatever piece of line had been destroyed. As time got on we had a long way to go to our jobs. Sometimes we got lifts in empty trains, but these frequently got shunted and detained so long that those who had trusted to their own flat feet got home first. We got a good deal of shelling while at work, and the Boche used gas shells to a considerable extent, which interfered seriously with work, as the hateful stuff hung about for so long.

A large number of Tanks were used in the attack of 31st July, but the ground was hardly hard enough for them, and the monsters were stuck all over the landscape. We did not much like them, for they had a nasty, careless habit while alive of waddling over our little line and making a nasty mess of it, and when dead the Boche delighted in shelling their corpses, so that their neighbourhood was unhealthy.

While in these parts we were visited by Captain R. O. Hall, now a Brigade Major, who had left us at Cramlington, and by Lieut.-Col. R. Stephenson, who with his Battalion was close by us for a time. From him we got an idea of a bathing plant, which Captain Nixon soon improved on and erected in the Head-quarters camp, so that we had hot baths without a long tramp. As one of the camps in which Battalions stayed on their last night before going into and the first night after coming out of the line was just alongside of us, they found our shower-baths very handy. After we had been some time established in our camp an inquisitive "Q" officer of an incoming Division accused us of being in his area, but he was advised by the "Q" officer from whom he was taking over to leave us alone, or his men would lose the convenience of our baths, so we were not disturbed. It was an awful thing to be out of your area; it was almost better to be in the Boche lines.

After some time operations were recommenced, and the Boche was gradually ejected from Poelcappelle and eventually from Passchendaele, and we pushed our line on to the far side of St. Julien. Our own Division came up, but alas! we did not join it. While in camp next door to us on its way up to the front one of our Battalions was badly bombed, losing a large number of men. That camp was singularly unlucky, many casualties from bombs occurring in it, while we, who were encamped on two sides of it, did not have one casualty from these horrid missiles. We had by now begun to think ourselves a lucky Battalion, for on several occasions when those near us suffered heavily we escaped.

At length our period of railway construction came to an end. With no great regret we turned our backs on the mud and desolation of the Wipers salient, and entrained at Peselhoek, close to Poperinghe, one moonlight night at the end of October. As we waited outside the station we formed a fine target for the night-flying Boche, but our luck held and none came. We detrained at Achiet-le-Grand and rejoined our Division, and were stationed at Henin. We are pleased to record the following message from Fifth Army :—

18th (Service) Battalion Northumberland Fusiliers

To 18th Northumberland Fusiliers.   26.10.17.

The 34th Division has shown the greatest pluck during its short stay in the Fifth Army. Ill fortune and bad weather have prevented its operations being rewarded with complete success, but despite this the Division has contributed to the successful course of the great battle now in progress. Not the least of its achievements has been the fine work of its Pioneer Battalion on light railway construction. I wish all ranks good luck in the future.

From Fifth Army.

The work at Henin[1] chiefly consisted in making preparations for a rapid advance should the Germans decide to retire in the event of the Cambrai push being successful.

On the 20th November we were again detached from Division and proceeded via Bapaume to Havrincourt,[2] to work with the Canadian Railway troops on a broad gauge line, which was to have gone through Havrincourt and joined up with the existing railway to Marcoing. We remained at Havrincourt until 5th December, and had a very trying time during our stay in this neighbourhood. The work was simple, but camping grounds were repeatedly changed and tents had to be repitched on ground that was hard and white with many days of hard frost. The camp also received a considerable amount of attention from a long range H.V. gun, which, however, failed to inflict any casualties. At one period it looked as if we were all off to Germany, for we were completely cut off owing to the successful counter-attack by the Boche, who had made a big advance on our right and held the only road available for our transport. The situation was relieved by the Guards Division, who were in or near Bapaume, and were brought up in buses. They attacked immediately and threw the Boche back a considerable distance. Orders were received the next day to proceed to Vaulx Junction where one night was spent previous to rejoining the Division at Henin. A wonderful change had taken place during our absence from the Division. Instead of preparing for an advance, everybody was working with feverish haste on new defences, as it was rumoured that the Boche might attack at any moment. The work consisted of digging new trenches and making wire entanglements on the entire divisional front. At first two companies were billeted at Neuville Vitasse, and two companies and Head-quarters at the Henin-Croisilles road, but later it was found necessary to send one and a half companies to Croisilles, where they were billeted in the huge underground chalk quarries. About the end of January the

[1] Henin sur Cojeul, 5 miles S.E. of Arras.
[2] Havrincourt Wood, 9 miles east of Bapaume.

Battalion went out of the line and rested at Boileux-au-Mont for four days, and afterwards continued their work on a three company strength, the fourth company resting at Battalion Head-quarters at Mory. One and half companies were billeted in huts on the Henin-Neuville Vitasse road, and one and half companies in St. Leger.

We had a very good Christmas in the Henin dug-outs. Many of us got passes to Amiens, and many and varied were the tales told by those who found the attractions of the ------ cathedral so great that they overstayed their leave.

Major F. Sweet, who had commanded " B " Company ever since Ripon days, was now haled away to be second in command of a Battalion of the Royal Welsh Fusiliers. He arrived late one night at the Battalion Head-quarters, which was in the trenches, and was greeted effusively by his new C.O., who quickly handed over the Battalion to him and promptly proceeded on leave. This Battalion was shortly after disbanded, and Major Sweet was sent to another Battalion of the same regiment. We are glad to see he has got through safely and has gained the D.S.O.

During this period another of our original officers was taken from us for the good of another unit, namely Major C. J. Francis, M.C., who was selected to be second in command of our 25th Battalion, later on he returned to us and held command during the C.O.'s absence from 18th to 31st March, 1918, and again after the C.O. was wounded. Eventually he had to quit the service on account of ill-health, but we hope we may meet him at our annual gathering for many years to come.

Extract from the diary of the late Private Wilson :—

On 20th Aug. we were working on a bridge, and about 20 of us was pulling a big tree along the road and one of the rollers happened to come forward with the tree and I slipped, and they pulled the tree right on to my ankle, so they got it off and put me on a stretcher and I went to hospital to the 46th C.C.S. Stayed there 2 days till Aug. 22nd, then we left there in a Red Cross train and travelled about 20 hours, then we reached Rouen, went into hospital there, stayed there till my ankle got better, then I got out of bed. But there was an old man in the same ward as myself and I mind he was very bad, too. It was a disgrace to the Army for having a man at his age out in France fighting and so many young men in England yet, this man was 59 years old and he had 13 years' service. But we were all pleased in the ward when the old man got marked Blighty on the 25th Aug. when he went over to Blighty. I left the 11 stat. hospital on the 12th Sept., after being there 3 weeks, and went to the Conval. Camp on that date, 12th Sept. On the 13th

Sept. we went to the Tivoli Music Hall in Rouen and it was great, half French and half English, and 100 artists took part in the Revue.

MEMORIES OF THE M.O.

November, 1917.—Of this period I cannot say much, for I have very few notes.

We left Henin sur Cojeul at 8.45 a.m. on the morning of 21st November and marched by Arras-Bapaume road to Grevillers. Had to turn back to Bapaume and we billeted there overnight. Next morning at 11 a.m. we left Bapaume Station by train, and eventually were dumped down east of Velu by the railway-side. The transport was the mystery, as it had been sent to Havrincourt and the road was closed. Ultimately it was found by runners on bicycles and it got in about 9 p.m. We got some food at 10.30— the first since breakfast. On the 23rd the Battalion went off first thing in the morning to work on broad gauge railway along the bank of Canal du Nord. Head-quarters marched up later and pitched camp in a field just behind village of Havrincourt. Transport was again very late. Shortly after we arrived at this point Walter Smith walked in wounded, and I was able to fix him up and send him on. On 24th we moved camp into Havrincourt Wood, and then began all sorts of building operations to put the place tolerably comfortable. All materials had to be salved from old Hun dug-outs, but we all worked hard all the time. The Battalion carried on with the railway right along the canal, then across and ultimately through Havrincourt. On 30th November came the big Hun counterattack. I was away for the day that day, but when I got back I found that there had been great excitement, and that the Hun had met with much success. Everything had been very hurriedly packed and all troops had been standing-to for most of the day. On the morning of 4th December at 4.30 a.m. a fellow stuck his head into the tent occupied by Major Bell and myself, and presented us with orders to vacate the camp by daybreak. Everybody was up at once, and there was much packing. We set off at 9 a.m. and marched by Canal du Nord, Velu, etc., to a camp on Bapaume-Cambrai road near Fremicourt. We had no mess kit, but managed to feed with a Labour Company that night. On 5th the withdrawal of our line took place, and we heard at night that it had been successfully completed.

We were having a heated discussion after lunch on the 6th when orders came for us to rejoin 34th Division. We packed at once and marched for Henin at 5 p.m. Got in at 9 p.m. to find all our old places absolutely destroyed. Made the most of a bad job and got to bed and to sleep at last. So ended our connection with the Cambrai battle.

CHAPTER XI

ON THE DEFENSIVE

ON 28th January, 1918, we were relieved by the 20th K.R.R.'s, and marched back to Avesnes le Comte[1] to enjoy rest and training with our Division. Here we were inspected by our Divisional and Corps Commanders, who paid us several compliments, but also gave us to understand that a tough time was coming, to prepare for which we Pioneers must " about turn " and march back to whence we had come, and labour under the Chief Engineer of the Corps; so after a rest of three days, which included the inspections, we found ourselves, with our Head-quarters and one company, at Mory,[2] the other companies being at St. Leger[2] and Henin.[2] Here we dug trenches and put up wire entanglements all over the countryside. We lived in huts and were very comfortable. Our work was mostly at night, for though it was far back the Boche was in a fretful mood and shelled any working parties he could see. We lost Lieut. Brown in this way, a promising officer who had joined us while we were in the Ypres salient.

After three weeks' sojourn here we again started for the back area in search of the rest of which we had heard so much and seen so little. We marched back to Menin in two stages, and were here inspected by the Corps Commander the very day after we arrived. We stayed here one more day, which was a sad day for " D " Company, for it was here broken up and divided among the other three companies. This was in accordance with a reorganisation scheme by which Pioneer Battalions were only to have three companies. We won't here discuss the merits of this new scheme, but we looked very suspiciously at it, as we thought it savoured of an idea of breaking up Pioneer Battalions and attaching the three companies, one to each R.E. Field Company of the Division. This we all knew meant ruin to us, and we were much relieved when our C.O. returned from a conference of Pioneer C.O.'s at Rouen and assured us that such a plan was not to be carried out. Having enjoyed two days' rest, on one of which we were inspected, we marched back with our Division, which had had a month's rest, to

---

[1] Avesnes le Comte is 12 miles west of Arras.
[2] Mory, St. Leger and Henin are all just east of Bapaume-Arras road.

the line again. This time our Head-quarters and "C" Company were at Moyenville, in a very pleasant little group of huts, and our transport lines just across the road. "A" Company went into shelters near to St. Leger, "B" going into that village itself, Mr. Van Hee and his platoon having a roving commission to help the gunners make gun positions.

We now spent a very busy three weeks. The Boche was expected to attack, and we came to the conclusion that preparing to be attacked was much worse than preparing to attack. In the latter case, from our experience, it was possible to foresee to a certain extent what was likely to happen, and to prepare accordingly, but when the rôle is reversed it is a very different pair of boots. "B" Company worked at deepening the Sensee reserve trench. "A" and "C" put up miles of wire entanglement and did many odd jobs, among others burying miles of cable for the Signalling Company, so that communications might not be severed by the bombardment, which was sure to accompany the attack and to be very severe. As time went on orders came out as to what was to be done on receipt of the word "Battle." Then our guns treated the Boche to a bombardment, and there was a feeling that possibly, after all, it was we, not the Boche, who were about to offend. Even this very severe bombardment apparently made no impression on the huge ammunition dumps which accumulated in the neighbourhood of the different batteries. Though it was evident that rough times were expected by those who ought to know best, we took matters very quietly, and in the intervals of our labours we played football, and the cheery call of "Housey, Housey, who'll 'ave a card" was heard in our huts, just as it had been in the ditch by the railway behind Albert in the last week of June, 1916, but alas! 18/886 Corporal Cowell who then raised it so constantly was with us no longer. We left him at Bienvillers, killed during the bombardment which greeted our gas attack.

At last about 10 p.m. on 15th March came the word "Battle," and all except transport and supernumeraries fell in and marched to the rendezvous at Boyelles, where we crowded into tents and huts as best we could, but the Boche did nothing. In fact, all this time the Boche was strangely quiet. His artillery in particular remained silent. His guns did not even register; the situation altogether was uncanny. If the Boche was on the eve of an offensive he certainly was proceeding on a new plan. We resumed our occupations. "B" was moved back to St. Leger and worked two platoons in each Brigade area, with orders, in case of attack, to act under orders of the G.O.C. 102nd Brigade. This Brigade held the right half of the Divisional front, and had the 59th Division on its right, holding Bullecourt.

We breakfasted at an unholy hour every morning, so as to be ready should we be called on to move off suddenly. Day after day passed and nothing happened. The official summaries told of prisoners being captured here and there, and all these statements pointed to an attack being imminent.

Then on 21st March, 1918, the attack did come, and there was a most awful din all round us. The morning was very foggy, and we could not get any information at all. At about dinner we were sent down to man a trench near Ervillers, but no sooner had we got there than we were ordered back to dig and man a trench very near where we were billeted so short a time before. On the 22nd we found this was the front line, but there was no sign of any Boche in front of us, so we had not much to worry us. The Guards took over our trench and we moved back and dug another line. Then we came out and set off on a four days' march of roughly 15 miles a day to Armentières, our usual " resting " place.

As above stated "B" Company was detached and placed at the disposal of G.O.C. 102nd Brigade. We append an account of its doings.

One of the most extraordinary things about the German offensive of March, 1918, was the uncanny silence which preceded it.

Our artillery pounded away at the enemy positions, but never a shell nor a rifle shot came in reply. The Germans—cunning devils—turned the other cheek! One felt like sending over a note of apology for having to use them so roughly.

The safety with which one could expose one's whole figure in the front line grew monotonous. Troops occupying the trenches wondered if the Hun had packed his kit and gone back to eat his sausage and smoke his ration cigar in some far distant rear position, leaving the British to carry on the war in a noisy solo.

What about this much-talked-of Boche offensive ? Never had it seemed more improbable to those whose duty it was to watch and wait!

Then suddenly at dawn on 21st March the heavens were rent with an appalling inferno of noise, and our trenches began to disappear into the air, 50 yards at a time.

General Head-quarters had not been wrong—here it was in all its frightfulness! " B " Company had been working for some time on the defences of both the 101st and 102nd Brigade fronts, and had erected incredible lengths of barbed wire entanglements in anticipation of the offensive, which, at last, had come. There was no doubt in any man's mind in " B " Company that they were up against it at last, and in a few minutes everyone was standing-to. " B " Company's position was in the St. Leger Valley, west of St. Leger, midway between the 101st and 102nd Brigade Head-quarters, to the latter of whom, it had been arranged, we were to look for orders in the emergency that had arisen.

On the tiptoe of expectancy the company waited under the St. Leger hillside, eager to participate directly the word came to move. As luck would have it, however, we were for the moment not wanted, and we had to possess our souls in patience as best we could.

The sun, meanwhile, had risen—it was a brilliant morning—and, as the day advanced, the general situation instead of simplifying itself became more and more obscure. One thing became certain, however, the Germans had broken through on the right and had captured not only Bullecourt, but Ecourt, but no one seemed to know how much else they had done. While, without doubting that the General would take the necessary precaution, we thought it wise to establish, under Mr. Petty, posts to our right to prevent any possible surprise from that quarter. Eventually orders were received to stand by ready to occupy a trench called Switch Hill, on Henin Hill. These were obtained by O.C. " B " Company at Brigade Head-quarters, where a curious assembly of staff officers, signallers, liaison officers and German prisoners were crowded together in a hubbub of what seemed very much like confusion. Standing enterprisingly at the General's elbow the O.C. " B " Company took the opportunity of translating for the General the many map references in the orders that were coming through the 'phone from the G.O.C. Division, thus solving the situation so far as " B " Company were concerned.

It was not until 11 o'clock the following morning that orders were received for " B " Company to evacuate their position in the St. Leger Valley, and occupy Hill Switch. By this time the enemy had got so far forward as to dominate St. Leger from the hillside immediately east of it, and it was not without anxiety that plans were made for the withdrawal from a position only hastily improvised overnight.

Under the very noses of the enemy the platoons moved back, half of them hugging the hillside for all they knew, and the other half proceeding slowly but surely along a dry river bed with high banks, affording concealment and protection. We breathed again when we reached the place where the valley turns and shuts out the view from the east. Although the shelling of the valley had been fast and furious not a man had been hit.

At this juncture orders came post-haste from the 102nd Brigade to occupy Hill Switch immediately. We climbed the hillside in half platoons, and as the crest was approached the Hun observers began to get a disconcertingly good view of us. The company hurried on, anticipating the worst but hoping for the best, but evidently the enemy had closed down for lunch, for we passed into the shadow of a friendly spur with a murmured thanksgiving.

As we came in sight of Henin Hill, near the top of which Hill Switch was located, we noticed landmarks of troops moving down the hillside to our left in artillery formation. For a moment they were thought to be Germans, but as they came nearer and binoculars were trained on them they proved to be British. We had been given instructions to get into touch with the 101st Brigade on our left, and there could be no doubt that this was the 101st withdrawing. As our instructions implied that the 101st would give support to our flank, it was painfully evident that this withdrawal was outside the programme. This circumstance was reported to advance Brigade Head-quarters, and we at length reached the system of trenches leading to Hill Switch. A runner dashed up and gave the information that progress was impossible as the enemy had machine-guns trained on the communications, which were only a foot deep. There certainly was a great volume of machine-gun fire, but we had heard these stories before.

We pushed on without mishap, providing good targets, although practically on all fours, and gained the front line, which had been dug down spasmodically to varying depths. Here were elements of the 102nd Brigade sleeping the sleep of exhaustion and blocking the trench with their recumbent forms. It was tedious work for "B" Company to pick and climb its way through as the trench in parts was so narrow as to make it almost impossible to squeeze past the sentries on duty, and always there was the horrid thought of that unprotected left flank which would have to be provided for when we got there.

Eventually Hill Switch was reached, and the company was stretched out to cover a distance of 700 yards. As the 101st Brigade had withdrawn, orders had been sent to form a defensive flank to cover advanced Brigade Head-quarters (No. 2).

The second Lewis gun was just getting into position when the enemy appeared in force to our left and opened machine-gun fire. Our Lewis guns replied, and the enemy was silenced for the time being.

Adopting different tactics the Hun endeavoured to creep along the shallow trench, and also to double from shell-hole to shell-hole in the hope of getting near enough for an assault. Our Lewis guns, directed by Mr. Petty, had good command, however, and a score of times they were brought to earth. At last, when we were congratulating ourselves that we had won on points, the German artillery took up the cudgels on our behalf, and a very heavy barrage settled down on the discomfited Hun. Disorganised and bewildered they scuttled back over the skyline to the accompaniment of Lewis gun and rifle fire, leaving us free to remove our few casualties. Half an hour later we had rather a gruelling with heavy shell fire, but by this time the men had dug themselves well in and we suffered only slightly.

Towards dusk, as our night position was being organised, we received orders to withdraw to a railway embankment, a mile in rear. This had become a necessity owing to the discovery that our right flank was also " in the air." To deceive the enemy we retired as a working party, six at a time with picks and shovels, conspicuously shouldered.

The night was spent at the embankment position, and in the morning we were relieved and marched back to Moyenville, where the remainder of the Battalion was stationed.

The Battalion reached Armentières on 31st March.[1] It felt like getting home, but alas, what a change we found. The town which we had left in such hurry in January, 1917, with its shops, estaminets and pâtisseries, was now deserted, not only by the friendly French folk but by our own troops, most of whom had been moved out in consequence of heavy bombardments during the preceding winter. A journey through the deserted streets was most depressing, miles of houses and not a soul in them.

" C " Company was billeted in Erquinghem. Battalion Headquarters and " A " were in a big jute mill on the right bank of the Lys, near the railway bridge. " C " was in another big mill, known as the Blue Factory, not far off. Divisional Head-quarters were at Steenwerck, and our transport was in Hollebeke Farm, not far from that place. The Divisional front was different from that we had formerly occupied ; roughly speaking, it had side-slipped a Brigade's frontage to the left. On our right was the 40th Division, which had been in reserve behind us at St. Leger. On the right of the 40th was the Portuguese Corps. The position held by the 34th Division was not a pleasant one in which to meet a heavy attack. On our left the line crossed the River Lys which was unfordable and not too well supplied with bridges from the point of crossing ; as you went southwards away from the river the distance between the line and the river increased steadily, but in the sector held by the 34th there was very little room between the lines and the river, so that there was great danger of the Division, if attacked in great strength, being forced back on to the river and unable to get across quickly enough to avoid capture, or if the attack were pushed home on our right we might be shut in between the river and the front line. The fact that the left Brigade's line of retreat lay through Armentières made its position all the more precarious.

[1] See Map at end of volume.

In the defence scheme one company of the Pioneer Battalion was allotted to defend each of the three bridge-heads in the Divisional area. "C" Company had the Erquinghem bridge-head; "A" Company looked after the railway bridge and the timber bridge by the jute mill; "B" was to guard the big bridge by which the main Bailleul-Armentières road crossed the Lys, known as the Pont de Nieppe. In order to facilitate the passage of infantry and to leave the permanent bridges free for guns and transport, a number of floating bridges were to be placed at various points on the river within the Divisional area. This job fell to us in the R.E. Yard at Erquinghem. A number of rafts had been prepared, made of timber frames, holding sheets of cork. Our job was to construct floating bridges out of these rafts and get them into position. The bridges were put together in the river which ran by the R.E. Yard, and varied in length according to the width of the river at the destined site of the bridge. They varied from 60 to 85 feet in length. The bridges for the sites furthest from the yard were put together first, and when several had been prepared, an officer and other ranks embarked on each and started off amidst considerable chaff to navigate their serpentine barque to her destination. Those that had to go to the far end of Armentières had no easy job, as there were many wires and other obstructions to be negotiated. Having reached its destination each party swung its bridge and moored it in position to make sure that it would fit, and then swung it back and fastened it close alongside the bank, covering it over with branches and herbage, so as to hide it from any flying Boche who might pass that way.

Trench work, wiring and burying cables were some of the other jobs which fell to our lot. The cable work was very different from what it had been by St. Leger, where the soil was chalky and dry, whereas here we got into water long before the stipulated depth of 6 feet was reached.

Erquinghem, where "C" Company was stationed, had not altered much since we were there last; the people were still there. The big factory was still working. In the country north of the Lys everything was as usual; the farms were fully stocked and inhabited, cultivation was in full swing and no one seemed to anticipate the coming disaster.

On the night of the 7th April, Armentières was bombarded with gas shells. The wind was blowing lightly from us towards the Boche, who therefore rained his shower of poisonous shells chiefly on the northern portion of the town, so that the gas would drift gently through the town and our lines, and become innocuous before it reached his own lines. The furthest limit of the shell shower was

Photo   *Lieut. Webb, M.C.*
ERQUINGHEM, 1919.

Photo   *Alfred Brewis.*
NEW BRIDGE AT NIEPPE, 1919.

the railway line running parallel to the Lys. Our Battalion Headquarters and " A " Company, north of this, escaped entirely, but " B " Company suffered severely. The men were in a huge building, the lower story of which accommodated the whole company. This was very close to the extreme limit of the shell shower. The officers were billeted close by in some houses, but further within the bombarded area. They suffered more than the men, partly because more shells fell in their neighbourhood and partly because most of them were in cellars. The shells falling here and there, sometimes in clusters, sometimes singly, liberated the poisonous gas in comparatively small quantities, which the light breeze soon carried away, so that the effects were not very noticeable at first, and until vomiting commenced no one appreciated the danger he was passing through, and it was not till early in the morning that medical aid was called. The men were then immediately moved across the railway line, where the air was clear. All the officers (ten in number) and some thirty-eight of the men had to be sent to hospital at once, and within the next forty-eight hours the casualties reached about one hundred. This was a bad prelude to a stiff fight. Captain Clements, who was second in command of " A " Company, took over " B," and supernumerary officers from " A " and " C " were hastily summoned. We suffered less than other units, owing to our being so near the northern limits of the shell shower. " B " Company was moved on the evening of the 8th to Pont de Niepppe.

Very early on the morning of the 9th the sound of very heavy firing far away on our right told us something was happening, and we all went to our battle stations. As " B " had been so weakened by the gas casualties, and as a company of the special branch of R.E. had been placed at our C.O.'s disposal, he attached No. 10 Platoon to " B " Company, and the R.E. Company took its place at the Erquinghem bridge-head with " C " Company, and Major Francis was sent to superintend the defence. The Battalion Headquarters moved to a camp north of the Lys, where the C.O. was in easy reach of all three companies.

Erquinghem and the road leading from Armentières through to Bac St. Maur were heavily bombarded, and the poor civilians who had clung to their houses had to beat a hasty retreat; several were wounded and Lieut. Collins rescued some from houses near the railway crossing at the entrance to Armentières. All he could do was to get them out of the houses and bring them back to the Jute Mill, and hand them over to the French police. Rumours of the progress of the Boche were plentiful. " B " at the Pont de Niepppe had to dig hard to get cover. The trenches defending the bridge-head had been marked out, but not excavated, so that they might not appear on any aerial photographs taken prior to the attack. All the foot bridges were swung into position and secured by parties from " B " and " C " Companies. " A " and " C " Companies occupied their trenches and made all preparations for defence. The Boche bombarded the neighbourhood of all three bridgeheads and the back area.

It was a very sad sight for us to see the French folk having to vacate their farms and houses in such a hurry. After having held the Boche at bay for so long, and enabled these plucky people to live in comparative comfort and safety, it went much against the grain to have to withdraw. Our Head-quarters Mess was established in a nice little house by the roadside; the owners were still there and had apparently made no preparations for leaving. They kindly welcomed our officers and produced coffee, but their hospitality was rudely interrupted by Boche shells. The poor folk had to decamp, taking with them what they could carry on their backs and on hand barrows. That night was an anxious one for everyone. Telephone communication between " A " and Head-quarters was intermittent, and there was none with " B " and " C." In order to enable the hourly reports to be sent into D.H.Q. the " runners " had to be constantly on the move. " Runners " deserve a paragraph to themselves. They were a fine lot of men who took a pride in their job and could be trusted to get a message to its destination through the worst weather and heaviest fire. It was a bad day when later on a shell hit Battalion Head-quarters and killed or wounded most of the runners who were there at the time. Daybreak on the 10th found us still in the same positions, but it was evident that the Boche was making quick progress on our right. An officer who had commanded a 15-inch howitzer detachment, somewhere on our right in front of the Lys, turned up at Battalion Head-quarters seeking for some means of reporting to his Head-quarters. He had been obliged to destroy his gun the previous evening, as the Boche arrived before the tractors which had been sent to remove it.

The C.O. and 2nd Lieut. Thorne set off to visit the companies and got to " A " and " B," but on their way to " C " received an urgent message from the Adjutant to the effect that the Boche were reported close to the transport lines, which were in a farm not far from Steenwerck. They therefore returned to Head-quarters so as to get into communication with the Division Head-quarters. On arrival there they were greeted with the news that the Boche were in Croix de Bac, and that D.H.Q. had moved to Outerscloore. The Adjutant had an order just ready for despatch directing the transport to remove itself with all speed to Nooteboom. This order only just reached them in time, for as they moved off from their lines the Boche machine-gun bullets began falling among them. Orders now came to demolish the foot bridges when all our troops were over, and for the three companies then to rejoin Battalion Headquarters as Divisional reserve. It was now about 2 p.m. Nieppe was selected as the Battalion rendezvous.

"A" Company report: "We remained at the bridge-head all night, 9th–10th, and most of the next day, April 10th, when our Division was ordered to retire over the Lys, to straighten out the salient, we to hold the bridge-head until all troops had passed over, and then, after blowing up the bridge, to retire ourselves as a rearguard. Before all our troops had got clear of the town the Boche was on the Armentières-Erquinghem road, within rifle-grenade range of our bridge-head, and later got a machine-gun in a building about 500 yards on our right. This building was once a laundry, and will be familiar to all who knew Armentières. This flank was protected by our company Lewis guns, so that the remainder of the troops passed over our bridge with comparative safety. Bang! Flop! went the bridge when our last man got over, and slowly we made for Nieppe, there to form a new line of defence. Our men were perfectly cheery, and one cannot speak too highly of the men of the 18th."

"B" Company, at the Pont de Nieppe, was the furthest removed from the Boche's main attack. When the sounds of the explosions warned Captain Clements that the railway and road bridges on his right had been blown up, he knew that "A" Company was retiring. This left his right flank unguarded, if the Boche should have crossed the Lys higher up. He could not withdraw his company, as troops of the left Brigade were still coming in from the front. He, therefore, threw out pickets to his right and waited. The troops arrived from the front in small parties by various routes, according to the portion of the front line they had been holding; it was therefore very difficult to tell whether all the troops had passed or not. Several parties reported that, as far as they knew, they were the last, but soon another party turned up. Captain Clements, therefore, held on. About 8.30 p.m. the 9th Northumberland Fusiliers arrived and passed over the bridge, and from them Captain Clements gathered that there were really no more of our troops to come. So, with a roar, the fine old bridge was sent to glory and "B" Company set out for Nieppe.

"C" COMPANY: DEFENCE OF ERQUINGHEM BRIDGE-HEAD

On the 8th of April, 1918, after a night of " standing to " owing to a German attack being expected, we reconnoitred some defensive positions, which were to be put in order, near Sandbag Corner,

Armentières. As there was a bit of gas hanging about in this part we decided to start the work next morning at about 5 a.m. There was no " stand-to " at night, so we all retired to our beds. Early next morning (9th), at about 4 a.m., we were all awakened by a very heavy bombardment on our front, and the shells began to fall very regularly on Erquinghem. We " stood-to " and didn't go out to our work. At 8 a.m. as the shelling was increasing the company was moved out of the factory in small parties to the fields near by, only Company Head-quarters remaining.

At 9 a.m., however, a direct hit on Head-quarters made us move to the R.E. Yard. Two G.S. wagons arrived from the transport lines and we managed to get our kits and some of the more valuable tools away. About this time a rumour got about that the manager of the factory was a spy, and that there were explosives in the building. He showed great keenness to be at the top of the factory where there was excellent observation, but he was forcibly prevented and after that closely guarded by two men who followed him round with fixed bayonets. (Later he was escorted from the place, but what happened after that I don't know.) At noon we began to get more definite news of the situation, and also orders to take up our battle positions. No. 10 Platoon was sent off to Armentières to join " A " Company. Great excitement prevailed amongst the civilian occupants of the village, many houses having been shattered and some set on fire by shell fire. Nothing of any importance happened during the remainder of the day nor during the night, except some shelling of No. 12 Platoon's trenches, which caused some casualties.

At 4 a.m. the next morning (10th) we " stood-to," and as the morning went on we learnt that Bac St. Maur was in the hands of the Boches. The party for the demolition of foot bridges over the River Lys was sent out with orders to destroy the bridges as soon as all British troops had crossed. 2nd Lieut. H. Rowe, with Corporal Cunningham, was in charge of this party, and they did their work well.

At this time the company was having some good shooting at parties of the enemy advancing against us. An order then came along for our Battalion to retire, and great was our surprise to see No. 9 Platoon withdrawing. I stopped the men who were near me and went along the trench to my right, but found no one. (On my right before this " withdrawal " were one company of R.E.'s and two Battalions of infantry.) No. 11 Platoon were formed up to make a defensive flank and then the real excitement began. The Boche advanced against us, but rapid fire from our small party made them get down. They then opened a machine-gun barrage on us, but as soon as they came on we managed to stop them by our fire. Evidently they didn't like us, for they next tried a light field-gun barrage and came on again, but the men re-opened fire and we managed to hold them off. Matters were now beginning to get serious, as we couldn't hope to keep them off indefinitely, and so a message was sent back to ask that some troops might be sent forward again to help us. A reply to this said that a Battalion was already in the village. I sent back and got in touch with them, and got some reinforcements for my line, and I do think we could have held on for quite a long time, but then, when things appeared to be going fairly well with us, an order came round that there would be a general withdrawal at 4 p.m., the remnants of " C " Company to act as rear-guard and destroy the one remaining foot bridge. Orders were sent round to this effect, and at 4 p.m. all the infantry successfully withdrew, leaving us alone. A small party, under Captain Parry and Lieut. Rowe (the demolition party having now returned), were guarding the bridge. This party noticed some Boches taking cover behind a pile of Mills bomb-boxes, apparently ignorant of their contents; their ignorance was their undoing, for a few shots from Captain Parry's men sent the bombs and the Boches to glory in a blaze. We were waiting for No. 11 Platoon to join us when some groups of men advanced along the main road about 100 yards distant, and dumped " something " on the road. This something was a machine-gun and we suddenly realised the Boche was practically on top of us. We were in a tight corner as we were on the wrong side of the river, and on the other side there was only one small gap in a belt of wire for us to get through. We withdrew very rapidly to the opposite bank and opened fire on the enemy. Small parties were ordered by me to withdraw through the gap, while the rest of us kept up covering fire. The bridge was cut in two—Private Havery doing the job; and then the few of us left made a dash through the gap. Unfortunately one or two men were killed or seriously wounded while getting through, as by this time the Boche had machine-guns in the factory and was keeping up a continuous barrage from our front, and enfilading us from each side. Half of No. 11 Platoon did not get away, as the Boche had succeeded in getting between them and the main party. 2nd Lieut. Turnbull, who was in charge, and the men with him were all taken prisoners.[1] Lance-Corporal Boaden and another man succeeded in hiding behind houses and swam across the river, rejoining us later. As we retired I was very thankful to see the factory burst into flames, as all the men's packs and blankets were dumped there, and this robbed the Boche of the use of them. We eventually arrived at Nieppe, where the Battalion was reorganised.

[1] See Appendix A, page 176.

During this time No. 12 Platoon had fared somewhat indifferently on the left flank of the company, as they were detached from us when the infantry withdrew. Owing to the enemy having advanced a considerable distance to the north on the west side of the river, and there being great danger of No. 12 Platoon being cut off, they withdrew upon the orders of Major Francis from their position east of the Erquinghem-Armentières road to the river, and received orders that they were responsible for the destruction of the two remaining foot bridges in this part after the whole of the Division had crossed over. At 6 p.m. a party of six machine-guns and riflemen from No. 12 Platoon were formed up on the bank to open covering fire while the bridges were being destroyed. (Lieut. Webb, who was in charge of this party, kept machine-gunners, who were returning, to help him.[1]) When the whole of the British troops and a number of civilians had crossed, the two bridges were destroyed with felling axes, and, while the work was proceeding, the Boche succeeded in mounting several machine-gun snipers on the ridge about 300 yards distant, and brought fire to bear upon the demolition and covering parties. This fire was greatly diminished by the activity shown by the covering party, thus enabling the bridges to be cut in two and floated down the river. At one bridge, near the church, the enemy machine-gun fire was so intense that three of the four men detailed for demolition took cover, but one man (Private T. W. Wainman, No. 57736), with great bravery, succeeded in cutting the bridge in two, working alone. (For this act of bravery and devotion to duty Private Wainman received the D.C.M.) After the main body and the demolition parties had got well to the rear, the covering parties, with one final burst of fire, got the order to cease fire and retire. They succeeded in getting safely away and rejoined the company at Nieppe about 8 p.m. No. 10 Platoon, who rejoined the company, was formed up in extended order and went forward in support to the advancing infantry, and dug a line which we held for the night.

When the Battalion Head-quarters reached Nieppe, various bodies of troops were arriving from different directions. The Boche machine-gunners, who had been pushed on far in advance of his infantry, were bringing a certain amount of fire to bear on the Bailleul-Nieppe road. Head-quarters were, therefore, moved in the direction of Neuve Eglise, whence they were recalled later on. The C.O. and the Adjutant, after going a short way, returned to Nieppe to meet the companies. " C " was the first to arrive. Nieppe then was in a state of considerable confusion. All three Brigades of the

---

[1] See also Appendix B, page 183.

18th (Service) Battalion Northumberland Fusiliers 87

34th Division were to rendezvous there, Divisional Head-quarters were a good way back, and communication was none of the best. The Boche were pushing up from the Erquinghem-Croix de Bac direction. A Major, whose name we never knew, appealed for troops to form a line in support of his own men, who were holding the Boche in check. General Chaplin, 103rd Brigade, who had arrived in advance of his Brigade, asked our C.O. whether he had any men available, and " C " Company, which was the only one in at that time, went out and took up a position to the south of the village. " A " Company was the next to arrive and occupied a road and ditch in rear of " C," in which position it was joined later by " B." It was with considerable relief that we saw Mr. Draper, cool, collected and smiling as usual, arrive with our rations, for we had not heard of the transport since it had left its lines in such a hurry.

The scene in Nieppe was very distressing, crowds of fugitives, with as many of their belongings as they could carry, were flocking down the road. One poor old fellow wandered about shouting wildly. Most of the women folk had arrayed themselves in their best clothes, with a view to saving them, at least. Nieppe itself had, up till then, not suffered at all, and all the houses were fully furnished. The inhabitants began evacuating as quickly as possible.

Early next morning (11th April) orders were received that we were to act under the orders of General Gore, commanding the 101st Brigade. As his Battalions were very weak, " A " Company was attached to the Royal Scots, " B " Company to the Suffolks and " C " to a composite Battalion, made of portions of various Battalions. During the 11th we remained in the vicinity of Nieppe, holding various positions. No serious attack was made by the Boche, but on account of his progress elsewhere orders were issued for all three Brigades to retire that evening. The 101st Brigade was to rendezvous at a cross-roads beyond Steenwerck Station, which was named as the Head-quarters of the 102nd Brigade. The rear was to be covered by the composite Battalion and " C " Company was detailed to be its rear-guard up to Steenwerck Station, after passing which place it was to rejoin Battalion Head-quarters.

No sooner had the movement started than a heavy artillery and machine-gun fire was opened on us. This necessitated small parties moving independently to escape heavy losses, and some parties of other Battalions lost their way in the dark.

It was rather a trying march, for none of us knew the country very well, and we only had small scale maps, and, further, the movements of the Boche were not known with as much accuracy as we should have liked. We were told that a Brigade of another

Division was holding a line on our left, but its whereabouts was somewhat uncertain. About midnight the Head-quarters of this Brigade were found close to the rendezvous, and the two Brigadiers consulted over matters, after which General Gore assembled his C.O.'s in an estaminet close by and issued the orders for the night. The estaminet staff rose to the occasion, and steaming cups of hot coffee were at once forthcoming, and apparently there was no limit to the supply, and the price was "as usual." The women moved about quietly and quickly, as if there were no Boche within 100 miles of them. We had been accustomed to think the French an excitable nation. We had several opportunities of modifying our opinions on this head. It was a curious scene in this estaminet, for custom was not restricted to those in authority, and many of all ranks had cause to be grateful to our kindly allies for very welcome refreshment that night.

"A" and "B" Companies rolled up intact and had suffered but little.

"B" Company was directed to rejoin Battalion Head-quarters; "A" Company, still with 15th Royal Scots, was on outpost duty, "B" Company carrying on the line to the left as far as the road by which we had come. Some anxiety was felt as regards "C," for it had been ascertained that Steenwerck Station had been occupied by the Boche and, as "C" had orders to act as rear-guard to this composite Battalion up to that spot, there was some danger of trouble ensuing. However, about 1 a.m., just as Head-quarters and what of "B" not on picket were squashing into a farm-house and attached barn, "C" Company came along, all going strong. Captain Vasey had, on approaching the station, seen houses burning and made a detour. So the Battalion had got through the very trying march with very little loss and practically no stragglers. Our only misfortune was that our rations had miscarried. This was the first and only time they had done so.

Early on 12th, the 15th Royal Scots advanced slightly and took up the line of "B" Company's outposts. "C" was placed in rear of "A," which was doing duty with 15th Royal Scots as close support. "B" remained in reserve. We had in front of us a Battalion of Worcesters holding the Pont d'Achelles, a bridge over a small stream. We remained in this position all the 12th and 13th, being bombarded from time to time and occasionally machine-gunned from aloft, for the Boche airmen waxed very bold. One very impudent Boche circled round us all the morning, regardless of heavy fire from all sources. However, he came once too often and was forced to come down, and in trying to land the machine turned a somersault, the pilot thus coming to the end of his flying days on

18th (Service) Battalion Northumberland Fusiliers 89

this earth. The farms in and around which we were, were still inhabited, and from in front came fugitives struggling along with their goods on their backs. We think we felt these pathetic sights more than anything else. We knew our retirement was only a temporary measure; we all knew we should get our second wind and come again; but for these poor fugitives it would be too late, for the Boche, when we drove him back, would leave them but little to come back to. The cattle grazed around us, hens fussed about, finding dainty morsels for their broods; was there ever such a curious mix-up of Peace and War? We got bad news on the evening of the 12th. Lieut. Collins, who was attached to the transport, arrived at Head-quarters early. He reported that he had come with Mr. Draper and the ration limbers as far as the far side of Bailleul, where the limbers had been left, while Mr. Draper and he set out along different routes to search for us and see how far the limbers could safely come. A place was pointed out and a party of " B " told off to meet the limbers there and bring up the rations. No rations arrived and we learnt later the reason. Draper and Collins met on the outskirts of Bailleul and were on their way to fetch the ration limbers when, as they crossed the square, a shell fell and wounded a number of machine-gun mules. The two officers went to put the poor beasts out of their agony and were both killed by another shell. Collins had only been with us a short time, but he had shown himself a good, energetic and resourceful officer. Mr. Draper's death was a sad, sad blow. Joining us very shortly before we embarked for France, by much hard work he got us thoroughly equipped, and, during all our time in France, he was always thinking of how best he could help us. No matter what our needs were we seldom went to Mr. Draper in vain. He got us things which other Battalions could not get, and yet he was popular with all the Supply Departments. Writing about him after his death a Staff Officer who knew him well said, " I always looked on Draper as an ideal Quartermaster." Alas! he lies in an unknown grave in Bailleul, for the Boche occupied the town before his resting-place could be marked in any way.

A platoon of " A " had been sent on the 12th to cover the retirement of a Battalion on our right. On 13th it had become, not only the front line, but the right flank of the whole " show," there being no one in sight on their right. We then sent a Lewis gun section up to strengthen their flank, until the gap which was then found to be 800 yards was filled by two platoons of " B " Company, in magnificent style, they having to come up in extended order under heavy machine-gun fire. It was just like a field day, and one felt very proud of the Pioneers of the 18th, for, by their cool behaviour, they not only kept brother Boche from being too curious, but encouraged others to follow their example. Our boys were fine.

On the 12th our Head-quarters had been moved back on to the Ravelsberg heights, in company with those of the Brigade, but our C.O. spent the night of the 12th–13th with the Head-quarters of the 15th Royal Scots, which was temporarily commanded by Major Osborne, who had been second in command of our 19th Battalion when we were all at Cramlington together. On the afternoon of the 13th he went up to Battalion Head-quarters and then on to Brigade Head-quarters. Here the Head-quarters of three Brigades were all crowded into one farm-house. Orders for a further retirement were expected. The situation seemed, in military parlance, decidedly obscure, and reports of Boches being seen in various directions came in.

There seemed to be some danger of the Head-quarters of the three Brigades being captured, so the personnel of our Head-quarters, together with some dozen runners from the Brigades, were utilised to form pickets on the four lines of approach, not only to look out for the enemy, but also to stop any parties of stragglers which might come along.

Later on a heavy bombardment of the Brigade Head-quarter farm commenced, and a shell, falling close to the wall, killed General Gore, commanding the 101st Brigade, and his signal officer. It also wounded Captain Gilbey, Brigade-Major 101st Brigade, and our C.O. The Boche was certainly one up on that shell.

General Gore had commanded the 101st Brigade since General Fitton's death in January, 1916. We had done a lot of work for the 101st and its Brigadier had frequently shown his appreciation of our efforts, so we heard of his death with great regret.

Major Francis took command of the Battalion. We were glad to hear that our C.O.'s injury, though severe, was not dangerous.[1]

At 2 a.m. on the 14th we withdrew according to orders to Bailleul Station, where we dug in, 9 and 10 Platoons in front and 11 and 12 in support. The enemy advanced against us with heavy shell fire; heavy shelling and sniping continued throughout the day, and we suffered considerable casualties. Our artillery retaliated, but caused a few casualties by firing short. There was no telephonic communication, so runners had to be sent back and eventually the artillery fire improved. Throughout the day extremely good work was done by the Lewis gunners; at one time they dispersed, with considerable casualties, a massing of enemy troops in a farm-yard. Later, some

[1] Even in November, 1919, Colonel Shakespear was not quite free from "hospital authority," but, to the joy of all, he was able to attend the dinner at Newcastle on the 22nd of that month, when about 400 of his old Battalion listened to his stirring words.

enemy machine-gunners advanced and caused us a lot of trouble and casualties, until Corporal Crellin got on to them with his Lewis gun and put them out of action, at any rate we had no more trouble from them. At this position, too, the enemy was fairly active with a light, high-velocity field-gun ; it fired on buildings from which observation could be made, and on our trenches. It was seen to fire several times, and our Lewis gunners advanced and fired on it. On the 15th, at 4 a.m., after waiting for some time, as our guides were knocked out by a shell, we were relieved by the South Staffs and marched back to a position about 1000 yards beyond Bailleul for a rest, but alas ! for our hopes, as soon as we got there we immediately started to dig a corps trench line and wire it. We occupied this trench all day on the 16th and, by the morning, everyone in front had retired, leaving us once again as the front line. However, we got many messages to hang on at all costs, and we were also officially informed that a large counter offensive would take place that night, which naturally made us, tired as we all were, much improved in every way. Nothing happened, so we settled down to hold our line. Officers' fighting patrols were sent out during the night. The next morning (17th) at 8.30 a.m. the Boche attacked with very heavy shelling on our frontage, with no result except one or two slight casualties. In the afternoon, for about two hours, the Boche turned on his Heavies and put down about the heaviest barrage we were ever in. Although we had a lot of casualties we were very lucky, as the trench was only 3 feet deep. (Lieut. Smurthwaite was killed, and 2nd Lieut. Charles Robson so seriously wounded that he died about nine months later.)

At midnight we were relieved by the 17th King's Liverpools, and the early morning of the 18th found us in a line near the Croix de Poperinghe. At 8.30 p.m., after a good day's rest, we moved back into Wolfhoek Wood for work under the C.R.E., and on the night of the 19th we wired the front line, which was holding when we left. On the 20th we had another rest, and on the 21st at 9 a.m. we marched out to Boeschepe, where we cleaned up for a day. At 10 a.m. on the 22nd we marched to St. Jan Ter Biezen,[1] and were accommodated in Road Camp. On the 23rd we began to reorganise, and we were inspected and thanked by General Nicholson, our Divisional commander.

During the above fighting " C " Company had about 100 casualties, including 5 officers, the Company Sergeant-Major Tallant and most of the sergeants.

Between the 7th and 21st the Battalion lost 27 officers (5 killed) and about 326 other ranks.

[1] Four miles west of Poperinghe.

Memories of the M.O.

April, 1918.—The C.O. was wounded on the night of 13th April. I ran down on the ambulance car with him to 103rd F.A. in search of a change of underclothing, for I was soaked to the skin. Could not get it so went on to transport lines, and got it there. Moved with the transport to Boeschepe. Rode up again to 101st Brigade Head-quarters. The acting Brigadier told me the Division was coming out that night—being relieved by 59th Division and that I was to remain at Head-quarters meantime. At 5.30 on the 15th I set off and found the Battalion again. We got settled in and all troops of the Division had to begin to dig new trench system with all possible speed along the bottom of the slopes of Mont Noir and Mont Rouge. The Boche began a very heavy bombardment that afternoon. We got orders to "stand-to," so I got R.A.P. established and all ready as the Battalion was in front line. On morning of 16th I managed to get in touch with field ambulance, and got two squads of bearers attached to carry to car post. There was a steady stream of wounded all day, and the Battalion was suffering heavily. On the morning of 17th early, Battalion Head-quarters was hit and the runners and signallers were caught. From 10.40 to 12 noon that day and again in the afternoon the Hun laid down a terrific bombardment and attacked time after time without making any impression. Hodgkinson and Smurthwaite were killed to-day. That night the Battalion fell back into support trenches. On the night of 18th we withdrew further up the slopes to reserve positions, and the men had a chance of some decent rest. C.-in-C.'s telegram to-day expressed the wish that he could meet all the men and shake each one by the hand. It would not have been too great an act of thanksgiving had he been able to do it. The 19th was spent cleaning up. Those who had no razor borrowed from those who had and we all enjoyed it very much. We got a huge mail that night—the first since 9th April. On the 20th we got orders to move, as we were being relieved that night by the 133rd French Division. Marched off at 4.15 on the 21st and got back to transport lines at Boeschepe at 6.30. There we breakfasted and got settled down. There was a huge sick parade which took 2 hours, mostly of men who were slightly gassed. The day was spent in the luxury of a hot bath and a clean change, and we all felt very pleased with life at night. Captain Wells rejoined the Battalion.

22nd.—Marched to Road Camp, St. Jan Ter Biezen, and got there at 3 p.m. and settled in.

23rd.—G.O.C.'s parade, at which he conveyed to us the messages of Corps and Army Commanders.

18th (Service) Battalion Northumberland Fusiliers

25th.—At lunch got orders to be ready to move at half an hour's notice. Nothing happened that day, but we slept in clothes and all ready.

26th.—Moved this afternoon to reserve positions south of Poperinghe. Then ordered to join 101st Brigade and moved to new positions. Next ordered to join 103rd Brigade and marched to Ouderdom. Battalion went into support trenches there on right flank of Brigade. Head-quarters and R.A.P. established in a house on roadside.

27th.—Very quiet. Casualties, two killed. At 6 p.m. got orders that 59th Division would relieve us, and that our Division would take over line on left of 59th. One company was attached to 101st Brigade and another to 102nd Brigade. The other company and Head-quarters went to School Camp, St. Jan Ter Biezen. Marched through Poperinghe during the night.

28th.—Absolute rest and quiet. Devoted day to sleep.

29th.—Moved from School Camp and ultimately got fixed up under canvas.

May 2nd.—" A " and " B " Companies back to Battalion.

5th.—" A " and " C " Companies went off to be attached to Brigades. At this time all were working hard on new trench systems, strong points, etc., in front of Poperinghe and around it.

10th.—Heard to-day of break up of Division and Battalion, but could get no word as to what would happen to me.

12th.—Moved at 8.30 a.m. and marched till 5 p.m. to billets near Rubrouck.

13th.—Off by bus to Harlettes and marched to Watterdal.

16th.—Saw A.D.M.S. who told me I would be reposted. O.C. had a parade to-day and told Battalion of the break up.

18th.—Handed in all medical equipment to 102 F.A.

19th.—Marched to Alincthun and got billeted there.

24th.—Got my orders to leave for 12th Division.

25th.—Left at 10 a.m. by ambulance car for Boulogne. It was a difficult job to say good-bye to all those whom I had known so well, whose life I had shared so long. But it had to be. Francis came with me and I dined with Renton and Pringle at night.

All will be glad to have these last words of our M.O. :—

" Since I left you all in May, 1918, I have seen Albert, where I rejoined you, and I visited it in August, 1918. Mons. Bomport's house is no more. Everything is desolation and destruction. Armentières I saw the other day and it is the same. ' C ' Company's billet there is flat, and shell after shell must have penetrated right into the cellars. Battalion Head-quarters near the station is a shell. The 'Au Boeuf' hangs together tolerably well, but 'the half-past 11 o'clock' is no more. I have strolled again among the gaunt spectres of Ypres. I have motored over the battle-fields of Arras. I have been through Wez Macquart, which few of you may have seen, and I have stood on the Aubers Ridge and gazed along the old lines you all helped to make. I have been through Nieppe and that area, and it, too, is blotted out. And I looked long at these places, and thought of all their old associations, for it was with the 18th that I first knew them all.

"My last touch with the 18th was made the other day. I was taking a sick parade of the 12th Division Machine-Gunners, and amongst the sick was P. G. Robinson, late of 'C' Company, who used to be G. A. M. Hall's batman. Naturally we talked of the old days, of the old folk and the old happenings, but I must have cured him for he disappeared too. Some-day I hope all these old associations will be renewed, and I look forward to that day with a wealth of anticipation and delight."

CHAPTER XII

CLEARING UP

OUR History is nearly complete. We quote from the diary of one of those who enlisted early and was with us to the end.

"*16th May.*—When we were told that the 34th Division was breaking up and, with our Battalion being in that Division, it meant the breaking up of our Battalion, the 18th Northumberland Fusiliers Pioneers, one of the best Pioneer Battalions in France, and I can say that all the men and officers that joined the Battalion in 1914 and 1915 took it badly with being in the Battalion so long. So it was on 18th May when we left Watterdal for Etaples."

It was a sad day for all that were left of us. The Battalion and Company Head-quarters were kept intact, but all other officers and other ranks were sent down to the Base, whence they were transferred to other Battalions. A large number went to the 14th Northumberland Fusiliers and others went to the 19th, both Pioneer Battalions.

Before we tell of the last days of the remnant of the Battalion, let us fill in a few gaps and gather up a few fragments. The following extract from a letter is vouched for as being an exact copy from the original :—

"I cannot tell you where I am, but I will venture to say I am not where I was before I left here to go to where I have just come from."

But little mention has been made of how we employed our leisure. We certainly had not much leisure, but football was our chief sport. Before we left England we had a good Battalion team and were successful in several matches, and it was with no misgivings that we accepted the challenge of a platoon of the 16th Royal Scots, but prior to the match the secret leaked out that our opponents were to be almost the best players of a crack Scotch team who had enlisted *en bloc* in the particular platoon. Our team played a plucky game, but sustained a severe defeat.

In France we were so broken up and so little time out of the line that we did not get a Battalion team together until we had been reduced to cadre strength, when, having less to do, we were able to organise a fair team, but each company kept a team going all the time, and " C " Company claim to have defeated all comers, except our own transport, who beat them at Moyenville while we were waiting for the Boche, but they avenged their defeat before this Push began.

We had some good runners, chief of whom was Dean, and our representatives got good places in the monster run on the Gosforth Park race-course early in 1915, and in the Divisional run at Sutton Veny.

At Rothbury, company concerts were very popular, and at various periods of our existence variety entertainments were got up.

There may have been a better behaved Battalion in the Army; if there was its men were " plaster saints." As far as we can remember, there were only three courts martial and Regimental entries were very few. Our conscience, however, pricks us as regards absence without leave in the early days, when our homes were near and we had not long donned khaki.

Lieut.-Col. J. A. Methuen, D.S.O.,[1] was posted to the command of the Battalion, which was employed in the instruction of American troops. The first move was to Alincthun, near Boulogne, and our job was to train the machine-gun units of the 28th American Division in musketry, physical drill, bayonet fighting and gas drill. This job occupied us from 19th to 31st May. Then we became Child's Guide to the 103rd American Engineers till the 22nd June, when they rejoined their Division and we were affiliated with 303rd American Engineer Regiment, with whom we moved to Oudereele area, a four days' march. We instructed our willing pupils in barbed wire work, laying out trenches and all the above-mentioned subjects till the 27th July, when they rejoined their Division—the 78th—and we were ordered to proceed to Licques to join the 39th Division. We thoroughly enjoyed our experience as instructors and made good friends with the Americans, who were keen and apt pupils.

A letter from the Colonel of the 303rd Engineers, N.A., to the G.O.C. 39th Division, thanking us for our assistance, gave us great pleasure.

Before we left Alincthun we fraternised with the townsfolk, and the following letter shows that our efforts were appreciated.

[1] Colonel Methuen was second in command of 1st Rhodesia Regiment during the South-West Africa campaign; afterwards serving in France with the King's Royal Rifle Corps.

LIEUT.-COLONEL J. A. M. METHUEN, D.S.O.

18th (Service) Battalion Northumberland Fusiliers

ALINCTHUN,
24.7.1918.

MY DEAR COLONEL,

I am very happy to express once again my warmest thanks for the fêtes which you kindly carried out with the assistance of the band.

I can assure you that we have all appreciated this kindly thought of yours. Our scholars in particular will always remember the good time they had. I am therefore certain that I am the interpreter of all in our village here in addressing to you our best thanks, and in expressing the wish that you will soon come back amongst us.

For my own part (personally) I should like to add that I have gladly welcomed the opportunity that was afforded me of making the acquaintance of your Officers and Men, who have left behind them a happy reputation in the Commune.

Kindly accept, my dear Colonel, this expression of my best wishes.

THE MAIRE OF ALINCTHUN,
MASSEN.

To :
    LIEUT.-COL. J. A. METHUEN, D.S.O.,
        Officer Commanding
            18th (S.) Battalion Northumberland Fusiliers.

At Licques we stayed three weeks and then moved to Abancourt, and after a fortnight we again moved to Haudricourt. In these places we worked at training malarial subjects, soldiers of various North-country Regiments which had come from the East.

We had more leisure these days than when in the line and, although diminished in numbers, we made good use of it. A theatrical troop was started and gave most excellent entertainments. Football was started and a good team got together. Officers' teams for lemon cutting and other equestrian exercises were formed, and altogether, though small in numbers, we were decidedly alive.

Armistice night found us at Haudricourt still training malarial troops, several drafts of whom we had despatched to 66th Division as reinforcements. That Division was operating on the Cambrai front and consequently were in the thick of the advance fighting. Hence the heavy call on us for reinforcements. The men went cheerfully, they all seemed to prefer fighting the Hun to sloping arms by numbers. A big draft, sent up on or about 1st November, soon became suitably dubbed the " Cease Fire Draft." There was one instance of a fellow returning to the camp within a fortnight of being sent up. He originally belonged to the East Yorks, and on posting as a reinforcement went to the 2nd Royal Munster Fusiliers.

A few days sufficed to bring on the malaria, and so again to hospital and from there back to the camp under our friends the 25th Northumberland Fusiliers.

Armistice night was celebrated in right high style. We had, of course, got news of the other armistices a few days ahead, so everyone was expectant. We carried on cheerfully, asking everyone who came along, " Any news ? " It was, however, left to Major P. C. Dodsworth, M.C., to announce the good news. In those days, as has been said before, we had our own concert party ; on this particular evening we had a " Go-as-you-please " concert going, and in the midst of it in came a runner to Major Dodsworth. He read the message to the troops from the stage and the applause was deafening. After that there was no lack of competitors for the sing-song. Discipline was relaxed for the time and everyone was out to enjoy himself. The camps there, which were laid on the inside sides of two hills, with a road up through the valley, soon became a blaze of light. Very lights went up, fireworks and huge bonfires with men parading with bugles, trumpets, drums, kettles, tins and everything else that could make a noise. There was not much sleep that night.

Next day was a Scale " A " Brigade Church Parade, and it was one of the best services of devotion and thanks one has ever had the pleasure of attending.

Soon after armistice we began losing our men, and no reinforcement arrived, till at last we had but two hundred left, and on 8th December, 1918, we attached them to another Cadre Infantry Training Station in the camp, and on the 10th proceeded to Havre. Here we started on demobilisation. First we lost our miners and then took on the work of demobilisation, and bit by bit our men gradually departed, leaving us with but a dozen of the old originals when we were disbanded in France on the 9th June and the Colours sent home to Newcastle the same date.

We had received our Colours on the 2nd May, 1919, the presentation of colours to eight Infantry Battalions of the 39th Division being made by Major-General Uniacke, C.B., C.M.G., commanding Lines of Communication Area. The 116th Infantry Brigade consisted of the following cadre Battalions :—

18th Battalion Northumberland Fusiliers (1st Tyneside Pioneers).
23rd Battalion Northumberland Fusiliers (4th Tyneside Scottish).
25th Battalion Northumberland Fusiliers (2nd Tyneside Irish).
14th Battalion Highland Light Infantry.

PRESENTATION OF COLOURS: 2ND MAY, 1919.
(18th Battalion's in foreground.)

Photo   *Newcastle Chronicle.*
THE COLOURS OF 18TH, 23RD, AND 25TH BATTALIONS
AT GUILDHALL, 12TH JUNE, 1919.

SPECIAL ORDER OF THE DAY

by

LIEUT.-COL. J. A. METHUEN, D.S.O.,

Commanding 18th (S.) Battalion Northumberland Fusiliers
(1st Tyneside Pioneers).

To the Officers, N.C.O.'s and Men of the
18th Northumberland Fusiliers.

As the Division is now being demobilised and I am returning to Rhodesia, I wish to thank you all for the splendid way you have worked and supported me all the time I have been with the Battalion.

I shall always look back with greatest pleasure to the happy time I spent with you all.

During my twenty-three years' experience in soldiering I must say I never came across a better lot of fellows.

Your Regiment has a splendid reputation which has been handed down to you by your forefathers. By your work and fighting you have kept up that glorious record with the greatest of success, and I am very proud to think I had the honour of serving with you.

When you go home do not get the feeling that you have finished your bit; there is a tremendous lot to do after the war in the way of Reconstruction. You must never try and forget the awful time you have gone through, because if you do you will lose sight of the ideal, the very purpose for which thousands of young lives were given that are not going home with you. We who have come through should live for those homes, which, taken together, spell Empire.

My very best wishes and good luck to you all.

J. A. METHUEN, Lieut.-Col.
Commanding 18th (S.) Btn. N.F.
(1st Tyneside Pioneers).

HAVRE,
26th May, 1919.

The last scene was enacted on the 12th June, 1919, when the Colour parties of the 18th, 23rd and 25th Northumberland Fusiliers were welcomed back to the town of their birth. Their welcome was enthusiastic and warm. The Lord Mayor,[1] the Sheriff and many others representing the Military Committee of the Chamber of Commerce, the Tyneside Scottish and Irish Committees, which had

---

[1] Mr. A. Munro Sutherland, our joint honorary treasurer.

raised the Battalions, besides crowds of friends, met them at the station and cheered them as they passed through the streets to the Exchange, where many speeches were made. Colonel Methuen, speaking on behalf of three parties, thanked the Lord Mayor for the cordiality of the reception, and asked him to accept an Iron Cross which had been taken from a German who had no further use for it. Captain Treanor, of the 25th Battalion, who had the proud distinction of being the only one present who had gone through the whole war with the Battalion, also spoke.

We were glad to hear from Colonel Methuen that the identity of the 18th, 23rd and 25th Battalions would be preserved in the Army, so that we trust this little chronicle is only a first chapter in a long and glorious record of the 18th Battalion Northumberland Fusiliers.

Farewell

And so our tale is told. I hope those of the old Battalion who read it will enjoy it as much as I have enjoyed getting the different accounts together.

It only remains for me to say farewell to you all, and to thank you for your loyal support and assistance. I came among you a complete stranger, only a poor southerner, but you took me to your hearts and were patient with my faults, and you never failed me. Officers, Non-Commissioned Officers and Privates, you all did your utmost to maintain the honour of the grand old Regiment to which we belonged and to add to its fame.

Farewell and the best of good luck to you. Your old Colonel will never forget you, the most faithful and cheery lot of comrades that ever a man had.

JOHN SHAKESPEAR, Lieut.-Col.,
18th Northumberland Fusiliers.

NORTHUMBERLAND FUSILIERS

16th (Service) Battalion (Newcastle)

In Command.
*Ritson, Lt.-Col. W. H., C.M.G., v.d. (Lt.-Col. ret. T.F.)   1 Sept. 14

Major.
(2nd in Command.)
Little, A. W. (temp.) (Lt. Unattd. List T.F.) (temp. Lt.-Col. 18 Feb. 16) 29 July 15
                      2 June 15

Majors.
*Archer, A.   29 July 15

Captains.
*Lindsay, D.   1 Apr. 15
*Graham, P. G.   20 Apr. 15
*Thompson, E.   27 Apr. 15
*Harvey, E.   29 July 15
*Young, A. C.   26 Aug. 15
*Dunglinson, V.   24 Oct. 15
*Worthington, R. H., Adjt.   8 Apr. 16

Lieutenants.
*Edwards, G. T.   1 Apr. 15
*Porter, C. W.   20 Apr. 15
*Lunn, W.   27 Apr. 15
*Irvin, D.   14 May 15
*Proctor, L. B.   2 June 15
*George, F. A.   2 June 15
*Leach, C. E.   1 Aug. 15
*Wake, T. H.   26 Aug. 15
*Falconer, R. W.   24 Oct. 15
*Southern, J.   24 Oct. 15

2nd Lieutenants.
*Brown, S.   4 Dec. 14
*Avery, W. E.   24 Mar. 15
*McLean, R.   24 Mar. 15
*Lucette, E. H.   3 Apr. 15
*Reed, R.   3 Apr. 15
*Watson, J.   18 Sept. 15
*Southern, G. S.   18 Sept. 15
*Park, A.   27 Sept. 15
*White, H. F.   23 Jan. 16
*Purchase, C. W.   23 Jan. 16
*Arnaud, F. C.   5 Mar. 16
*Harris, W.   5 Mar. 16
§*Klean, M. G.   28 Apr. 16

Adjutant.
Worthington, Capt. (temp.) R. H.   24 Oct. 15

Quarter-Master.
*Richardson, W. T., hon. lt.   1 Mar. 16

18th (Service) Battalion (1st Tyneside) (Pioneers)

Hon. Colonel.
Cowen, J.   5 Dec. 14

In Command.
Shakespear, Lt.-Col. J., C.I.E., D.S.O., ret. Ind. Army   22 Dec. 14

Major.
(2nd in Command.)
*Porch, C. P. (Capt. Res. of Off.)   9 Sept. 15

Majors.
*Stephenson, R.   1 Dec. 14

Captains.
*Reay, T.   22 Oct. 14
*Sweet, F.   1 Dec. 14
*Francis, C. J.   16 Feb. 15
*Fortune, G. S.   16 Feb. 15
*Wilson, F. G.   16 May 15
*Smith, N.   31 May 15
*Drury, P. B.   16 June 15
*Dodsworth, P. C.   16 June 15

Lieutenants.
*Smith, W., Adjt.   16 Feb. 15
*Wood, R.   1 Apr. 15
*McQuillen, W. T.   15 Apr. 15
*Vasey, J. W.   16 May 15
*Coombs, H. W.   16 May 15
*Hall, G. A. M.   16 June 15
*Robson, John E.   16 June 15
*Bean, H. H. W.   16 June 15
*Armstrong, H. J.   16 June 15
*Nixon, J. B.   16 June 15

2nd Lieutenants.
*Dodds, W. M.   15 Feb. 15
*Holbrook, W. S.   10 Mar. 15
*Parkinson, E. M.   22 Mar. 15
*Renton, A.   1 Apr. 15
*Caswell, G. F.   3 Apr. 15
*Cook, S. E.   3 Apr. 15
*Parry, G. H.   3 Apr. 15
*Fletcher, S.   3 Apr. 15
*Genner, L.   Apr. 15
*Makepeace, W.   25 Apr. 15
*Crichton, T. S.   7 May 16
*Flinders, G. F.   19 Aug. 15
*Reid, J. L.   28 Aug. 15
*Nicholson, J. A.   3 Sept. 15

Adjutant.
Smith, Lt. (temp.) W.   15 Apr. 16

Quarter-Master.
*Draper, A. R. O., hon. lt.   22 Nov. 15

19th (Service) Battalion (2nd Tyneside) (Pioneers)

In Command.
Daniell, Maj. (temp. Lt.-Col.) F. W., ret. Ind. Army   15 Apr. 15

Major.
(2nd in Command.)
*Renwick, G. A.   15 Apr. 15
                16 Feb. 15

Majors.
*Renwick, W. H.   15 June 15

Captains.
*Dawson, H. S.   20 Feb. 15
*Fawcus, W.   15 Mar. 15
*Storar, J.   15 Mar. 15
*Fawcett, J.   15 May 15
*McIlwaine, A. L., Adjt.   15 May 15
*Muir, A. W.   16 June 15
*Noyes, T. R. A. H.   16 June 15
*Todd, F. W.   17 Jan. 16
               16 June 15

Lieutenants.
*Hunter, G. D. L.   10 Apr. 15
*Tudor-Hart, W. O. T.   10 Apr. 15
*Anthony, M. S.   15 June 15
*Roberts, H. H.   16 June 15
*Jeffreys, A. H.   17 June 15
*Morton, W. H.   5 July 15
*Stabell, A.   1 Aug. 15
*Watson, H. R.   1 Aug. 15
*Marr, L. E.   2 Aug. 15

2nd Lieutenants.
*Blayney, B. W.   7 Dec. 14
*Carrick, A. D.   25 Dec. 14
                30 Dec. 14
*Middleton, R. W. S.   18 Jan. 15
*Davies, W. R.   3 Apr. 15
*Pretheroe, E. O.   3 Apr. 15
*Jones, A. P.   3 Apr. 15
*Mould, H. A. H.   3 Apr. 15
*Simon, G. N.   3 Apr. 15
*Cooke, C. H.   27 May 15
*Cheffins, O. H.   29 May 15
*Davies, J. R.   25 June 15
*Roberts, V. C.   20 Aug. 15
*Willis, J. I.   28 Aug. 15
*Lawrence, A. K.   28 Aug. 15
*Watts, C.   14 Sept. 15

Adjutant.
McIlwaine, Capt. (temp.) A. L.   15 May 15

Quarter-Master.
*Hill, G. H., hon. lt.   31 Mar. 16

---

* Temporary.   § On probation.

The permission of the Controller of His Majesty's Stationery Office has been obtained to reproduce the above extracts from the columns of the Army List of July, 1916.

34TH DIVISION:

INFANTRY BATTALIONS

JANUARY, 1916.

Commander: LIEUT.-GEN. INGOUVILLE WILLIAMS, C.B., D.S.O.

101ST INFANTRY BRIGADE.
Commander: BRIG.-GEN. H. G. FITTON, C.B., D.S.O., A.D.C.

15th Batt. Royal Scots. 10th Batt. Lincolns.
16th ,,   ,,   ,,   11th   ,,   Suffolks.

102ND INFANTRY BRIGADE (TYNESIDE SCOTTISH).
Commander: BRIG.-GEN. TREVOR P. B. TERNAN, C.M.G., D.S.O.

20th Batt. Northd. Fusiliers.   22nd Batt. Northd. Fusiliers.
21st ,,   ,,   ,,   23rd ,,   ,,   ,,

103RD INFANTRY BRIGADE (TYNESIDE IRISH).
Commander: BRIG.-GEN. N. J. CAMERON, C.M.G.

24th Batt. Northd. Fusiliers.   26th Batt. Northd. Fusiliers.
25th ,,   ,,   ,,   27th ,,   ,,   ,,

PIONEER BATTALION.
18th Northumberland Fusiliers.

MARCH, 1918.

Commander: MAJOR-GEN. C. L. NICHOLSON, C.B., C.M.G.

101ST INFANTRY BRIGADE.
Commander: BRIG.-GEN. R. C. GORE, C.B., C.M.G.

15th Batt. Royal Scots.   11th Batt. Suffolks.
16th ,,   ,,   ,,

102ND INFANTRY BRIGADE.
Commander: BRIG.-GEN. N. A. THOMSON, D.S.O.

22nd Batt. Northd. Fusiliers.   25th Batt. Northd. Fusiliers.
23rd ,,   ,,   ,,

103RD INFANTRY BRIGADE.
Commander: BRIG.-GEN. J. G. CHAPLIN, D.S.O.

9th Batt. Northd. Fusiliers.   1st Batt. East Lancs.
10th ,,   Lincolns.

PIONEER BATTALION.
18th Northumberland Fusiliers.

Personal Notes

EMBARKATION ROLL
18TH NORTHUMBERLAND FUSILIERS
7TH JANUARY, 1916

HEAD-QUARTERS

†Lieut.-Col. J. Shakespear, C.I.E., D.S.O.		C.M.G.
Major C. P. Porch, second-in-command		D.S.O. & Bar. Lieut.-Col. 23rd North. Fusiliers.
†Captain T. Reay, Adjutant		D.S.O. Major. 2nd Comd. 25th North. Fusiliers.
†Lieut. and Qr.-Mr. A. R. O. Draper		**Died of wounds.**
Lieut. W. Smith, M.G. Officer		Transferred to 4th T.C.
†Lieut. R. W. Shegog, R.A.M.C. (attached)		**Died of wounds.**

222	Sheperd, R.	Regt. Sergt.-Major	
815	*Willey, W.	Reg. Q.M.S.	
1377	*Kidd, M.	Orderly Room Sergeant	
47	*McFarlane, G. F.	,, Clerk	
109	Rainey, C. G.	H.Q. Sergeant	
662	**Edgar, A.**	**Sergeant Cook**	**Killed.**
176	†Armstrong, M.	Sergeant Shoemaker	
91	Routledge, B.	Pioneer Sergeant	
1928	*Young, A.	Staff-Sergt. A.O.C. (attached)	
143	Yates, G.	Band Sergeant	

TRANSPORT

925	*Nicholson, W. E.	Sergeant	To England for Commission.
843	*Arkless, H.		
956	†Aiston, A.		
1050	*Allan, H.		
420	*Bamburg, C.		To 14th Battalion.
936	*Bell, C.		To 14th Battalion.
571	Bewick, W.		
795	*Blake, G.		
592	Brewis, J.		
407	Carr, H.		
106	*Cowen, J.		To 19th Battalion.
60	*Cowings, G.		To 14th Battalion.
238	***Curry, R.**		**To 14th Battalion. Killed.**
565	*Donkin, J. E.		To 14th Battalion.
12	†Drinkald, G.		
912	Dunn, A. E.		

Those marked * were still with Battalion May 1918.
Those marked † were wounded.

Personal Notes

62	*Fletcher, J.	Lce.-Corpl.	With 1st Batt.	Wounded.
931	**Foster, L.**		**Killed.**	
524	Galloway, J.			
968	*Gaynor, J.		To 14th Battalion.	
763	Gowland, R.		To 19th Battalion.	
400	Hardy, A.		To 19th Battalion.	
236	*Heron, O.		To 14th Battalion.	
1026	*Hogg, J.		To 1st Battalion.	
971	*Holland, J. E.			
481	†Jefferson, T. E.			
1001	*Johnson, R.			
972	Kay, J.			
388	Kershaw, E.			
1174	††**Kyle, J.**		**Killed.**	
490	McLean, W.		Lieut. 4th N.F.	
61	*Marshall, W.			
121	Mordue, W. S.			
871	Muirs, G. E.			
164	*Noble, W.			
163	Roberts, T.			
120	Roberts, H.			
711	*Robson, R.			
897	†Reay, J.			
1015	*Reay, R. E.			
110	*Ridley, O.			
506	*Sanderson, G.	Lce.-Corpl.		
824	*Straughan, J.			
640	*Turnbull, R. H.		To 14th Battalion.	
239	*Wailes, S.	Sergeant.		
591	Wand, A. B.			

MACHINE-GUNNERS

186	†Charlton, W. R.	Sergeant	
112	Thompson, R.	Sergeant	Commission.
142	Bell, C.	Corporal	
1043	Elgey, M.	Lce.-Corpl.	
141	*Williams, J. H.	Lce.-Corpl.	Sergeant.
1042	*Barron, W. V.		
652	†Crellin, G.		
73	†Dawson, A.		
679	Hunter, C. W.		
118	Johnson, T.		
616	Kay, E.		
78	Nichol, W. J.		
131	Sanderson, R.		Also with 19th Battalion.
1009	†Small, E.		
929	**Smith, E.**		**Killed.**
178	†**Stephenson, J.**		**Killed.**
146	Watson, W.		
488	Willis, E.		Commission. [Corps.
581	**Yarrow, E.**		**Died of wounds with Tank**

Personal Notes

SIGNALLERS

No.	Name	Rank	Notes
948	Harley, W. S.	Sergeant	To England for Com. (cadet).
246	*†Young, A.	Corporal	
85	*Walton, S. W.	Lce.-Corpl.	Sergeant.
938	††Bell, W.		Instr. with 2nd West Yorks.
37	†Dickinson, A.		
814	Gray, A. D.		To 19th Battalion.
976	**Gray, J.**		Lieut., 2nd West Yorks Regt. Died of sickness.
789	*Hardy, G.		
589	*Horn, G.		Lance-Corporal.
932	**Jackson, W.**		**Awarded M.C. Lt. 3rd Batt., attached 15th D.L.I. Killed.**
434	*Knox, H.		
648	*Lee, S.		
570	*Moll, E.		
781	*Stephenson, W.N.		
602	Stonehouse, D.		Commission.
852	**Storey, T. W.**		**Killed.**
249	*†Tennant, J.		

"A" COMPANY

Major R. Stephenson, O.C. . . . . Lieut.-Col. 9th S. Staff. Regt., C.B.E., D.S.O.

*Captain P. C. Dodsworth, second in command . Major, awarded M.C.

| 101 | *Scorer, J. A. | Coy. Sergt.-Major | R.S.M., awarded M.C. |
| 601 | Spraggon, A. E. | Coy. Q.M.S. | Flight cadet, R.A.F. |

NO. 1 PLATOON

Lieut. H. Bean, Platoon Commander.

No.	Name	Rank	Notes
215	Forsyth, J.	Platoon Sgt.	Awarded D.C.M.
89	*Balmain, H.	,, Sgt.	A/C.S.M.
99	*Walker, J. N.	,, L/Sgt.	
1311	**†Agnew, J.**		**Died of wounds.**
1244	†Armstrong, J.		
1139	Arnison, F.		
167	†Askew, J.		
46	Bremmer, J. M.	Corporal	
1222	*Bell, G.		
1219	Brookes, T.		
44	*†Brown, O.		
1142	Bruce, C.		
130	*Cook, J. S.		Sergeant.
210	*Cowans, R.		
9	Craig, R.		
135	Craigie, B.		
179	*Dixon, J.		
81	**Dixon, W.**		**Killed.**
1131	Dixon, C.		
1220	†Elliott, A.		
1335	Emmerson, G.		

"A" COMPANY.

Personal Notes

110

111	Errington, R.		
136	Fairless, F.		
35	*Forster, G.		
128	France, W. P.		
1558	Goodwin, J.		
1280	Henderson, T.		
133	*Hind, J.		
1369	†**Hinton, J.**		**Killed.**
980	Hough, D.		
26	*†Matthews, P.		
122	Mason, T. R.		Also with 19th Battalion.
1119	**McGowan, J.**		**Died of wounds.**
96	Ormston, W.		To 9th S. Staffs. with Lieut.-Col. Stephenson.
560	Parkinson, P.		
104	Partis, T.	Lce.-Corpl.	
1028	**Pearson, P.**		**Died of wounds**: attached 7th Royal Fusiliers.
129	Porteous, J.		
108	†Potts, J. W.	Lce.-Corpl.	
43	**Quinn, J. E.**		**Accidentally killed**: Flight-Cadet, R.A.F.
28	*Relph, J.	Corporal	Sergeant Cook.
102	**Russell, E.**		**Killed : Lieut. 20th D.L.I.**
1291	*Rutherford, W.		
1344	†Simpson, W.		
207	†Smith, J.		
50	*Stewart, T. S.		
1287	*Storey, E.		Awarded M.M.
1088	*Storey, H.		
42	*Tindle, E.		
36	†Telford, J.		
34	**Thompson, J.**		**Killed.**
31	**Travis, W. H.**		**Killed.**
1229	**Wilson, H.**		**Killed.**

NO. 2 PLATOON

†Lieut. R. W. Wood, Platoon Commander.

145	Mawston, A.	Platoon Sgt.	
97	†Wood, R.	,, Sgt.	
117	Allan, G.		
216	†Arthur, W.	Corporal.	
95	†Ashworth, C.		
105	Askew, J.		
93	**Bailey, C.**	Corporal	**Died of wounds.**
119	Barrasford, G.		
1002	†Bell, G.		
86	Daley, J.		
87	*†Davies, R.		
998	**Dent, J.**		**Killed.**
94	†Dixon, G. W.		

Personal Notes

112

165	†Dixon, W. S.		
76	England, H.		
992	*Gillait, F.		
1375	*Grey, A. E.		
970	†Grey, W. J.		
851	†Hands, J.		
973	†Hedley, W.		Also with 19th Battalion
70	**Heron, J.**		Killed.
1048	Hindmarsh, J.		
1008	Hindmarsh, T.		
1255	*†**Hitcham, S. P.**		To 14th Batt. Died of wounds.
68	Lawson, T.		
1520	Lombard, E.		
84	McKay, J.		
132	McQueen, R.		
1108	*Moyes, R.		
155	Nelson, J. R.		
157	†Nicholls, J. H.	Lce.-Corpl.	
1084	Nobes, E. G.		
1061	O'Connor, R.		
144	*Parker, W.		
1029	†Parmley, J. H.		Sergeant.
1052	Percival, A.		
98	Quinn, G.		
16	Robson, S.		
1022	Rowell, P.		
88	†Russell, J. F.		
182	**Russell, R.**		Killed : with 12/13th Batt.
1018	**Rutherford, F.**	Lce.-Corpl.	Killed.
79	**Short, W.**		Killed.
137	†Stewart, T.		
1031	*Stobbs, D.		
1007	†**Tones, J.**		Killed.
67	Tweddle, W.		
1365	**Walton, W.**		Killed : with 4th K.O.Y.L.I.
977	Wardhaugh, T.		
66	**Weddell, W.**		Died of wounds.
168	†Wilson, T. J.		Died of wounds.

NO. 3 PLATOON

†Lieut. H. Coombs, Platoon Commander . Died of wounds.

271	**Hall, A.**	Platoon Sgt.	Killed.
233	Phillips, J.	„ L./Sgt.	D.C.M. Commission.
175	Barnes, L.		
191	†Beazley, R.		
302	†Brabhan, W.	Corporal	
156	**Brannan, J.**		Died of sickness.
174	*†Brewis, J. H.		
1073	†**Brown, J.**		Killed.
584	Brown, W. B.		
1158	**Carter, J. J.**		Killed : with 14th N.F.

Personal Notes

48	Clark, A.		
53	†Clark, B.		
77	*Clark, D.		Also with 19th Battalion.
195	*Clark, J.		To 4th K.O.Y.L.I.
205	†Clark, J.		
1262	De Leuw, R. H.		
993	*†Downey, E.		Also with 19th Battalion.
1353	Foreman, W.		
194	*Friend, J.	Corporal	
1211	*†Gavine, P.		
1475	*Gilhespy, S. K.		
1848	Gill, E.		
1154	†Hargreaves, J.		
150	*Henderson, L.		
858	†Heron, F.		
1212	Hird, J.		
209	*†Jeffrey, R.		
225	Knight, S.		
1141	Lawes, M. R.		
1151	*Liddle, G.		
265	Lock, J. S.		
1309	Lowe, S.		
201	Lowe, W.		
1590	Lowes, W.		
153	Marley, J.		
190	†Palmer, A.		Corporal.
184	*†Pearson, H. E.	Corporal	
231	*Pearson, J. F.		
1260	Purvis, W. P.		
177	Pyle, S.		
257	*Salkeld, M.		
144	Scott, H.		
204	Simpson, W.		
83	Smith, H. B.	Lce.-Corpl.	
107	*Stephenson, J.		
198	†Stephenson, J. H.		
151	**Stott, J. T.**		**Died of wounds.**
206	Temple, T. S.		
171	†Waddington, J.		
1216	Wall, F.		
229	Williams, T.		
213	†Winship, S.		
283	*Wood, J. T.		
254	†Wood, R. W.	Lce.-Corpl.	
180	*Wrightson, F. S.		

No. 4 PLATOON

2nd Lieut. E. Parkinson, Platoon Commander.

29	†Rowe, A.	Platoon Sgt.		Lieut., 53rd Battalion.
193	*Stott, J. W. D.	,,	Sgt.	Coy. Sergt.-Major.
335	*Arnold, J.			

Personal Notes

937	Ashton, J. W.	Lce.-Corpl.	Killed.
103	*Atkinson, W.		
267	†Avery, R.		Died of sickness.
240	*Baker, G. W.		
211	*Bowman, T.		
220	*Brass, A.		
1277	†Brown, S. P.		
323	Carey, F.		Commission.
224	*Carr, D. E.		
203	*†Carrot, J.	Corporal	
877	Chisholm, M.		
1178	†Churchill, W.		Sergeant D.C.M.
158	†Dunn, E.		
232	Dunn, J. B.		
1	*Dunn, N.		
13	Dunn, W.		
169	†Elliott, E.		
147	*Elliott, R.		Killed : with 4th K.O.Y.L.I.
1065	Fletcher, L.		Commission. M.C., M.M. 23rd Northumberland Fusiliers.
1078	†Gardiner, A.		
909	Gentles, W. S.		
154	†Green, P.		
245	Hewitt, I.		
217	Hogg, C. E.		
63	†Holmes, F. W.		
1080	*Hunter, N.		Lance-Corporal.
125	*Jobling, D.		Lance-Sergeant,
1012	*Johnson, I.		
1226	†Keir, O. L.		
1063	*Knox, H.		
36	†Leblique, L.		
234	*McDermott, G.		
1336	†McDougall, T.	Lce.-Corpl.	
212	Milburn, W.		Killed : with 10th Battalion.
21	Moore, C.		
557	†Moore, G.		
188	Moore, W. T.		
218	†Mortimer, G. H.		
227	Naylor, R.		
1183	Oxley, J.		Killed.
199	*Price, R. G.		
221	Richardson, H.		
1281	†Richardson, R.		
152	†Robinson, J.		
258	Robinson, R.		
1356	Robinson, R.		
166	Robson, J.		
253	Salkeld, R.		
10	Sanderson, W.		Commission.
708	Savory, W.		
208	*Shiel, A. C.		
259	Stoker, R.		

Personal Notes

118

5	*Strawbridge, W.	Lce.-Corpl.	
116	Swift, J.		
1200	†Tait, M. S.		
18	Thompson, R. B.	Corporal	Sergeant.
997	Thompson, R.		
252	*Tomlinson, J.		
228	Walsh, J. M. P.		
149	*Ward, W.		
19	†Watson, G. A.		2nd Lieut. 3rd Battalion: attd. R.A.F.
230	*Watson, S. T.		
251	**Watson, T.**		**Died of wounds.**

" B " COMPANY

Captain F. Sweet, in command . . Maj. 13th R. Welsh Fusiliers, awarded D.S.O.
Captain F. G. Wilson, second in command M.C.

534	†Ayre, W. H.	Coy. Sgt.-Major	
394	†Todd, F. D.	Coy. Q.M.S.	

No. 5 PLATOON

Lieut. W. T. McQuillen, Platoon Commander.

288	Farrage, C.	Platoon Sgt.	Lieut. Tank Corps.
235	††Ross, H.	,, ,,	England for Commission.
467	Armstrong, T.		
306	†**Atkinson, H.**		**Died from wounds.**
1206	**Baker, W.**		**Killed.**
276	Bramble, H.		
319	**Briggs, E.**		**Killed.**
618	*†Brydon, N. A.		
1278	Burnell, J.		
314	*†Burns, W.		
298	†Charlton, J.		
243	†Clarke, R. J.		
1403	†Clennan, J. R.		
1556	†**Clennan, W.**		**Died of wounds.**
248	*Cummins, N.		
80	*†Curry, F. B.		
294	*†Davidson, J.		
311	†Dracup, R. H.		
1275	Douglas, W.		
287	**Elliott, J.**		**Killed.**
1378	Ensell, E.		
51	**Fenn, R. W.**		**Killed.**
273	Finnigan, W.		

Personal Notes

303	Gibson, A.	Corporal	Commission.
290	*Graham, W. T.		
1300	**Graham, J.**		**Killed.**
244	†Gregan, C.		
274	**Gustard, T.**		**Killed.**
301	†Hutchinson, W.		
1241	†Johnson, D.		
197	†Johnson, J. J.		
295	†Kirsop, A.		Transferred to R.A.M.C.
296	**Maltby, T.**		**Died from wounds.**
277	†Mason, N.		
447	Matthew, E. G.	Corpl.	
279	†**Mortimer, A.**		**Killed.**
264	†Newton, R.		
1113	†Nichol, J.		
308	††Ostle, R.	Lce.-Corpl.	
315	Quickmire, J.		Lce.-Corpl.
285	*†Robinson, J.		To 4th K.O.Y.L.I.
1628	Ryder, G.		
281	Saxby, F.		
317	Scott, A.		
1167	††Scott, A.		
269	*†Scott, B.		
1087	*Shanks, J.		
280	Sheader, R. A.		
284	†Sheader, H. J.		
266	†Simm, E.		
1199	**Short, J.**		**Killed.**
1182	Shotton, J.		
278	**Stephenson, P.**		**Killed.**
260	Storey, A. B.		Transferred to R.E. Father
1380	†Storey, E. G.		,, 18th Lab. Co. & son
286	*Sutherland, J.		Pioneer Sergt.
305	***Vasey, J. R.**		**Killed**: with 1st Royal Fuslrs.
291	**Walton, I. G.**		**Died of sickness**: att. R.A.F.
292	†Walton, J.		
312	*†Warren, A.		
263	†Watson, W.	Lce.-Corpl.	
1201	†Wells, D.		
247	††Welsh, R.		
324	†Wright, G. T.		
1202	Wright, J.		

No. 6 PLATOON

*Lieut. J. B. Nixon, Platoon Commander   .   Captain and Adjutant, M.C.

262	**Harris, W.**	Platoon Sgt.	Commission. **Killed.**
440	††Parkin, J.	,, ,,	
342	Anderson, W.		Lce.-Corpl.

Personal Notes

289	Ash, C.	Corporal	Killed.
363	Bates, J.		
365	Barker, T. P.		Died of wounds.
318	†Best, W. S.		
391	†Blanch, W. L.		
332	Blythman, W.		Died from wounds.
1343	Brittain, C.		Commission.
1298	†Brown, J. R.		
368	Carr, G.		
349	Chapman, W. A.		
339	*Coxon, W.		
183	†Cutting, J.	Corporal	
331	†Day, J.		Killed.
354	*Devlin, D.		Also with 19th Batt.
403	*Dixon, M. B.		Died of wounds: with 1st Batt.
1314	Elliott, R. A.		Killed.
388	†Emerson, J. W.		
1341	*Emmerson, J.		
1299	†Farrar, W.		
393	Finlay, W.		
1312	†Forrest, J.		
409	Freeman, G. E.		Died of sickness.
377	*Greenhall, W.		Corporal.
334	*†Greenwell, T.		Lance-Corporal.
340	†Greenwell, W.		
322	††Hall, R.		Died of wounds: with 14th Batt.
1605	Hamilton, D. M.		Killed.
320	Hutchinson, R. W.	Lce.-Corpl.	
1464	Imeson, J. B.		
1137	*Lee, E.		
350	*†Lewis, T.		Lance-Corporal.
346	*Lister, J.	Corporal	Sergeant.
326	†Longstaff, G.		
1317	†Marshall, J. W.		
189	*Mitchell, A.		
357	*Monaghan, P.		
1177	*Murphy, J.		
367	Newman, S.		Awarded M.M.
341	†Nicholson, R.		
1271	*Patterson, J.		
344	*†Pearson, J.		Sergeant.
371	*Powell, R. D.		
1296	†Ridley, J.		
1534	*Robinson, H.		
1145	†Robson, E.		
684	†Robson, S.		
330	†Smith, T. B.	Lce.-Sergt.	Area Employment Co.
1322	*†Smith, W.		Served with 12/13th N. F.
404	Waldie, H.	Lce.-Corpl.	
389	†Walker, J.		
384	*Walker, W.		Corporal Cook.
1329	Wardle, H.		

Personal Notes

364	†White, J. R.		
345	**Winwood, J. N**		**Killed.**
369	†Wonnocott, W. G.		

No. 7 PLATOON

2nd Lieut. Caswell, G. E., Platoon Commander . Captain, M.C.

329	†Charlton, N.	Platoon Sgt.	
299	Phipps, A.	,,	Commission.
471	*Adamson, P.		Awarded M.M. with 14th N.F.
464	*Alderson, A.		7th Royal Fusiliers.
1372	*Arrowsmith, G.		
1109	**Beck, D.**		**Died of wounds.**
555	†Bell, A. W.	Corporal	Sergeant, awarded D.M. Belge.
373	Brown, J.		
355	Brown, J.		
1307	**Coulson, A. E.**		**Died of sickness.**
398	*†Cubin, R.		
1607	Dodds, F. C.		
441	†Dunn, D.		
358	*Foster, T.		
462	†French, J.		To 19th Battalion.
472	†Gair, E.		To 19th Battalion.
429	Gair, W.		
316	*Goodfellow, G.		Corporal.
1135	Guthrie, G.		
455	†Haddon, H.		
473	*Hall, G.		
361	*Harmison, W.		Corporal.
432	†Hogg, J.		
459	†Holmes, T.		
1160	††Hooker, B.		
1282	Hooker, R.		
448	**Imeson, E.**		**Killed.**
1470	*Irving, W.		To 14th Battalion.
419	Jacques, S.		
386	†Johnson, R. J.		
452	*Lowry, J.		To 14th Battalion.
442	†Luke, T.	Corporal	
360	†McKay, E.		
1486	†Mooney, J.		
1321	More, J.		
1339	Mounsey, J.		
486	Petrie, J.		
487	**Potts, W.**	Lce.-Corpl.	**Killed.**
461	Proudlock, T.		
1242	Read, J.		
382	*Reay, J.	Lce.-Corpl.	
370	*Richardson, P.		

Personal Notes

359	†Robson, M.		
709	Robson, R.		
1239	†Robson, R.		Also with 19th Battalion.
444	Rogers, W.		
476	†**Roper, J. H.**		**Killed.**
427	**Ross, H.**		**Killed.**
1121	†Smith, C. M.		[wounds.
1323	*†**Smith, J. W.**		To 12/14th Battalion. **Died of**
351	†Smith, R.		
1444	†Snowdon, A.		
468	*†Stephenson, J. G.	Lce.-Corpl.	To 19th Battalion.
1597	Stokor, T. D.		
380	Storey, A. G.		
1136	†**Stoves, J.**		**Died from wounds.**
458	**Sutherland, J.**		**Killed.**
411	†Telford, F.		
1163	†Thompson, R.		
352	†**Wood, E.**	Lce.-Corpl.	**Killed.**

No. 8 PLATOON

†2nd Lieut. S. E. Cook, Platoon Commander.

511	Harris, T. W.	Platoon Sgt.	Commission.
139	Tomlinson, F.	,,	Awarded M.M.
533	Adams, G.		
548	Aikman, D. W.		Awarded M.M.
425	†Arnison, S.		
1187	†Bailey, N.		
1263	Baillie, D. T.		
415	†Baker, A.		
513	Banham, T.		
536	Barnes, W.		
338	*Boag, J.		Promoted Sergeant.
547	Bowman, E.		
451	*Clarke, G. A		
470	†Dawson, J.		
1198	*†Deighton, D		
423	**Dixon, F. A.**		**Killed.**
414	†Drady, D. R.		
512	*†Falcus, J.		
282	†Farrell, E.		
523	†Ferguson, W.		
499	†**Garrity, J.**		**Killed.**
1279	Gibbon, G.		
510	Harper, S.		
325	*†Healey, J.		
501	Henderson, G.		
519	†Hodgin, J.		

Personal Notes

1176	Howe, T.		
412	Hughes, J.		
475	†Longville, J. B.		
516	*†Lyon, W. M.	Lce.-Corpl.	Corporal.
480	McLaurin, A.		
431	Noble, J.	Lce.-Corpl.	
446	O'Neil, A.		
428	*Richardson, W.		
528	Robson, C.	Lce.-Corpl.	
1097	†Robson, P.		
515	†Robson, R.		
322	Ruth, T.		Corporal.
550	Skeock, A.		
478	*Smith, A.	Corporal	
502	†Smith, J. R.		
521	Sutherland, R.		
1034	†Taylor, J.		
514	†Thompson, T. A.		
590	†Tully, S.		
433	†Varty, A.		
469	*Ward, W.		Awarded M.M.
1294	Wann, A. G.		
553	*†Watson, R.		
527	Watson, W.		
1264	Weir, H. W.		[Diary Writer.)
1288	*†**Wilson, I.**		**Killed :** att. 9th R.F. (The
375	*Witherley, J.		
435	†Wood, J.		
437	Wood, J.		
556	†Wood, W.		

"C" COMPANY

*Captain C. J. Francis, Company Commander . Major. M.C.
Captain N. Smith, second in command . . Transferred at own request to R.E.

348	Surtees, W. M.	Coy. Sergt.-Major	Commission.
678	Peacock, J. C. M.	Coy. Q.M.S.	Commission. Missing.

No. 9 PLATOON

Lieut. H. J. Armstrong, Platoon Commander . Capt., Naval Acont.

564	**Coulson, A.**	Platoon Sgt.	Lieut. 5th N.F., **M.M. Died in Germany.**
641	**Hodgkinson, J.**	Platoon Sgt.	2nd Lieut. with Batt. **Killed.**
677	†Tallant, J. W.	,, L./Sgt.	C.S.M.
1104	*Barkhouse, R. C.		
1240	†Barwick, H.		
1462	**Batie, J.**		**Killed.**
503	**Beadling, J.**		**Killed.**
624	†Brewis, J. G.		
603	Brown, J.		

Personal Notes

587	Brown, W.		
1387	**Brunton, J.**		**Killed.**
500	Carr, G. B.		
579	Chapelow, I.		
492	*Collings, W.		
1274	Coxon, E.	Lce.-Corpl.	
612	†Cummings, F.		
593	Dean, C.		
1077	*Dixon, R.		
694	*Elliott, J.		
422	*Emmerson, A. G.		
496	†Featherstone, J.		
625	Hall, J.		
1234	†Hudson, T.		
647	Hughson, S.		
520	Jackson, T.	Lce.-Corpl.	
783	*†Lambert, J.	Lce.-Corpl.	
1400	**Lamberton, J.**		**Killed.**
621	**Liddell, J. T.**		**Killed.**
1153	*Logan, J.		
577	†Lough, J.		
566	Lyall, G.		
1221	*†Martin, J.		
657	Milne, A.		
582	†Parker, J. T.		
586	Price, W.		
1195	Pybus, C.		
544	Railston, W.		
658	Richardson, E.		
1318	*††Richardson, H.W.		Also with 19th Battalion.
1115	Ridley, J.		
772	†Robinson, A.		
1415	Robson, R.		
642	*Smith, J. H.		
1522	†Snaith, R.		
599	Stephenson, J. W.		
610	Sutherland, D.		
1107	†Thompson, M. W.		
518	*Thompson, T. A.		
1500	Thompson, T.		
1105	Tozer, T.		
489	*Turnbull, R. H.		Also with 17th Batt.
509	Walker, J.		
1122	Watts, C.		
1411	*Weir, G. T.		
525	Woodhead, C. M.		
609	†Young, J.		

No. 10 PLATOON

Lieut. G. A. M. Hall, Platoon Commander, 17th Corps School.

701	*Fairnington, P.	Sergeant	
606	**McInnes, R.D.**	**Sergeant**	2nd Lieut., Lancs. Fus. **Killed.**

Personal Notes

915	Abbott, F.		
1531	Akers, J.		
1223	Arkley, J. E.		
1228	†Batey, W.		
1459	*Bean, G. W.		
633	††Beaumont, R.		
628	†Beckworth, E.		
632	Begg, L.		
1190	**Brown, G.**		Died of sickness.
623	*Cowans, A.		
696	*Davidson, R. B.		Corpl.
1503	†Dodd, E.		
666	†Dwyer, J.		
629	Dunn, R.		
667	*Ekin, J.		Died of wounds: with 14th N.F.
1171	†Fairbairn, T.		Died of wounds.
691	Fawcett, B.		
1165	†Forster, G. H.		
1127	*Georgeson, H.		Lce.-Corporal.
1347	Gibson, A.		Also with 4th K.O.Y.L.I.
600	†Good, R.		
561	*Hardy, J.		
646	**Havelock, J. A.**		M.M. Corpl. Killed in action.
1270	†Horan, I.		
563	*Jameson, J.		With 7th Royal Fus. Killed.
660	†King, D.		
722	**Lancaster, W.**		Killed: attached 13th Batt.
655	Mason, T. R.		
493	*McCallum, J. H.		C.Q.M.S.
775	McCutcheon, T.	Corporal	
1478	†McLaren, H.		
1249	***Mercer, J.**		**Killed: with 4th K.O.Y.L.I.**
710	*Nicholson, A.		To 14th Battalion.
703	*†Plantin, R.		
631	†Purvis, J.		
665	*Reay, W.		
1258	Roy, J. T.		
567	*Robinson, J.		
494	Robinson, R. V.		
1162	*Shannon, D.		To 14th Battalion.
1247	*Shannon, T.		To 14th Battalion.
637	Smith, H.		
615	*Steele, J. T.		Corporal with Battalion.
1155	Tilney, F.		
670	Turnbull, S.	Corporal	Commission.
1161	*Waite, J.		
650	†Wallace, B.		
697	**Watson, M. L.**	Lce.-Corpl.	**Killed in action.**
668	*Welch, R.		Corporal.
1413	Wilson, I.		

Personal Notes

No. 11 PLATOON

†2nd Lieut. W. S. Holbrook, Platoon Commander. Capt. M.C. and Bar.

638	Roy, E. G.	Platoon Sgt	Commission.
517	Thompson, S. R.	,, ,,	Commission.
645	†Adams, J. N.		
1315	Allsopp, N.		
685	†Armstrong, R.		
1342	†Atkinson, A.		
718	Bell, J. C.		
1473	*Boaden, E.		
636	Bonner, H. V.	Lce.-Corpl.	M.M. Lieut. 16th Battalion.
1313	*Bould, T. N.		
1355	Brady, M.		
1346	*†Brown, A.		
700	†Burlinson, J.		
64	**Cheesman, W. D.**	Corporal	**Sergeant. Killed in action.**
686	*†Clough, J. R.		
720	*Davidson, W.		
1421	Davison, T. R.		Prisoner of war.
1383	†Dow, J.		
1492	Edgar, T. W.		
653	†Forrest, T.		
375	Garthorne, J. G.		
715	*†Georgeson, J.		
619	*Gleghorn, J. A.		
1069	Gray, J.		
774	**Hall, J.**	Lce.-Corpl.	**Died of wounds.**
1310	Handcock, T.		
699	†Heads, T. C.		
1310	†Heslop, R.		
1316	†Hindmarsh, J.		
717	*Holmes, G.		
681	**Home, W.**		**Killed: with 13th W. Riding R.**
576	*†Jones, H.		
1133	Lamming, W.		
395	**Leach, J. G.**		**Lce.-Sergt. Killed in action.**
1567	†**Lowes, G.**		**Died of wounds.**
1351	†**Lumsden, J.**		**With 2nd West Yorks. Killed.**
546	March, W.		
682	Martin, C.		Prisoner of war.
620	*Mather, J.		
1545	†McCaulay, T.		
1424	McManus, J.		
328	*Minto, G.	Corporal	Sergeant with Battalion.
405	Nisbett, G. C.		
418	*†Pinckney, T.		
669	†Reed, E.		
562	Renwick, G.	Lce.-Corpl.	
1225	†Richardson, E.		
644	Ridd, R.		
1543	**Riddle, W.**		**Killed.**
1207	†Riddle, W. H.		

Personal Notes

136

596	*†Robertson, J.		
1203	Roche, R.		
505	†Rogerson, R. D.		
688	†Simms, D.		
507	†Spencer, R.		
763	Storey, R.		
597	†Thirlwall, T.		
397	*Turnbull, S. R.		
574	Waddell, J.		
661	Welch, J.		Corporal
551	Yeeles, W.		
680	Yendell, J. H.		

No. 12 PLATOON

*†Lieut. J. W. Vasey, Platoon Commander . Captain. M.C.

580	†Rees, W. H.	Platoon-Sgt.	
762	**Sibbit, G. B.**	,, ,,	**Killed. Lieut. 1st Battalion.**
651	**Cowell, T. H.**	,, Lc.-Sgt.	**Died of sickness.**
763	Gowland, R.		
1054	**Blackshaw, H.**		**Killed in action.**
761	Brogan, J.		
758	*Burn, D. H.		
726	*Carr, J.		
740	†Carter, H.		
736	*Cockerton, W. G.		
771	†Corbitt, R.		
729	Craig, F.		Awarded M.M.
760	Davison, J.		
750	*Devlin, J.		
1245	Donkin, D.	Lce.-Corpl.	
1360	†Dowson, R.A.		
748	**Dufour, G.**		**Killed in action.**
741	**Duggin, C. H.**		**Killed in action.**
743	Farbridge, A.		
787	†Farrell, M.	Corporal	Awarded M.M.
779	†Fisher, F.		
735	**French, W.**		**Killed in action.**
792	**Greenwell, A.**		**Died of wounds.**
1257	†Green, J.		
1350	Hall, N.		
1357	Hill, R.		
751	*Hindmarsh, R.		**Killed: with 7th Royal Fusiliers.**
737	*Hope, E.		To 4th K.O.Y.L.1.
745	Hunter, J.		
769	†Hunton, J.		
572	*Johnson, T.		To 19th Battalion.
744	**†Johnstone, T.**		**Killed in action**
777	*†Jones, E.		Awarded M.M.
722	†Law, A.		
617	†Lillicoe, A.		
773	†Lillicoe, J. H.		
759	Lishman, J.		

Personal Notes

757	†McGuire, G.		
635	**Malone, T.**		Died of wounds.
791	**Malone, J.**		Killed in action.
733	**Margetson, F. A.**		Died of sickness.
627	Miller, R.		
689	†**Mole, A.**		Died of wounds.
1354	Palmer, J.		
770	*Parker, G. P.		
719	Pearcy, G. W.		
731	Pritchard, T.	Lce.-Corpl.	
784	†Reed, R.		Also with 14th N.F.
753	Reed, W.		
1058	Scott, F. H.		
654	Scott, T.		
1335	Scott, W. J.	Lce.-Corpl.	
674	*Snowdon, G.		
793	**Snowdon, R.**		Killed in action.
749	*Stewart, J.		
767	**Taylor, R.**		Killed in action.
776	Wake, R.	Corporal	
766	*Wright, O.	Lce.-Corpl.	Corporal.

"D" COMPANY

Captain G. S. Fortune, Company Commander
Captain P. B. Drury, second in command . Died in England.

25	Davison, A. S.	Coy. Sergt.-Major	Commission.
831	Hawson, W. B.	Coy. Q.M.S.	

NO. 13 PLATOON

2nd Lieut. A. Renton, Platoon Commander.

920	Cowan, J.	Platoon Sgt.	
878	Simm, D.	,, Sgt.	C. de G. (Belgian).
839	†**Atkinson, R.**		Died of wounds.
796	**Barnes, J.**		Killed.
808	**Barringer, C. A.**		Died of wounds: with K.O.Y.L.I.
1244	*Bell, A.		To 14th Battalion.
1091	Bone, R. A.		
1266	Bonney, J. L.		Also with 19th Battalion.
727	Callaghan, A.		
752	Callaghan, T.		
1017	**Charlton, T.**		Killed.
768	Clarkson, J. H.		
886	**Cowell, J. T.**		Corporal. Killed in action.
860	Crankshaw, R. T.		
807	*†Devere, E.		
1076	*Douglass, J.		
829	†Everson, R. L.		
827	†Frampton, J. S.		

140

1130	*Gibson, S.		
785	Green, E.		
816	†**Haley, F.**		Died of wounds.
1595	*Hall, H.		
712	**Hammell, G.**		Killed.
1577	*Harris, E.		
819	Hutchinson, S.	Corporal	
853	Innes, J.		
1301	†Irving, J.		
1483	**Jeffrey, J.**		Killed.
822	†Johnson, J. W.		
817	†Jopling, G.		
1246	Lewis, R.		
1521	†Liddle, W.		
813	Lincoln, C.		
811	*Lobley, A.		
849	***Lowry, W.**		Killed : with K.O.Y.L.I.
1398	†McElwane, E.		
27	Patterson, T.		Also with 19th Battalion.
800	†Phillipson, T. H.		
1330	**Proudfoot, A. S.**		Died of wounds.
825	*Proudlock, R.		
1128	Pyle, J.		
780	†Quickmire, A.		
847	†Robinson, J.		
1011	Ross, W.		
844	Rycroft, J.		Also with 19th Battalion.
845	†Shipley, A.		
952	**Stoves, A.**		Died of wounds.
742	Sunter, S.		
1243	†Taylor, J. F.		
1157	Temperley, G.		
1129	Temperley, J. W.		
826	†Toole, E.		
765	Tynemouth, W.		
1126	Voyzey, G.		
820	†Wallace, R. W.	Lce.-Corpl.	
859	Wannop, W. D.	Lce.-Corpl.	Pioneer Sergeant.
846	†Watson, J.		
895	Watts, C.		
815	*†Willey, C.	Lce.-Corpl.	R.Q.M.S.
1402	Young, J.		

No. 14 PLATOON

†**2nd Lieut. W. M. Dodds, Platoon Commander . Died in Germany.**

855	Armstrong, A.	Platoon Sgt.	M.M., M.C. Lieut. 19th
690	Green, R. B.	,, Sgt.	[Battalion.
889	Asprey, V.		
803	Bateman, J. F.		
958	Batie, J.		
960	***Blakey, E.**		Killed : with 4th K.O.Y.L.I.
916	Cairns, F.		

Personal Notes

1049	*Chisholm, G. A.		C.Q.M.S.
882	Connell, J.		
1027	†Cowey, T.		
891	*Cunningham, W.		Corporal.
1237	**Dick, J.**		**Killed.**
1025	Dickinson, J.		With 7th Royal Fus. Killed.
965	Dolman, E.		
921	Elliott, A.		
857	Franklin, T.		
854	*Garbutt, R.	Lce.-Corpl.	
914	†Grainger, W. T. A.	Lce.-Corpl.	
905	†Hardwick, E.		
875	Harrison, E. W.		
930	Harrup, J.	Lce.-Corpl.	
1067	Harvey, W.		
804	*Hey, L.		Lance-Sergeant.
906	Hiftle, J.		
873	Hindmarsh, J.		
1014	*Jackson, J. W.		
1081	†Lowry, A.		
1056	McCourt, T. L.		
869	†McDougall, R.		
949	†Pargeter, T.		
1116	Proud, J.		
1117	*Proud, Jos.		
1248	Purvis, J.		Missing.
1289	Purvis, G. S.		
1096	Robinson, R.		
950	†Robson, R.		
940	*Rowell, E.		
1408	Stobes, J.		
961	*Telford, N.		
790	**Thompson, J. B.**		**Killed.**
962	*Totton, P.		
1306	**Urwin, F.**		**Killed.**
834	†Walton, J.	Lce.-Corpl.	
928	Watson, S.		Also with 19th Battalion.
939	Wilkie, W. S.		
934	Woodhouse, J. W.		
867	Wright, J. R.		
1396	Wright, J.		

No. 15 PLATOON

††2nd Lieut. G. H. Parry, Platoon Commander . Captain.

202	†Hill, A.	Platoon Sgt.	
538	Philipson, N.	,, Sgt.	
1045	Barry, D.	Sergeant	
866	*†Bell, E. D.		Corporal.
943	†**Blakey, C.**		**Killed.**
1053	*Charlton, W.	Corporal	Sergeant.

Personal Notes

887	**Clark, G. W. W.**		**Killed.**
1005	Clark, G.		
907	Cook, P. S.		
967	Cooper, R.		
901	Davison, J.		
1004	†Dixon, J.		
919	*Dixon, J.		To 1st Battalion.
917	†Dorman, R.		
1138	Errington, P.		
1325	†French, A.		
1057	**Glen, J. A.**		**Died of wounds.**
953	Goodman, R.		
904	†Gray, J.		
876	Green, R.		
910	*Guy, R.		
925	Hare, J. M.		
543	Hobson, A.		
1236	*†Hodge, J.		
881	†Hodgson, J.		
1386	Hodgson, R.		
855	Howarth, A.		
964	Howarth, R.		
863	Hunter, A.		
1147	*†Johnson, S.		
799	Johnson, W.		
951	*Kirtley, A.		
594	†Lancaster, J.		
935	†Lowes, C.		
1064	Marr, R. S.		
1218	**Meggison, J.**		**Died of wounds.**
893	**†Morpeth, A.**		**Died of wounds.**
1102	†Murray, A.		
1095	Musgrove, J. W.		
541	*O'Neill, S.		
908	†Prim, R.		To 19th Battalion.
539	*Prower, F.		
549	Prower, W. A.		
879	†Ridley, C.		
883	*Ritson, J.		
1047	**Robson P. J.**		**Killed.**
540	†Roughton, L.		
933	Scott, J. H.	Lce.-Corpl.	
965	†Shepherdson, S.		
874	Symonds, W.		
1089	**Taylor, T.**		**Killed.**
1148	†Ullathorne, G.		
894	Walton, F.		
1238	†Whiteside, J. T.		
1608	**†Wiffen, G.**		**Killed : Attached 10th N.F.**
911	Wilkinson, R. D.		
972	Wood, C. C.		

Personal Notes

No. 16 PLATOON

*††Lieut. J. E. Robson, Platoon Commander . Captain.

755	Dellow, R.	Platoon Sgt.	2nd Lieut. 19th N.F. Died in Hospital.
902	Fisher, N.	,, Sgt.	Commission.
1185	†Adams, L.		
990	Alexander, J.		
1227	Allsopp, J.		Lance-Corporal.
1495	†Anderson, J.		With 14th Batt.
1111	Armstrong, E.		
1260	†Armstrong, H.		
983	*Baillie, G. G.	Lce.-Sergt.	C.S.M., awarded M.S.M.
1013	Baptist, J.		
1440	Barras, J.		
1114	*†Baxter, T.		
832	†Brown, J. R.		
1196	Carlisle, J.		
1624	Cherry, W.		
1105	Collinson, J.		
1010	Cooper, T. G.		
1259	†**Clydesdale, W.**		Died of wounds.
898	†**Coulthard, E.**		Died of wounds.
1037	†**Croudace, J.**		Killed : attach. 12/13th N.F.
1472	†**Douglas, J.**		Died of wounds.
1570	*Fox, T.		
1619	**Harbit, J. W.**		**Killed.**
542	Hedley, J. W.	Corporal	
1327	†Heslop, G.		
1000	Hill, W. A.		
1003	†Hornsby, J.		
1205	Hughan, H.		
862	Johnson, A. G.		
1250	*Johnson, J. S.		
1205	Keeghan, H.		
1306	*Lee, J. H.		
987	†**Mafhan, J.**		**Killed in action.**
1052	McParlin, W.		
818	Milne, F. B.		
985	*†Mitchell, G.		
903	Nicholson, S. R.		
1046	Nisbet, J.		
984	†**Reed, C. E.**		**Died of wounds.**
1030	Reed, J. S.		
1569	†Richardson, D.		
880	*Richardson, N.		
1320	Robertson, J.		
1060	†Robinson, W. A.		
981	†Robson, J.		
1064	†Robson, J. W.		
944	Robson, C. J.		
999	*Rowbotham, E.		Lance-Corporal.

Personal Notes

1252	††Rowntree, M.		
995	†Scorer, T. L.		
802	Smith, T. H.		
996	*Steel, G.	Lce.-Corpl.	
1118	Thompson, F.		
1044	Thompson, G. R.		
692	Totton, W.		
1265	**Wake, H.**		Killed.
1019	†Walpole, B.		
869	Ward, J.		
1168	Ward, J. R.		
1016	*Wilde, H.		To 12/13th Battalion
1021	†Wilde, T. H.		
1038	Wilson, G. T.		
801	†Wood, J. F.		

Those marked * were still with the Battalion in May, 1918.
Those marked with † were wounded.
All regimental numbers are 18/—.

CASUALTIES, 1916–1918

	Officers	Men
Killed	3	89
Died from wounds	7	52
Died from sickness		4
Missing	1	24
Wounded	27	632
	38	801

This total of 839 is for casualties while serving with the Battalion; the roll on page 170 shows that out of those who had sometime served with the Battalion, at least 27 officers and 221 other ranks laid down their lives.

Personal Notes

A LIST OF OFFICERS WHO SERVED IN THE BATTALION BETWEEN JANUARY AND APRIL, 1918

Lieut.-Col.	J. Shakespear, C.M.G., C.I.E., D.S.O.	Wounded.
Major	P. Bell	
,,	C. J. Francis, M.C.	
,,	P. C. Dodsworth, M.C.	
Captain	J. W. Vasey, M.C.	Wounded
,,	J. B. Nixon, M.C. (Adjutant)	
,,	W. S. Holbrook, M.C. (Bar)	Gassed.
,,	G. H. Parry	Wounded.
,,	J. S. Clements	Wounded.
,,	G. E. Caswell, M.C.	Wounded.
,,	A. Renton	
Lieut.	J. E. Robson	Gassed.
,,	F. R. G. Webb, M.C.	Wounded.
,,	C. A. Murray	
,,	F. L. Crawford	
,,	**T. E. Keenlyside**	**Killed.**
,,	J. M. Johnson	
,,	**N. Futers**	**Afterwards killed with 1st Battalion.**
,,	**G. R. Brown**	**Killed.**
,,	**O. Smurthwaite**	**Killed.**
,,	**A. R. O. Draper (Quartermaster)**	**Killed.**
2nd Lieut.	R. H. Van Hee	
,,	W. H. Pringle	Wounded.
,,	J. P. Hillhouse	Gassed.
,,	**J. Hodgkinson**	**Killed.**
,,	W. Mole	Gassed.
,,	J. T. Petty	Gassed.
,,	**E. Veitch**	**Afterwards killed with another Batt.**
,,	J. S. Wilson	Wounded.
,,	M. H. Wilson	
,,	A. Rowe	Wounded.
,,	C. E. Thorne	
,,	E. Turnbull	Prisoner.
,,	J. D. Corbitt	Wounded.
,,	**C. H. T. Collins**	**Killed.**
,,	E. Dance	
,,	W. Meadows	Wounded.
,,	J. Jackson	Gassed.

Personal Notes

2nd Lieut.	T. O. Harding	Gassed.
,,	**F. P. McCormick**	Wounded, afterwards killed with 9th Batt.
,,	B. R. Gribbon	
,,	H. Spiller	
,,	F. W. Rutter	Gassed.
,,	W. Rough	
,,	R. W. Silk	
,,	J. J. Ambler	
,,	C. Logan	
,,	**C. Robson**	Died of wounds.
,,	E. Stephenson	
,,	G. Morton	Gassed.
,,	W. J. Mills	
,,	G. R. Schooling	
,,	J. Wright	Gassed.

ATTACHED

Captain	J. Graham, R.A.M.C.	
,,	The Rev. L. Pigott, C.F.	

The following also served with the Battalion :—

Lieut.-Col. E. L. Chambers	12th Yorks. L. Infantry	
Captain J. M. Needham	2nd Sherwood Foresters	
Captain S. C. Wells		
Captain L. N. Rogers		Killed.
Lieut. Hunn		
†Lieut. R. G. Helsby		
†2nd Lieut. J. H. Nicholson		
†*2nd Lieut. C. S. C. Russell		
†2nd Lieut. H. Spiller		
2nd Lieut. I. Spain	C. de G. Belgian	

18/28	Moffitt, W.		
82	Bell, G.	Also with 19th Battalion	
96	Bruce, G.		
110	†Blackett, E.		
115	*Kennedy, J. H.		
148	†Clark, J.		
161	†Spoors, R.		
162	Scribbings, F.	Also with 19th Battalion	
187	*Welsh, J. R. F.	Awarded the D.C.M.	
199	*Price, R.		
214	*Simpson, W.		
220	*†Watson, S. T.		
222	*Carr, D. E.		
225	Proudlock, R.	Also with 19th Battalion	
237	**Atkinson, R.**	**With 11th Battalion**	Killed.
242	Cole, S. J.	C.Q.M.S. with 9th and 12th Battalions	
258	Turnbull, C. R.		
259	*Stoker, R.		
261	Skeoch, N.		
270	†Little, G.		

Personal Notes

285	†Robinson, J.		
290	*Graham, W. T.		
300	**Lawson, E. G.**	Lieut. with 7th Batt.	Killed.
302	†Warren, A.		
304	**Armstrong, T.**		Died of wounds.
308	Turnbull, G.		
321	*Hall, J.		
333	Hall, R.		
346	Anderson, L.		
357	†Smith, R.		
378	*Hunter, R.		
391	†Barnwell, T.		
394	†Chapman, W.		
401	**Moffitt, J.**	With 5th Lincoln Rgt.	Killed.
433	†Poctrous, W. H.		
445	†Coleclough, W.		
450	McDonald, J.	Sergt. with 19th Batt.	
463	†Dodds, S.		
471	†Hall, T. L.		
485	Atkinson, A. T.		
509	*Furness, J.		
522	†Ruth, T.		
532	†Sewell, A.		
537	†Moore, G.		
543	†Atkinson, D.		
550	Lee, J. T.	Prisoner of war	
558	†Carr, G. D.		
576	Pinkett, T.		
588	McMahan, M.		
596	Robertson, J.	Also with 19th Batt.	
619	†*Kelley, J. W.	To 14th Battalion	
630	†*Harvey, A.		
634	Cole, F.		
640	†King, D. R.		
671	Hardy, J. R.		
672	**Kennedy, W. H.**	With M.G. Corps	Died of sickness.
695	Watts, C.		
721	†Pritchard, T.	Sergeant	
724	Ferguson, D.		
793	†Lillice, J.		
803	†Barrass, J. H.		
810	***Scott, J. H.**	**With 1st Battalion**	**Killed.**
833	*Watson, A. S.	With 19th Battalion	
840	**Belshaw, W.**	**With 19th Battalion**	**Killed.**
865	Dolman, E.		
890	†*Crosby, W.		
893	†McDougal, R.		
915	*Donnelly, F.		
928	†Turnbull, J.		
934	Howorth, R.		
947	King, G.		
991	Wilde, J.		
1006	*Wood, E. E.		

Personal Notes

1001	Hunter, C. S.		
1012	*Johnson, I.		
1028	**Pearson, F.**	With 7th Royal Fus.	Killed.
1033	*Johnson, A.	Sergt., awarded M.M.	
1036	†Wilson, G. T.		
1074	**Brown, R. L.**		Killed.
1079	*Guthrie, G.		
1083	†Miles, E. W.		
1090	**Brownless, L. E.**	Sergt. with 12th and 25th Battalion	Killed.
1100	Clough, R.		Died of sickness.
1101	Hunter, C. S.		
1103	**Moore, H.**	C.S.M. 9th South Lancashire Regt.	Killed.
1112	**Angus, J. T.**		Killed in action.
1120	*Alderson, D.		
1124	*Sherrington, J. N	C.Q.M. Sergt.	
1166	†Weatherhead, H.		
1173	Armstrong, J. W.		
1180	**Fisher, N.**	With West Yorks Rgt.	Killed.
1184	†Nesbitt, E.		
1186	†Thompson, R.		
1179	Price, J.		
1194	Proud, T.		
1209	Corder, J.	With 19th Battalion	
1213	**Barrie, A. J.**	With 14th Battalion	Killed.
1247	†Coxen, E. H.		
1251	Gregory, R.		
1254	Johnston, C.		
1267	†Archer, H.		
1273	**Gibson, J.**	Lce.-Sergt. with 12/13th Battalion	Killed.
1297	†Gibbon, G.		
1300	*Urwin, F.		
1313	†Cothics, R.		
1319	Bennett, J.		
1328	†Wills, J.		
1331	Newall, A.		
1334	**Urwin, A.**		Killed.
1338	**Rutherford, W. C.**	With 1st Battalion	Killed.
1340	Binney, W.		
1345	Dobbins, T.		
1352	Chambers, R.		
1361	Bone, G. W.		
1371	Taylor, G.		
1385	**Stephenson, E.**	Sergt., M.G. Corps	Died of wounds.
1388	*Platten, H.		
1390	**Brunton, H.**	With 5th Battalion	Killed.
1393	*Robson, J. W.		
1397	**Milburn, T. W.**	With M.G. Corps	Killed.
1401	*Hunter, N.		
1410	Wright, J. W.		
1416	Fall, A.		

Personal Notes

1425	Tomilson, T.		
1427	Chipperfield, D.		
1437	Gunn, B.		
1443	**Parkin, F. W.**		Died of wounds.
1449	Milne, D.		
1455	†Wilson, T.		
1456	†Hall, R.		
1458	†*Charlton, J.		
1465	*Jackson, H.		
1469	**Monkhouse, T.**		**Killed.**
1476	*Huston, A.		**Killed.**
1478	**Jeffrey, T.**		**Killed.**
1481	**Robertson, J. W.**		Died of wounds.
1485	Teasdale, J.		
1486	†Watson, H. W.		
1488	*Brown, G.		
1493	Dixon, A.		
1494	*Anderson, J. R.		
1498	Emslie, G.		
1501	**Jude, E. J.**		Died of wounds.
1504	Rawson, W.		
1505	Higham, J. S.		
1510	Hancock, T.	Prisoner of war	
1514	Vost, J.	In India with 2nd Garrison Batt.	
1518	Philips, G. S.		
1525	*Canning, J.		
1526	**Merrillees, S.**	With 11th Battalion	**Killed.**
1530	**Lightfoot, T.**	With 11th Battalion	**Killed.**
1536	Banks, W.		
1538	*Rutherford, W.		
1539	Bath, W.		
1542	Reay, G. T.	With 9th Battalion, awarded M.M.	
1544	*Goodrich, A.		
1549	*Anderson, A.		
1562	**Carr, J. R.**	With 12/13th Batt.	**Killed.**
1568	**Johnson, J.**		Died of wounds.
1572	*Ward, M.		
1576	Keigham, G. A.		
1579	Young, G.		
1580	Crawford, W. F.		
1584	*Brown, W.		
1585	*King, J. E.		
1586	Charlton, J.		
1597	White, B.		
1591	Gilbert, M.		
1593	McTaggart, A.		
1600	Willey, C.		
1603	†Hopson, J. E.		
1609	†Cairns, J.		
1614	Makepeace, F. G.	With 19th Battalion.	
1616	*Brown, J. S.		

Personal Notes

1617	Thomas, J. G.		
1618	**Gibson, R.**	With 7th Battalion	**Killed.**
1620	*Brodie, J.		
1621	Wardle, J.		
1629	Straughan, J.		
1630	Robinson, H.		
1635	Tomlinson, J.		
1639	Walton, A.		
1662	†Jones, N.		
1666	Fitzpatrick, J.		
1668	Wilkie, J. T.		
1675	Palmer, R. R.		
1679	Jenson, J. L.	With 14th Battalion	
1690	**Elliott, N. L.**	With 1st Battalion	**Died of wounds.**
1691	**Gair, J. E.**	With 7th D.L.I.	**Killed.**
1693	†Urwin, J. C.		
1696	Forsyth, C. N.		
1697	Watson, W. H.		
1700	Charlton, T.		
1704	Tait, R.		
1709	Laben, C.		
1710	Hetherington, R.		
1714	**Gallagher, J.**		**Killed.**
1719	Atkinson, W.		
1727	Coakley, J.		
1728	Emmerson, A.		
1730	*Gregory, C.		
1731	**Charlton, W.**	With 14th Battalion	**Killed.**
1732	Thompson, J.		
1735	**Charlton, R. H.**		**Killed.**
1746	Hope, T. T.		
1756	Kennedy, W. B.		
1760	†Jackson, T. W.		
1761	**Hart, J.**		**Killed.**
1764	**Williams, W. A.**	With 13th Battalion	**Killed.**
1766	†Newton, H.		
1768	**Aitchison, W. J.**	With M.G. Corps	**Killed.**
1771	Turner, T. S.		
1776	**Gallirher, G. W.**	With 7th Battalion	**Killed.**
1777	*McPeak, A.		
1779	Peel, J.		
1781	Hinds, G. E.		
1792	**Rodham, J.**		**Killed.**
1804	Robson, A.		
1807	Burns, R. B.		
1809	Brown, P.		
1812	Cowlic, A.		
1814	Marshall, J.		
1816	Buchan, J.		
1819	Moore, A.		
1820	Hamilton, R.		
1821	Thompson, G.		
1822	Stanley, G. S.		

Personal Notes

1828	Laverock, N.	
1827	Brooks, S.	
1832	Wilson, R.	
1837	Hadaway, J. W.	
1838	Forster, J. J.	
1840	Whiteman, R.	
1847	*Brand, G.	
1850	**Laing, P.**	**Died of wounds.**
1855	*Chandler, T.	
1889	†Darmody, J.	

Personal Notes

ITINERARY :
QUO FATA VOCANT

16/10/14	Newcastle	First recruits arrive County Cricket Ground. Major R. Temperley, T.D., in command.
21/10/14	,,	Lieut.-Col. Sir Campbell Kirkman Finlay in command.
4/11/14	,,	Battalion complete.
17/11/14	,,	Part of " Emergency Battalion."
21/12/14	,,	Entrain to
22/12/14	Rothbury	Lieut.-Col. J. Shakespear, in command. Part of 122nd Brigade.
8/2/15	,,	Become 1st Tyneside Pioneers.
3/4/15	,,	Inspection at Felton.
21/4/15	Cramlington	Moved into Camp.
20/5/15	,,	Reviewed by the King at Newcastle.
/6/15	,,	122nd Brigade broken up.
21/7/15	Kirkby Malzeard	Left Cramlington for Ripon. Part 34th Division.
10/8/15	Totley	Musketry course.
30/8/15	Salisbury Plain	Divisional training.
28/9/15	Sutton Veny	Divisional training.
4/11/15	,,	Battalion taken over by War Office.
28/12/15	,,	Embarkation preparations.
7/1/16	Southampton	Battalion embarked.
8/1/16	Havre	In rest camp.
9/1/16	Staple	Billets.
21/1/16	Les Ciseaux	Billets.
10/2/16	Armentières	" A " and " C " attached to 9th South Staffs. " B " in Nieppe Forest, " D " attached to 8th Division.
8/4/16	Erquinghem	Battalion in The Line, first casualty. En route for Rest. Four days' march to
	Boisdinghem	Rest. Squad and platoon drill.
18/4/16	St. Omer	Entrained for the Somme.
	Albert, etc.	Battalion attached to 8th Division.
23/4/16	,,	St. George's Day.
10/5/16	,,	The 34th Division arrive. Preparing for offensive.
23/6/16	" The Ditch "	Battalion in bivouac.
	" The Glory Hole "	" C " opposite La Boisselle.
1–5/7/16		Battle stations ; 101 casualties.
6/7/16	Henencourt, Pas	Transferred to 37th Division. Embussed to about 12 miles north of Albert.
11/7/16	Bienvilliers	In trenches as infantry—gas attack. Three days' marching to Verdrel.

Personal Notes

18/7/16	Verdrel	Ten miles west of Lens.
	Bois de Bouvigny	Attached to 63rd Division. Returned to 37th Division.
26/7/16	Villers au Bois	Working with 9th Division.
	Zouave Valley	Trench digging.
23/8/16		Marched 12 miles to railway, entrained for
24/8/16	La Gorgue	Marched another 12 miles for
	Erquinghem	Back to the 34th Division.
25/8/16	Merville	Embussed to Merville, train to
	Albert	Again. Attached to 15th Division.
28/8/16	Martinpuich	In the Line with 103rd Brigade.
12/9/16	Albert	For Rest. Attack delivered.
15/9/16	Back to Line.	Tanks first used; Battalion consolidate and make roads.
22/9/16	Armentières	Back to the 34th Division. Half-way House, Pig Farm. Hurried move out of Line to
27/1/17	Meteren	and south to Arras, arriving
2/2/17	Etrun	Attached to 9th Division. Hard frosts; working in Roclincourt Valley. Major P. Bell in command.
	and	
	St. Catherine	
9/4/17	,,	Battalion in attack; Arras offensive.
16/4/17	Old German Line	With 4th Division, in deep dug-outs.
28/4/17	Rœux	Attack with 101st and 102nd Brigade on Chemical Works.
1/5/17	Beaudricourt	Rest with 34th Division.
7/5/17	Candas	Training near Doullens.
28/5/17	Hindenburg Line	N.E. of Arras.
5/6/17	Greenland Hill	The 34th Division attack.
19/6/17	Hermaville	Rest. Entrained for
30/6/17	Poperinghe	and marched to
1/7/17	Crombeke Wood	With 5th Army; on light railway work.
6/7/17		Colonel Shakespear rejoined.
31/7/17	Dawson's Corner	Ypres offensive.
	" P " Camp	One company at a time in rest.
29/10/17	Poperinghe	Leaving Belgium for
30/10/17	Henin	Back with the 34th Division, till
21/11/17	Bapaume	En route for
22/11/17	Havrincourt	Cambrai offensive; work on broad gauge railway.
4/12/17		German counter-attack.
6/12/17	Henin	Back to the 34th Division.
/1/18	Mory and St. Ledger	Preparing defensive line.
/2/18	Moyenville	Exit " D " Company.
15/3/18	Boyelles	In battle positions.
21-27/3/18		The German Offensive.
28-31/3/18	Armentières	Marching back to
1/4/18	Erquinghem	Preparing bridges.
	Nieppe	
7/4/18		Gas attack.
9/4/18		German offensive.
10/4/18		Divisional retirement—bridges blown up.
11/4/18		On the defensive.
14/4/18	Bailleul	Colonel Shakespear was wounded. Major C. J. Francis in command.

Personal Notes

18/4/18	Mont Noir	Battalion relieved, having lost 27 officers and 326 O.R. since the 7th.
22/4/18	Road Camp	Inspected by General Nicholson.
26/4/18	Poperinghe	In the support trenches.
18/5/18	Watterdal	Battalion reduced to Cadre establishment.
	Alincthum	Lieut.-Col. J. A. Methuen, D.S.O., in command. Training 28th American Division.
27/7/18	Licques	Battalion with 39th Division.
11/11/18	Haudricourt	Armistice: training malaria reinforcements.
10/12/18	Havre	Demobilisation.
2/5/19		Presentation of Battalion Colour.
9/6/19		Cadre left France.

Personal Notes

ROLL OF HONOUR

THIS roll commemorates those who, at the call of King and Country, left all that was dear to them, endured hardness, faced danger, and finally passed out of the sight of men by the path of duty and self-sacrifice, giving up their own lives that others might live in freedom.

LET THOSE WHO COME AFTER SEE TO IT THAT THEIR NAMES BE NOT FORGOTTEN.

Officers and other ranks who have been killed in action, or died from wounds received in action, or other causes :—

Captain P. B. Drury.
Captain L. N. Rogers.
Lieut. and Quartermaster A. R. O. Draper.
Lieut. G. R. Brown.
Lieut. H. W. Coombs.
Lieut. T. E. Keenlyside.
Lieut. C. Robson.
Lieut. O. Smurthwaite.
2nd Lieut. C. H. T. Collins.
2nd Lieut. J. Hodgkinson.
Major R. Worthington, 16th Cheshire Regiment.
Lieut. W. M. Dodds, 25th Northumberland Fusiliers.
Lieut. N. Futers, 1st Northumberland Fusiliers.
Lieut. E. Russell, 20th Durham Light Infantry.
Lieut. R. W. Shegog, R.A.M.C.
Lieut. G. B. Sibbit, 1st Northumberland Fusiliers.
2nd Lieut. A. Coulson, M.M., 5th Northumberland Fusiliers.
2nd Lieut. R. Dellow, 19th Northumberland Fusiliers.
2nd Lieut. Gray, 2nd West Yorks Regiment.
2nd Lieut. W. Harris.
2nd Lieut. R. D. McInnes, Lancashire Fusiliers.
2nd Lieut. W. Jackson, M.C., 3rd N.F. (attached 15th D.L.I.).
2nd. Lieut. E. G. Lawson, 7th Northumberland Fusiliers.
2nd Lieut. F. P. McCormick, 9th Northumberland Fusiliers.
2nd Lieut. J. C. M. Peacock.
2nd Lieut. E. Veitch, Northumberland Fusiliers.
Cadet J. E. Quinn, R.A.F.

306 Pte. H. Atkinson.
289 Cpl. O. C. Ash.
1311 Pte. J. Agnew.
937 J. W. Ashton.
45375 Pte. J. W. Allan.
28/377 Pte. T. R. Atkinson.
304 Pte. Thos. Armstrong.
839 Pte. R. Atkinson.
237 Lce.-Cpl. R. Anderson (attached 11th N.F.).
1768 Pte. Wm. J. Aitchison (attached M.G.C.).
1113 Pte. J. T. Angus.
206 Pte. R. Avery.

Photo *Lieut. Webb, M.C.*
TO THE GALLANT MEN OF THE 34TH DIVISION: LA BOISSELLE.

18th (Service) Battalion Northumberland Fusiliers

156 Pte. J. Brannon.
93 Cpl. C. Bailey.
1054 Pte. H. Blackshaw.
1073 Pte. J. Brown.
332 Pte. W. C. Blythman.
503 Pte. J. Beadling.
1462 Pte. F. Batie.
1387 Pte. J. Brunton.
319 Lce.-Cpl. E. Briggs.
1206 Pte. W. J. Baker.
202900 Pte. S. Bell.
28/96 Pte. M. T. Bruce.
1090 Sergt. L. E. Brownless, with 12th Battalion.
840 Pte. Wm. Belshaw (attached 19th N.F.).
796 Pte. J. Barnes.
1190 Pte. G. Brown.
365 Pte. Thos. Pringle Barker.
6234 Pte. George Beavis.
32 679 Pte. W. H. Bell.
943 Pte. Chas. Blakey.
37532 Cpl. T. Brown.
27/834 Pte. G. W. Brown.
47564 Pte. W. Blackley.
808 Cpl. Chas. A. Barringer (attached K.O.Y.L.I.).
1074 Cpl. R. L. Brown.
1109 Pte. Douglas Beck.
960 Lce.-Cpl. Ed. Blakey (with 2/4th K.O.Y.L.I.)
1390 Pte. Henry Brunton (attached 5th N.F.).
1213 Pte. Arthur John Barrie (attached 14th N.F.).
886 Cpl. J. T. Cowell.
651 Pte. T. H. Cowell.
1017 Cpl. T. Charlton.
887 Pte. G. Clark.
1735 Pte. R. H. Charlton.
64 Sergt. W. Cheesman.
1100 Pte. R. Clough.
1259 Pte. W. L. Clydesdale.
898 Lce.-Cpl. E. Coulthard.
1307 Pte. Atherley E. B. Coulson.
238 Pte. Ralph Wm. Curry (with 14th Batt. N.F.).
Pte. John Clasper (with Tyneside Scottish).
1562 Pte. J. R. Carr (transferred 12/13th N.F.).

1158 Pte. John J. Carter (transferred 14th N.F.).
1731 Pte. Wm. Charlton (attached 14th N.F.).
1566 Pte. Wm. Clennan.
1037 Pte. J. Croudace (attached 12/13th N.F.).
748 Pte. J. Dufour.
741 Pte. C. Duggan.
1025 Lce.-Cpl. J. Dickinson (attached 7th Royal Fusiliers).
998 Pte. J. Dent.
1237 Pte. J. Dick.
1472 Pte. J. T. Douglas.
81 Pte. W. Dixon.
423 Pte. F. Dixon.
331 Lce.-Cpl. J. Day.
403 Pte. M. B. Dixon (attached 1st N.F.).
35385 Pte. R. Dickenson.
1314 Pte. R. Elliott.
t62 Sergt. A. Edgar.
287 Pte. J. Elliott.
3/421 Pte. S. Emmerson.
1690 Pte. N. L. Elliott (attached 1st N.F.).
667 Pte. J. C. Ekin (attached 14th N.F.).
147 Lce-Cpl. R. Elliott (attached 2/4th K.O.Y.L.I.
735 Pte. W. French.
51 Pte. R. W. Fenn.
1171 Pte. T. Fairbairn.
1180 Pte. W. Fisher (attached W. Yorks.).
409 Pte. G. E. Freeman.
931 Pte. L. Forster.
1273 Lce.-Sgt. J. Gibson (transferred 12/13th N.F.).
792 Pte. A. Greenwell.
274 Pte. T. Gustard.
1714 Pte. J. Gallagher.
1057 Pte. J. Alex Glen.
1776 Pte. G. W. Gallirhir (attached 7th N.F.).
1300 Pte. J. Graham.
499 Pte. John Garrity.
1691 Pte. John Ed. Gair (attached 1/7th D.L.I.).
1618 Pte. R. Gibson (attached 1/7th N.F.).

774 Cpl. J. Hall.
1761 Pte. G. Hart.
712 Pte. G. Hammell.
816 Pte. F. Haley.
1605 Pte. D. Hamilton.
271 Sergt. A. Hall.
70 Pte. J. Heron.
1619 Pte. J. Harbit.
203926 Pte. A. Hulbert.
1369 Pte. J. Hinton.
646 Cpl. J. A. Havelock, M.M.
1476 Cpl. A. E. Huston.
322 Pte. Robt. Hall (attached 14th N.F.).
631 Pte. Wm. Home (attached 13th W. Riding Regt.).
751 Pte. Robt. Hindmarsh (with 7th Royal Fus.).
1255 Pte. Septimus Hitcham (attached 14th N.F.).
448 Pte. E. Imeson.
1201 Pte. E. J. Jude.
1483 Pte. J. Jeffrey.
1478 Pte. T. Jeffrey.
1568 Pte. J. Johnson.
563 Pte. Jas. Jameson (transferred 7th Royal Fus.).
45341 Lce.-Cpl. A. A. Jee.
744 Pte. T. Johnson.
1174 Pte. J. G. Kyle.
672 Pte. W. H. Kennedy (attached M.G.C.).
1400 Pte. J. Lamberton.
1850 Pte. P. Laing.
45325 Pte. T. G. Labbett.
621 Pte. T. J. Liddell.
45392 Pte. W. Lathey.
1533 Pte. J. R. C. Lovett (attached 11th N.F.).
57796 Pte. T. Levitt.
1351 Pte. J. H. Lumsden (attached 2nd W. Yorks).
1567 Pte. Geo. Lowes.
395 Lce.-Sergt. J. G. Leach.
722 Pte. Wm. Lancaster (attached 13th N.F.).
1530 Pte. Thos. Lightfoot (attached 11th N.F.).
849 Pte. W. E. Lowery (transferred K.O.Y.L.I.).
1469 Pte. T. Monkhouse.
1218 Pte. J. Meggison.

119 Pte. J. McGowan.
45367 Lce.-Sergt. G. A. Miners.
689 Pte. Alex. Mole.
791 Pte. J. Malone.
635 Pte. T. Malone.
205198 Pte. C. F. Morris.
987 Pte. J. Mafhan.
733 F. A. Margetson.
Pte. Jas. McPherson (attached 7th N.F.).
1397 Pte. Thos. W. Milburn (attached M.G.C.).
893 Pte. Anthony Morpeth.
401 Pte. Jas. Moffitt (attached 2/5th Lincolns).
1249 Pte. John Mercer (attached K.O.Y.L.I.).
279 Lce.-Cpl. Andrew Mortimer (attached K.O.Y.L.I.).
212 Cpl. Wm. Milburn (transferred 10th N.F.).
1526 Pte. Sam Merrilees (attached 11th N.F.).
1103 C.S.M. H. Moore (attached 9th South Lancs).
296 Pte. T. Maltby.
59467 Pte. F. R. Norman.
1183 Pte. J. Oxley.
26/1191 Pte. R. O'Neill.
1443 Pte. F. W. Parkin.
487 Lce.-Cpl. W. Potts.
45400 Pte. F. W. Puddicombe.
36299 Pte. R. Preston.
1330 Pte. A. S. Proudfoot.
1028 Pte. Percy Pearson (attached 7th Royal Fus.).
45340 Pte. A. W. Paumier.
1543 Pte. C. W. Riddle.
1018 Lce.-Cpl. F. Rutherford.
1792 Pte. J. Rodham.
476 Pte. J. H. Roper.
1047 Cpl. P. J. Robson.
1481 Pte. J. W. Robertson.
427 Cpl. H. Ross.
984 Pte. C. E. Reed.
202688 Pte. F. Robson.
45279 Pte. F. Rush.
57768 Pte. G. F. Rolls.
1338 Pte. Wm. Chas. Rutherford (attached 1st N.F.).
182 Lce.-Cpl. Robert Russell (attached 12/13th N.F.).

18th (Service) Battalion Northumberland Fusiliers 173

793 Pte. R. Snowden.
178 Pte. J. Stephenson.
151 Pte. J. T. Stott.
1199 Pte. J. Short.
278 Pte. T. Stephenson.
458 Pte. J. Sutherland.
79 Pte. W. Short.
852 Lce.-Cpl. T. W. Storey.
952 Pte. A. Stoves.
57693 Lce.-Cpl. F. Singer.
19/1515 Cpl. R. H. Straughier.
810 John H. Scott (attached 1st N.F.).
1136 Pte. J. Stoves.
1323 Pte. J. W. Smith.
920 Cpl. E. Smith.
31 Pte. W. H. Travis.
790 Pte. J. B. Thompson.
1089 Lce.-Cpl. T. W. Taylor.
19/1472 Pte. T. G. Thompson.
34 Pte. J. D. Thompson.
1007 Pte. J. Tones.
767 Pte. R. Taylor.
1334 Pte. A. Urwin.
305 Pte. J. R. Vasey (attached 1st N.F.).

697 Lce.-Cpl. M. L. Watson.
45336 Pte. V. Wiltshire.
1608 Lce.-Cpl. Geo. Wiffen (attached 10th N.F.).
345 Pte. J. Winwood.
1265 Pte. H. Wake.
1229 Cpl. H. H. Wilson.
241252 Pte. G. W. Wells.
352 Pte. E. Wood.
66 Pte. W. Weddell.
35739 Pte. E. Wall.
30163 Pte. G. C. Wilson.
291 Pte. Isaac G. Walton (attached R.A.F.).
1288 Pte. Isaiah Wilson (with 9th Royal Fusiliers).
1365 Pte. W. Walton (attached 2/4th K.O.Y.L.I.).
251 Pte. Thos. Watson.
168 Pte. T. J. Wilson (attached 10th N.F.).
1764 Pte. Wm. Alex. Williams (attached 13th N.F.)
581 Pte. Ed. Yarrow (transferred Tank Corps).

HONOURS AND AWARDS

LIST OF HONOURS AWARDED TO OFFICERS AND OTHER RANKS WHO HAVE SERVED WITH THE 18TH (S.) BATTN. NORTHUMBERLAND FUSILIERS (PIONEERS)

Companion:

Most Distinguished Order of St. Michael and St. George.
Lieut.-Col. J. Shakespear, C.I.E., D.S.O.

Most Excellent Order of the British Empire.
Commander: Military Division:
Lieut.-Col. R. Stephenson, D.S.O.

Distinguished Service Order.

Lieut.-Col. J. A. Methuen, King's Royal Rifle Corps.
Lieut.-Col. C. P. Porch, 25th Northumberland Fusiliers.
Lieut.-Col. R. Stephenson, C.B.E., 9th South Staff. Regt.
Major T. Reay, 25th Northumberland Fusiliers.
Major V. B. Rogers, M.C. (Divisional Staff).
Major F. Sweet, 13th Royal Welsh Fusiliers.

Bar to Distinguished Service Order.

Lieut.-Col. C. P. Porch, D.S.O.

Military Cross.

Major P. C. Dodsworth.
Major C. J. Francis.
Major R. O. Hall (Divisional Staff).
Major V. B. Rogers (Divisional Staff).
Capt. J. B. Nixon.
Capt. W. S. Holbrook.
Capt. G. E. Caswell.
Capt. J. W. Vasey.
Capt. F. G. Wilson.
Lieut. A. Armstrong, M.M., 19th Battalion.
Lieut. F. R. G. Webb.
Lieut. W. Jackson, 3rd. Batt.
Lieut. L. Fletcher, M.M., 23rd Batt.
Regt. Sergt.-Major J. A. Scorer.

Bar to Military Cross.

Capt. W. S. Holbrook, M.C.
Major R. O. Hall, M.C.

18th (Service) Battalion Northumberland Fusiliers 175

Distinguished Conduct Medal.

18/215 Sergt. J. Forsyth.
57736 Pte. J. W. Wainman.
18/187 Cpl. J. R. F. Welsh.

18/1178 Sergt. W. Churchill
18/233 Sergt. J. Phillips

The Military Medal.

18/584 Sergt. A. Coulson, Lieut. 5th Battalion.
18/636 Cpl. H. V. Bonner, Lieut. 16th Battalion.
18/646 Lce.-Cpl. J. A. Havelock.
18/1542 Pte. G. J. Reay (attached 9th N.F.).
18/777 Pte. E. E. Jones.
18/729 Pte. F. A. Craig.
18/139 Sergt. F. Tomlinson.
18/367 Pte. S. Newman.

18/1065 Pte. L. Fletcher.
45307 Pte. F. Surtees.
18/855 Sergt. A. A. Armstrong, Lieut. 19th Battalion.
18/787 Cpl. M. Farrell.
18/1033 Sergt. A. Johnson.
41291 Sergt. G. R. Peart.
18/469 Pte. W. Ward.
18/548 Pte. D. Aikman.
18/1287 Pte. E. Storey.
18/471 Pte. P. Adamson.

Meritorious Service Medal.

18/983 C.S.M. G. G. Baillie.

Croix de Guerre.

Lieut.-Col. J. A. Methuen, D.S.O. (French).
Major V. B. Rogers, D.S.O., M.C. (French).
Lieut.-Col. R. Stephenson, C.B.E., D.S.O. (Italian).
2nd Lieut. I. Spain (Belgian).
18/878 Sergt. D. Simm (Belgian).

Decoration Militaire (Belgian).

18/555 Sergt. A. W. R. Bell.

APPENDICES

APPENDIX A

EXPERIENCES OF A PRISONER OF WAR

April 9th, 1918.—No. 11 Platoon, " C " Company, took up a position in front of Erquinghem about 10 a.m., and immediately began to entrench between the railway and a strong point previously prepared. No. 9 Platoon was on our right and detachments of other units of the Division were on our left, linking us up with No. 12 Platoon. During the day we were shelled intermittently by field guns, and were several times fired upon by aeroplanes flying low.

April 10th.—The night passed quietly, the advance posts which were out having nothing unusual to report. These were withdrawn at daylight and our time was occupied in improving our hastily prepared positions. Early in the forenoon (Wednesday, 10th) the infantry on the right front retired and were collected to reinforce our positions. No. 9 Platoon was then withdrawn from our left and with two sections of No. 11 Platoon took up a position at right angles to us and between ourselves and the River Lys, as the Germans were reported to be advancing on our right. We garrisoned the strong point and the Royal Scots filled up the gaps between us and the railway.

Soon afterwards the Germans appeared over the rising ground (half right from our position) and occupied the farm buildings about one thousand yards away. From there they skirmished in the direction of the river. Although they suffered several casualties we were unable to prevent them carrying out this manœuvre, as they took every advantage of the good cover afforded by the nature of the ground. They were well supplied with machine-guns, which they carried upon what at that distance appeared to be stretchers.

They occupied some farm buildings immediately on our right and from where they could enfilade our trench.

Just prior to this we had been reinforced by some of the Duke of Wellington's. The Boche in front caused us little annoyance, as our field of fire in that direction was good, and they showed no indication of making a frontal attack. From the right, however, we suffered several casualties ; but eventually we obtained superiority in that direction too, and matters remained in this condition until about 4 p.m. Soon after that time Bruce and Davidson, at great personal risk, succeeded in getting through with orders to the effect that after the infantry were clear we were to withdraw through the engineer yard and across the river.

During the withdrawal of the infantry the enemy put down a heavy machine-gun barrage on our trench and immediately this lifted I ordered

Corporal Boaden and the men to make their way across the river. With a few Lewis gunners and Sergeant Kye of the Duke of Wellington's we tried to keep the Boche occupied during this withdrawal. The remainder of us then left the trench and tried to make our way to the river. The Boche, however, had broken through behind us and caught us in the open. As two of the men were wounded and the Boche had us covered an attempt to get away meant useless sacrifice of life, so we were obliged to surrender. We found that some of the men who had left with the first party had also been captured, together with some machine-gunners.

The Boche officer—a Prussian—tried to get information, but in spite of his threatening attitude he was unsuccessful and eventually sent us down the Erquinghem road under an escort. We had two or three wounded with us, and these were attended to at a dressing station where we had to leave them. While waiting here a box of Army biscuits was discovered, from which we supplied ourselves. It was fortunate that we did so as the first meal provided by the Boche was on Friday.

From here the men were compelled to carry wounded until we came to a village which we supposed to be Levante. Here we had our first taste of Boche coffee—a concoction made from acorns or chestnuts—which was supplied after some grumbling. We were then taken to a billet—very much knocked about—where we spent the night.

April 11th.—Next morning we were early on the move, the men again having to carry wounded for several kilometres to a light railway. This was arduous work as the only substitutes for stretchers were "duck-boards," and waterproof sheets hung from poles. During this part of our journey we passed many Uhlans and enormous numbers of infantry going up the line. The roads in this part—near the old front line—were very bad and the German transport was in a wretched condition.

Eventually we came to a village, behind the old German line, which was supposed to be a collecting station for prisoners, and here we had to give up any papers we possessed. We had taken the opportunity before this of destroying any papers we may have had, so we had nothing of any value to the enemy. There were already many prisoners here, and after a rest the men were given work to do. That night the officers were sent on to Lille, the men following next day.

April 12th.—We arrived in Lille about 1 a.m. on Friday morning, and were imprisoned in the fortress there. Three of us were put in a room already inhabited by Portuguese, but were promised fresh quarters for the night. From here we could send a field card, which would be immediately forwarded to England—mine arrived some three months afterwards.

The meals here consisted of soup at midday, made from horseflesh and barley—coffee morning and evening and one-fifth of a loaf of black bread. The men of the 34th Division left Lille on the Saturday and were taken to work behind the Boche lines, where they had a bad time during their imprisonment.

With a draft of about eighty British and a number of Portuguese officers, I left Lille on Sunday, April 14th, for Rastatt in Baden. While going to the station the French tried to show their sympathy by handing small things to us, but the Boche, of whom they seemed very much afraid, were very harsh with them. We had each been supplied with two loaves of bread to serve for the journey and a pail of jam was served out to supply several compartments. This jam resembled only in the slightest degree its English namesake, discolouring the mouth and especially the teeth. On our journey we passed through Valenciennes, Strassburg, Metz and Karlsruhe, and arrived at Rastatt about 2 a.m. on Wednesday the 17th.

This camp was pleasantly situated, but that is all that could be said in its favour. It had previously been used as a Russian "lager" and was divided by barbed wire fences into several compounds. We were allotted to Block 2, which consisted of from twelve to twenty large huts, each to accommodate about eighty persons. There were wooden erections for beds and we were scantily supplied with bedding. The sanitary arrangements, too, were very bad; perhaps for this reason we were inoculated for typhus, typhoid, and cholera.

The meals consisted of Boche coffee in the morning and soup at midday and in the evening. These with one-fifth of a loaf of bread formed a day's rations. Life here was very trying; we were without many of the necessities of life. We had only the clothes in which we were captured and were without the means of keeping ourselves clean. Finally the Germans provided a small canteen where we could purchase a substitute for soap, a few cigarettes at twopence (20 pfennigs) each, etc. But the next difficulty was want of money, as those who were fortunate enough to have some when captured had by this time spent it. The Boche provided a number of cheques, but not nearly enough to give one to each officer, and by this means we could draw upon our Army agents through a Dutch bank. The soonest we could get the money was ten days, but some of the cheques were not cashed until July or August.

The days at Rastatt seemed very long, as there were practically no means of occupying our time. Gradually, however, we were provided with a few books and a series of lectures were arranged. These were delivered by various officers on different subjects, but almost brought to a premature conclusion by the Germans taking exception to something that was said in one lecture—they always had an interpreter present.

Rastatt was an overflow camp for officer prisoners of war, and about twice a week drafts left for other camps via Karlsruhe. Most of the 34th Division left on Monday, May 13th, for Karlsruhe. During the short walk to the station many of us felt the results of the lack of nourishment and of the privations of the last month.

Arriving at Karlsruhe we were taken to the hotel "Europaishof," four to a room with the windows barred and doors bolted. Some were kept in this place a week, but about twenty of us left for the camp during the afternoon. This camp which, we were informed, stood in the part of the town bombed by the Allies a year previously, was a great improvement on Rastatt. The huts here were divided into four parts, each to accommodate eight people, and an orderly was responsible for each part. These orderlies were chiefly men who had been captured in the early days of the war and were unfit for harder work. This camp was quite cosmopolitan in character—there were officers of the French, Portuguese, Serbian, Belgian, Italian and British armies, as well as a number of Russian orderlies.

Here we were able to cash cheques and receive the money at once—the value of five pounds being now one hundred and five marks as against one hundred at Rastatt. The greatest boon, however, was the supply of British Red Cross emergency food, and it is almost impossible to describe the feelings with which we sat down to partake of our first meal of English tea, Berne biscuits, butter and cheese. The Boche meals were

18th (Service) Battalion Northumberland Fusiliers

as usual—midday and evening—but facilities were given for the cooking of emergency rations.

There was quite a good library, too, at Karlsruhe besides a billiard-table, otherwise there was nothing to do to pass the time. We stayed at Karlsruhe about three weeks, during which time there was an air raid on the town. This occurred about 8.30 in the morning and from the camp the aeroplanes were easily visible.

On Saturday, June 1st, two hundred of us left Karlsruhe for Graudenz, West Prussia. We travelled through Frankfurt, Heidelberg, Halle, Berlin and Bromberg. From Berlin to Graudenz—about four hundred kilometres—the country had a bleak appearance and we skirted many pine forests.

We arrived at Graudenz about 9 a.m. on Tuesday, June 4th, and were taken to the camp, which consisted of two blocks of buildings and a part of the parade ground wired off from the rest of the barrack buildings, which were inhabited by Boche soldiers. Here we were searched by the Germans, who confiscated many articles. This camp was already peopled by about four hundred officers whom we had left at Rastatt, so that in all there were six hundred of us. The food conditions here were as bad if not worse than at Rastatt, and from our arrival until the appearance of the Red Cross parcels about the end of July was about our worst period in Germany. At Rastatt though the nourishment we received was insufficient our reserve of energy helped us. At Karlsruhe the extra food supplied by the British Red Cross had been invaluable to us, but at Graudenz we had nothing but the German rations, and as we were already in a weak state the next two months were a great trial of fortitude and strength. At roll call which was held morning and evening it was a common thing to see men faint through weakness, very few had energy for anything and most of our time was spent in lying upon our beds. The penalty for this—if caught—was three days' cells, and very soon there was a waiting list—for after all it saved one going down to the roll call.

After a time official permission was given to use our beds in the afternoon, and a few who suffered most from weakness were granted extra rations—in some cases a fifth of a loaf extra per week, and in others an additional supply of semolina soup—which was really made from maize. Appeals had been made to other camps for help, and in answer several packages of foodstuffs arrived from Ruhleben. Soon afterwards bread arrived from Copenhagen, but as this had followed us round by Rastatt and Karlsruhe it resembled the rainbow in colours. All that we could do was to pick out the best and with very great reluctance the remainder had to be consigned to the refuse heap. Finally the parcels began to arrive and our spirits rose correspondingly. Sufficient food and changes of clothes made a wonderful difference, and soon we were engaged in various games and exercises to regain our fitness for any emergency.

Plans were next made for escapes, and a tunnel was begun from the cellars of Block 2 to go under the barbed wire and the wall surrounding our prison. We had to improvise tools for this work as the tools used in the camp to make a tennis-court and theatre were only allowed us on giving our word of honour that they would not be used for any other purpose than that for which they were supplied. Fortunately the soil was chiefly sand and with the exception of a concrete wall was easy to work. Timbering was done with bed boards, and the material excavated was stowed away in various parts of the cellar, being carried in kit-bags and haversacks. The work was done chiefly just before and after lights out. When the tunnel was finished seventeen officers, who were all well shod and had been plentifully supplied with provisions, attempted an escape. The first two were soon discovered on the main road, but they kept the Germans busy talking until the remainder had time to get out. The difficulties of getting clear away were too great as we were too far from any neutral country, and all who tried to escape on this occasion were back within ten days. As soon as the Germans were aware of what was going on they came round the rooms to discover how many were missing, but by putting pillows, etc., in some of the beds they did not find out the exact number until next day. For aiding those escaping the members of the whole camp were confined to their rooms for three days and the issue of parcels stopped. Next night (Sunday) at roll call not going straight to our rooms the guard was turned out and we were driven in, many being struck by the butt ends of rifles. The officer in charge of the Boche urging the men on with his sword drawn.

The next attempt at escaping was also by a tunnel—this time from a cook-house beneath the mess-room—but unfortunately the excavation was too near the surface and the German sentry while parading up and down that part came through—much to his surprise.

Next three officers tried by getting over the barbed wire and the wall, but at that time influenza was prevalent and although they succeeded in getting clear within a few days they were brought back suffering from that complaint.

Another attempted to escape by concealing himself in the cart going out with the washing, but was discovered before the cart left the German portion of the barracks.

The last attempt was to be made by two Captains, by going along some wires which stretched from our portion of the barracks to the German quarters. The first was seen by a German sentry who ran round to inform the guard. In the meantime the officer got clear, but whether he escaped or not we were unable to find out. He was never brought back to camp.

After the arrival of parcels schemes were instituted to enable us to pass away the time. Educational classes were formed and such subjects as languages, shorthand, book-keeping, etc., were taught. We had also a good library. Various games were played, including hockey, football and badminton. Sports were held and were very entertaining. One drawback was that cheering was forbidden, and it was a bit of a shock on one occasion when an exciting hockey match was stopped by the Commandant and not allowed to proceed unless we stopped cheering.

An attempt was made to run a newspaper. This consisted of a double sheet of paper, containing the official communiques translated from the Dantzig paper and was in great demand during the Armistice negotiations. It was also intended to have a magazine, and two copies were issued before the signing of the Armistice, which turned our thoughts to other channels.

The mess-room we had turned into a theatre, and we had several good variety performances. The dresses were all made in the camp, many of them from paper.

During the month of October and November influenza was very bad in the camp—about five-sixths of the officers and orderlies suffered from

18th (Service) Battalion Northumberland Fusiliers

it and six officers died. They were buried with military honours in the cemetery at Graudenz, about one hundred of us being allowed to attend their funerals.

When we first arrived in this camp there were no British orderlies, but within a few weeks forty arrived and these were augmented a few weeks afterwards by sixty others. These latter were men who had been captured in March, 1918, and kept to work behind the German lines. When they arrived they were little better than living skeletons, the result of the treatment they had received during their captivity. They were allowed a good rest by the Brigadier, and with the extra food—supplied from the British Red Cross parcels—their condition greatly improved.

After the signing of the Armistice the camp was handed over to the Senior British Officer, who was advised by the Soldiers' and Workmen's Council then in charge of the town. We were allowed to go into the town, but were advised by the Brigadier to be in camp by nine o'clock in case of friction with the Boche soldiers then returning from the Front. There were also four hundred French officers imprisoned in this town with whom we fraternized. They were not so well supplied with food as we were and we gave them what aid we could. The first draft of two hundred left our camp for home about the end of November and the remainder on December 13th, arriving in Leith on the 18th December and proceeding to Ripon, when after a medical examination we were granted two months' leave.

APPENDIX B

(These notes were received too late for incorporation in the main narrative)

LINES: ON ARRIVAL IN FRANCE

The " Commercials " from Newcastle town
    Came full of fight to France,
And every man resolved that he
    Would make the Kaiser dance.

They landed at an old French port,
    The crossing—it was rotten!
Then there came the beastly train—
    It really was a hot 'un.

Poor 18th were bundled in
    A truck once made for horses,
Their food, breakfast, lunch and tea,
    Was bully-biscuit courses.

At length, when they had disentrained,
    They'd visions of the Marne—
But they were quite surprised to find
    A billet in a barn!

When bed-time came the fun would start,
    The rats were overbearing,
They'd exercise upon our beds
    Amidst the general swearing.

Some days elapsed and then there came
    The word to leave the barn,
The firing line at last, we thought.
    Alas! it was but a yarn.

We marched along for miles and miles
    And saw an old château,
The boys said, " My, it is a hole,"
    The sergeants said, " What ho! "

The boys into *another* barn were packed
    That really looked so fearful,
But the sergeants had found a room
    And made *themselves* quite cheerful.

And so we go on day to day,
    We've heard there *are* some trenches,
But we remain and pass our time
    In writing to our wenches.

But we no doubt will get our turn
    And show the Boche our muscle,
And let them see they *have* to face
    The 18th from New-Custle!

January, 1916.
                                            SIGNALLER.

18th (Service) Battalion Northumberland Fusiliers

THE STORY OF A BRAVE GERMAN TOLD BY A TANK CREW NEAR BAPAUME, 22.11.17.

WE halted between Fritz's support and front line near a couple of stranded tanks, and I entered into conversation with their crews. They were very proud of their souvenirs, two machine-guns, whose crews they had killed and a dead German, who had shot and killed the Captain of their section. The story was that this man, a young and good-looking fellow, who must have been a clever shot, had lain down in the open field and had managed to get a shot right through the spy-hole of the tank, where their Captain was, killing him instantly. A shot brought the man down, but he continued to fire, and by means of special bullets he set the petrol supply of both the tanks on fire and the crews had to come out on account of the heat. From behind the tanks, one fellow hit him again, and even then he shot a Highlander "Then," they continued, "a Jock went up and prodded him a dozen times with his bayonet." Even after this he was alive. Here is a specimen of British chivalry. Despite the fact that he had shot their Captain before their eyes, had put their tanks out of action, and accounted for several infantry men, these tank chaps went to him with water to drink and had endeavoured to bandage him up a bit, but he died while they were attending to him. "'E got some pluck, 'e 'ad," was their verdict. A party of our transport men on hearing the story the following day dug a grave for him and made a rough cross, on which they wrote : "Here lies a brave German."

SOME NOTES ON THE FIGHTING AT ERQUINGHEM AND IN THE RETREAT IN APRIL, 1918

10th April.—Now that the attack was on, the Boche sent a real rain of shells on Erquinghem, and when I walked through, back to my platoon, the road seemed full of bricks from the houses on each side, all mixed up with dozens of dead men and horses. It looked horrible, and I would run a few yards then lie down to dodge a shell, and then run again a little way and so on. . . . After I had been back with my platoon a few minutes a runner arrived with a dirty little scrap of paper addressed to me, and on it was written :—

> You will attend to the destruction of the two foot bridges at H.4.d.15.90 and H.4.b.50.550, but these bridges must not be destroyed until all the British troops have passed over them, as they are the only ones remaining over the river.
>
> C. FRANCIS,
> *Major.*

I took my men through one of the houses into the street and across the fields about 500 yards to the river ; marched them across the bridge and divided them into two parties, gave instructions for the demolition of the two bridges, which was to be immediately proceeded with on receiving my signal. . . . The Divisional Infantry were all this time coming across our foot bridges, and each party which came across assured me that they were the last party of the Division. However, further troops kept appearing from somewhere or other and we continued to wait about till we were spotted by the enemy, and a machine-gun from the direction of the factory commenced to use the party at the first bridge, viz. near the church, for its target. This was, of course, not at all comfortable, and I gave orders for the bridge to be at once demolished. Our Lewis gun blazed away in the direction from which the enemy guns seemed to be firing, while four men attacked the bridge with the choppers.

The enemy machine-gun, apparently, saw a good chance of distinguishing itself, and commenced operations with vigour. It was ably assisted by another gun which seemed to be firing through the church window. One was therefore enfilading the river, the other enfilading the bridge. It was really rather disconcerting when one saw the splashes which the bullets were making in the water round about, and the way they were splintering the woodwork of the bridge. In fact, it disconcerted three of the four men so that they turned tail and ran off the bridge, leaving it only half destroyed.

One man, named Wainman, stood and cut the bridge through alone; how he was not hit goodness only knows. Anyhow, he managed it somehow or other, and on my recommendation got the D.C.M. shortly afterwards for this brave deed. When the moorings of the bridge had been cut and the bridge in two parts floated down-stream the party retired in double time to the other bridge, I began to realize that the enemy would be getting uncomfortably near by the time the last got over. I therefore set on my four axemen to commence cutting down as much of the bridge as possible, but so that it would still bear the strain of the last few men crossing it. I collected six Lewis guns with their teams from the infantry which were coming over the bridge, and told them that I should require them to give covering fire while I cut the bridge down. . . . I lined them up in the end with my own Lewis gunners in the best position I could think of.

I detailed four men for the cutting down of the bridge, and the rest of my platoon I placed behind a hedge and a wall. About this time I was surprised to find a number of civilians, including my old landlady and some other people that I knew from next door, on the other bank. They had hastily collected together their money and valuables and had waited almost until they had seen the enemy in the back garden before they had decided to quit. I helped them across the bridge, although we had some trouble with the female portion. There was one girl who *would* run across the bridge about twelve times, because her aged father was coming along and had not yet reached the bridge. She was weeping bitterly, and I had nearly to carry her across the bridge and put her on the other side, as she was hindering some soldiers who wanted to cross. The old man, carrying apparently half the household goods on his back, then came across and the party moved off.

A few minutes later we noticed that the white Véry lights, which the Germans fired to show their artillery the position of their most advanced troops, were going up just over the ridge in front of us, only about 300 yards away. I was just about to give the order for the bridge to be cut down when another party of soldiers started to roam slowly round the laundry 400 yards away, blissfully ignorant of the proximity of the enemy. We yelled over to these folk to "get a move on" and to "look sharp," which they did; the last few men were just coming across when we saw the enemy coming over the crest of the hill. Then we had a good time.

18th (Service) Battalion Northumberland Fusiliers

According to the Musketry Regulations, Part I, I should have here given the order in something of this style :

" Sight 250, direct front, enemy advancing over ridge,—— Dis—trib—u—tive——*Fire*."

Had I been on Salisbury Plain, I should probably have said this ; as it was, I am afraid that Musketry Regulations, Part I, " went to pot." My order, as far as I can recollect it, ran :—

" There are the beggars (?). Let 'em have it ! "

Both sides opened fire, but I rather fancy that with our seven Lewis guns we got the best of the bargain. At any rate the enemy who crossed the ridge either fell or ran back. After a while their fire slackened and we got the bridge cut in two. Then it was discovered that I had made no arrangements for cutting the rope which held the bridge to the bank.

There then ensued a frenzied hunt for knives, and one man tried in vain to sever the rope by firing at it. At last the writer had an inspiration. I got one man to hold the butt of his rifle under the rope whilst I brought a chopper smartly down on the top of it which severed the rope and the bridge floated away. We threw all the axes into the river ; half the party ran back, whilst the remainder kept up a covering fire. Then while one Lewis gun fired as hard as it could, the remainder of the men rushed back up the road leading north ; then I and the last Lewis gun team also took to our heels. Despite the fact that bullets were still whizzing round, everybody started to laugh very heartily, apparently at the hiding which we all considered we had given the Boche.

Unfortunately there were several casualties, and it was impossible to remove the severely wounded ; in fact, there was no time to ascertain who were only wounded and who were dead. Strange to say, all these casualties were among the teams that had been pressed into the defence ; the Battalion's luck held and not a man of ours was hit.

About 8.30 a.m. on the 17th a terrible bombardment began [the writer says] Everybody lay in the bottom of the trench crouched up, and, if they spent it as I did, they spent nearly the whole day saying their prayers. I had never been so frightened during the whole of the war as I was during these bombardments. Shells were falling in front and behind the trench, all very near. Occasionally one would fall into the trench, killing one or two men. It was terrible to lie there and hear those shells so near, then see a shell burst in front of you. When the smoke had cleared away and you had shaken off the earth that had been thrown on top of you, to see a couple of men just in front lying all smashed up in a great pool of blood. The worst of it was that one was so powerless to do anything in defence. . . . The shelling stopped for a short time about noon, and we saw crowds of Germans coming towards us. They seemed to think that we could not possibly be in these trenches after such a terrific bombardment. When we opened a sharp fire they quickly ran back and took cover. Their artillery started again, and continued till it suddenly stopped about 5 o'clock in the afternoon.

The Division never budged till relieved during the following night.

APPENDIX C

18TH NORTHUMBERLAND FUSILIERS COMRADES' LEAGUE
(Founded 20th July, 1918)

LIST OF OFFICIALS FOR 1919-20

President:
Lieut.-Col. JOHN SHAKESPEAR, C.M.G., C.I.E., D.S.O.

Vice-Presidents:
Sir C. KIRKMAN FINLAY.
Lieut.-Col. C. P. PORCH, D.S.O. and Bar.
Lieut.-Col. ROBERT STEPHENSON, C.B.E., D.S.O.
Lieut.-Col. J. A. METHUEN, D.S.O., C. de Guerre.
Major R. TEMPERLEY, O.B.E., T.D., D.L.
Major P. BELL.

Hon. Treasurer:
Lieut. G. A. M. HALL,
St. Matthew's Vicarage, Newcastle.

Hon. Secretary:
Ex-C.Q.M.S. J. COLE,
19 Cramer Street, Gateshead
(to whom all communications should be addressed).

Committee:

Major P. C. DODSWORTH, M.C.	Ex-Sergt. J. H. PARMLEY.
Capt. H. ARMSTRONG.	Ex-Cpl. SANDERSON.
CAPT. J. B. NIXON, M.C.	Ex-Pte. T. L. COWEY.
Ex-Sergt. W. SIMM, C. de Guerre.	
Lt. G. A. M. HALL } *ex-officio.*	
C.Q.M.S. J. COLE	

OBJECTS OF THE LEAGUE

1. To maintain comradeship amongst those of all ranks who have served in the 18th (Service) Battalion Northumberland Fusiliers.

2. To hold a Reunion at least once a year.

3. To take such steps in the interests of Past Members of the Battalion and their dependents as may be found desirable.

RULES

1. The Society shall be known as the 18TH NORTHUMBERLAND FUSILIERS COMRADES' LEAGUE.

2. All who have served in the 18th (Service) Battalion Northumberland Fusiliers shall be eligible for membership.

3. Members and Officials of the Newcastle and Gateshead Chamber of Commerce Military Committee, and other gentlemen who have been intimately associated with the raising and administration of the Battalion during the Great War, shall be eligible for Hon. Membership.

4. Except so far as otherwise provided in these Rules or by resolution of a General Meeting, the affairs of the League shall be managed by a

18th (Service) Battalion Northumberland Fusiliers

Committee to be appointed annually by the members at the Annual General Meeting of the League, the Committee to hold office until the next Annual Meeting.

5. The Committee shall consist of not less than 5, nor more than 9 members, exclusive of *ex-officio* members, and shall have power to add to its numbers up to the limit of 9 ordinary members.

6. All applications for Membership of the League to be sent to the Hon. Secretary for approval of the Committee.

7. Each Member shall pay an annual subscription of 2s. to the Funds of the League (in addition to cost of Suppers, etc., which he attends).

8. The Funds shall be vested in and controlled by the Committee, which shall have full power (subject to any directions of a General Meeting) to apply them as they may think fit for carrying out the objects of the League.

9. A General Meeting of the Members shall be held in Newcastle in each calendar year.

10. The Officers of the League, consisting of the President, the Vice-Presidents, Hon. Treasurer and Hon. Secretary, shall be elected by an Annual General Meeting, and shall be *ex-officio* Members of the Committee.

11. The Committee shall present an Annual Report and Balance Sheet at each Annual General Meeting.

12. The Committee shall appoint its own Chairman.

The League has a membership of 422 members, and all past members of the Battalion are cordially invited to join the League.

APPENDIX D
NEWCASTLE AND GATESHEAD INCORPORATED CHAMBER OF COMMERCE

President: The Right Hon. LORD JOICEY, D.L., D.C.L., J.P.
HERBERT SHAW, D.L., J.P., Secretary, Chamber of Commerce.

THE MILITARY COMMITTEE, 1914—1919.

MAJOR R. TEMPERLEY, O.B.E., T.D., D.L., Chairman.
GEORGE RENWICK, D.L., J.P., M.P., Vice-Chairman.
[THE LATE C. W. C. HENDERSON, First Hon. Treasurer.]
A. MUNRO SUTHERLAND, J.P. } Joint Honorary Treasurers.
H. E. ANDERSON }

DANIEL STEPHENS, Chairman, Finance Committee.
F. B. FENWICK, Chairman, Clothing Committee.
H. E. ANDERSON, Chairman, Dependents Committee.
ROBERT EELES, Chairman, Reception Committee.
F. CARRICK, Chairman, Comforts Committee.
ALFRED BREWIS, Chairman, Histories Committee.

WALTER ARMSTRONG.
J. H. BECKINGHAM, J.P.
E. L. BECKINGHAM, J.P.
MAJOR B. BRYANT, M.C.
T. M. CLAGUE.
F. CLARK.
[THE LATE W. CROSSING.]
R. S. DALGLEISH.
COL. H. A. ERSKINE, C.B.E., C.B., C.M.G., T.D.
EVANS FAWCUS.
A. J. FENWICK.
GERALD FRANCE, M.P.
L. GEIPEL.
R. M. GLOVER, J.P.
W. R. HEATLEY, O.B.E.
J. S. HINDLEY.
REUBEN HODGSON.
CHARLES IRWIN, J.P.
F. W. KINGSTON.
G. DE LORIOL.
SIR GEORGE LUNN, J.P
E. R. NEWBIGIN, J.P.
MAJOR GEORGE PARKINSON.
CAPTAIN C. E. PUMPHREY, M.C.
J. REAH.
LIEUT.-COL. W. H. RITSON, C.M.G., V.D.
RICHARD ROBSON.
A. SCHOLEFIELD, J.P.
CLARENCE SMITH.
LIEUT.-COL. R. STEPHENSON, C.B.E., D.S.O.
R. M. SUTTON.
MAJOR J. TALBOT.
RIDLEY WARHAM.
T. E. WEBB.
L. E. WOODS.

Committee Secretary: T. M. MCBRYDE.
Hon. Secretary (1919): CAPTAIN R. H. WORTHINGTON, M.C.

THE LADIES' WORKING PARTY (COMFORTS COMMITTEE)

MRS. GEO. RENWICK.
„ ALFRED BREWIS.
„ F. CARRICK.
„ ROBERT EELES.
„ ROBERT HARRISON.
- MRS. G. S. HUNTER.
- „ GEORGE JOICEY.
- „ J. T. LUNN.
- „ H. J. RICHARDSON.
- „ W. H. RITSON.

MISS MARY ADAM, Hon. Secretary.

THE WORK OF THE MILITARY COMMITTEE

On the 2nd September, 1914, at a meeting of the Council of the Newcastle and Gateshead Incorporated Chamber of Commerce Mr. George Renwick, referring to the grave national situation, proposed that the Chamber should ask the Lord Mayor to raise a Battalion among the citizens of Newcastle for the Northumberland Fusiliers of the New Army. Major Robert Temperley suggested that the Chamber could intervene most usefully by appealing direct to those classes of young men with whom it was most in touch, and that application should be made at once for authority to raise, organise and equip a battalion of infantry from amongst the young commercial men on the Quayside and "Upstreet," who would be eager to join a unit in which they could serve side by side with their comrades. The Quayside Company raised for the 3rd Volunteer Battalion—now 6th Battalion—Northumberland Fusiliers during the South African War had shown the desirability of this basis of recruiting. Mr. Renwick cordially accepted the suggestion and on his proposal the Council decided that a telegram be sent at once, to the War Office putting forward the offer and asking for authority to commence recruiting, and a Committee—the Military Committee —was appointed to carry out the undertaking on behalf of the Chamber.

Day followed day without the authority being received. But nothing could restrain the impatience of the young commercial men of Newcastle. Under the leadership of Mr. Robert (now Lieut.-Col.) Stephenson some 400 had already been provisionally enrolled. They would wait no longer— and on the 7th September a full company of 250 accepted enlistment in the 9th Battalion Northumberland Fusiliers and left Newcastle to join that Battalion, then in training at Wool, Dorsetshire. The history of this fine Company, a very large number of whose members ultimately became officers in various units, forms one volume of the present series.

The very next day, the 8th September, 1914, the War Office acceptance of the Chamber's offer was received and recruiting at once commenced for the first Battalion raised by the Chamber. This Battalion, afterwards numbered the 16th (Service) Battalion (Newcastle) Northumberland Fusiliers, was completed by the 16th September.

The training of the 16th Battalion commenced at the grounds of the Royal Grammar School, Newcastle, under the command of Lieut.-Col. W. H. Ritson, V.D. (now C.M.G.), late 6th Battalion Northumberland Fusiliers, who had for the previous month been in command of the Citizens' Training League, with Head-quarters at the Grammar School, a circumstance which facilitated the initial drill and early organisation of the new Battalion. The Battalion moved into huts at Alnwick in December, 1914, and after further training at Cramlington and Salisbury Plain went to France under Colonel Ritson on 22nd November, 1915, as part of the 96th Brigade, 32nd Division.

The 16th Battalion having been successfully raised, the Chamber pressed for authority to raise a second Battalion, but it was not until

October 14th that the request was granted, the authority from the War Office in this case being addressed along with those for the first Battalions of the Tyneside Scottish and Irish, to the Lord Mayor as nominal raiser. Recruiting commenced on 16th October, 1914, and was completed on 4th November. The history of this Battalion, originally known as the Tyneside Battalion and afterwards as the 18th (Service) Battalion Northumberland Fusiliers (1st Tyneside Pioneers), is the subject of the present volume.

On the 16th November, 1914, the Chamber obtained War Office authority to raise a third Battalion, and the numbers were completed on 1st December. This was the 19th (Service) Battalion Northumberland Fusiliers (2nd Tyneside Pioneers). It had its first Head-quarters at 20 Osborne Avenue, Newcastle, Major Robert Temperley, T.D., in command, and after training at Morpeth, under Lt.-Col. L. E. Fawcus and Lt.-Col. F. W. Daniell, and under Col. Daniell at Cramlington and Salisbury Plain, went under his command to France on 28th January, 1916, as the Pioneer Battalion of the 35th Division.

The Military Committee also recruited Depot Companies for each of the three Battalions; the reserves of the 18th and 19th Battalions trained at Cramlington and Harrogate under Lt.-Col. L. E. Fawcus, they formed the 28th (Reserve) Battalion Northumberland Fusiliers, while those of the 16th Battalion trained at Cramlington and Catterick Bridge and formed the 31st (Reserve) Battalion Northumberland Fusiliers.

The troops raised by the Chamber of Commerce thus numbered in all about 5550.

The *Military Committee* (Chairman, Major R. Temperley; Vice-Chairman, Mr. George Renwick) carried through the prolonged and arduous work of raising, organising and providing for the Battalions by means of a series of Sub-Committees, as follows :—

The Recruiting Committee (Chairman, Major Robert Temperley), whose success was largely due to the energy of Mr. George Renwick and to the management of the Chamber's Recruiting Officers by Mr. Lionel Woods and Mr. Walter Armstrong.

The Clothing Committee (Chairman, Mr. Fred B. Fenwick), which in circumstances of great pressure and difficulty, owing to the phenomenal shortage of supplies, carried through or advised on the purchase of clothing, equipment, etc., amounting to some £50,000, which sum was in due course almost entirely recovered from the War Office.

The Billeting and Camp Committee (Chairman, Major Robert Temperley).—This Committee, of which Mr. Richard Robson, Mr. Robert Eeles and Mr. A. M. Sutherland were very active members, arranged the Head-quarters for the three Battalions while stationed in Newcastle, the hutments at Alnwick for the 16th and billeting schemes for the 18th at Rothbury, and the 19th at Morpeth, including the installation of cooking and sanitary requirements, baths, rifle-ranges, etc.

The Dependents Committee.—As soon as recruiting commenced this Committee was formed " To arrange that all dependents of soldiers in the Battalions shall be properly looked after during the breadwinner's absence on military service," and the great success of its operations is due to its original Chairman, Mr. W. R. Heatley, to his successors Mr. J. S. Hindley and Mr. H. E. Anderson, and to the Secretary, Mr. T. M. McBryde.

18th (Service) Battalion Northumberland Fusiliers

The assistance given has in the main been to supplement the Army Separation Allowance where such assistance was considered necessary. At one time there were as many as fifteen hundred cases on the books, involving a weekly expenditure of about £240 or over £12,000 a year. The total expenditure of this Committee has been about £38,000, this sum being provided out of the Guarantee Funds subscribed by the members of the Chamber of Commerce and others.

The payments to dependents have been made through the post, except in large areas where the grants were personally distributed by lady voluntary workers. The Committee have kept in the closest possible touch with all the recipients of grants and have been able to advise the dependents on many points of difficulty. The Committee have been much gratified by the very numerous letters which have been received from both the dependents and soldiers expressing appreciation for the help received.

An important feature of this Committee's work has been their efforts to obtain for dependents (where known to the Committee) the maximum possible allowance from State Funds, and it may be mentioned that similar assistance has been given to dependents of men in other Battalions than those raised by the Chamber of Commerce.

With the demobilisation of the three Battalions this work has naturally diminished, although in many cases the Committee continue to give relief to widows and dependents of men who have fallen in action where circumstances are especially hard.

The Finance Committee (Chairman, Mr. D. Stephens; Joint Hon. Treasurers, Mr. H. E. Anderson and Mr. A. M. Sutherland).—Under the Chairmanship originally of the late Mr. Charles Henderson, the first Hon. Treasurer, this Committee acted as Paymaster on behalf of the Government for the clothing, equipment, stores, and other provisions for these troops until taken over by the War Office, and has also been responsible for the judicious disposal of the " Guarantee Funds " raised by the Chamber (largely through the instrumentality of Mr. R. M. Glover and other Committee men), by voluntary subscriptions, which amounted to about £44,653.[1]

---

[1] The contracts for clothing, equipment, stores, etc., were made by the Sub-Committees concerned on the authority of the Military Committee, which, on behalf of the Chamber, guaranteed any excess which might ultimately not be authorised by the War Office. The monies for these expenditures were in due course drawn from the Army Paymaster and all items originally disallowed were eventually approved by the War Office, and where these had been paid by the Committee out of the " Guarantee Funds " the amount was refunded from Army Funds.

Thus though the Chamber incurred a great initial financial responsibility during the period of formation of the Battalions, its ultimate unrecovered expenditure in respect of this period only amounted to about £5294, which had been expended on outlay which may be legitimately regarded as outside the scope of War Office responsibility, viz. :—Officers' Kits, Gifts to Officers and Men, Travelling Expenses for Men, Extra Accommodation at Training Head-quarters, Clothing and Equipment Extras, Extra Expenses of Recruiting, Salaries, Printing, Stationery, Postages and Sundries. The Balance (about £38,000) of the total " Guarantee Fund " (about £44,000) thus became applicable for grants to dependents, etc. *See under the " Dependents Committee."*

The 16*th Battalion* kept its own accounts; the Battalion only once approached the Committee to get War Office authority for unauthorised expenditure (£380 for extra undervests), which was obtained.

The Comforts Committee (Chairman, Mr. F. Carrick ; Hon. Treasurer, Mr. Alfred Brewis ; Hon. Secretary, Mr. Herbert Shaw) was formed in October, 1915, to send out to the men at the Front comforts as required and a regular supply of magazines and newspapers, etc. These, and the special gifts sent out at Christmas and St. George's Day, have been much appreciated by the men. During four years the Ladies' Working Party (Miss Mary Adam, Hon. Secretary), with the assistance of numerous workers, including relatives of all ranks of the Battalions, were able to send out 37,426 pairs of hand-knitted socks, in addition to other useful woollen articles. The sum of £1860 was spent in the purchase of wool and £1178 in the purchase of goods and in cash grants to the three Battalions and to the " Quayside " Company of the 9th Northumberland Fusiliers. These sums were provided by special subscriptions.

The Entertainments Committee (Chairman, Mr. Robt. Eeles ; Hon. Secretary, Mr. T. M. McBryde) organised during the summer months (1915 to 1919) a series of garden parties and river trips (the latter on the launch lent by the Tyne Improvement Commission) for the wounded soldiers stationed at the local military hospitals.

To enable this scheme to be successfully carried out a sum of £790 was collected. The Committee have every reason to believe that both the greatest possible enjoyment and the highest beneficial effects were derived by the soldiers from these outings. They were conveyed to the garden parties in motor-cars provided by local ladies and gentlemen.

During the winter months, through the courtesy of the management and with the gratuitous assistance of the artistes of the local theatres, weekly indoor entertainments were provided at the Armstrong College and the Northumberland War Hospitals.

The total number of soldiers for whom entertainment was arranged is about thirty-one thousand.

The Reception Committee (Chairman, Mr. Robert Eeles ; Hon. Secretary, Capt. Worthington).—This Committee was founded in 1919 to make arrangements for entertaining in a suitable manner the returned Officers, Non-Commissioned Officers and Men of the units raised by the Chamber.

The 18*th Battalion* kept its own accounts until April, 1915, when, as large sums had been disallowed by the Paymaster, they were handed over to the Committee, which ultimately received approval of this previously disallowed expenditure. On this Battalion's account the Committee has drawn from Army Funds £11,192.

The 19*th Battalion* accounts were kept by the Committee throughout the period of formation, the total sum received from Army Funds being £17,139.

The funds administered by the Comforts, the Entertainments and the Reception and Histories Committees were raised by special subscription and were independent of the " Guarantee Funds."

The principal funds raised and administered by the Military Committee and its Sub-Committees may therefore be summarised as follows :—

	£
The " Guarantee Funds "—	
Formation Expenses unrecoverable from Government	5294
Grants to *Dependents* and Soldiers	39,359
Comforts Fund	3038
Entertainment Fund	790
Reception and Histories Fund . about	2000
Total	£50,481

Sundry minor subscriptions raised for purposes not here recorded will bring the aggregate up to about £51,000.

Through the instrumentality of Lieut.-Col. R. Stephenson, Major Bryant and Mr. H. E. Anderson, a substantial sum has been collected from the members of the Chamber for this object and that of the Histories Committee.

The Histories Committee (Chairman, Mr. Alfred Brewis) undertook the arrangements for the publication of the Histories of the three Battalions raised by the Chamber and of the " Quayside " Company of the 9th Northumberland Fusiliers and the presentation of these volumes to the returned men and the next-of-kin of those who have fallen. These Histories are to be compiled under the general editorship of the Chairman of this Committee.

Secretarial. On obtaining a post in a Government Department in London, Mr. McBryde resigned his position of Committee Secretary and also the honorary secretaryships of the three Comrades' Leagues, founded in connection with each Battalion. Thereupon Captain R. H. Worthington, M.C., late Adjutant of the 16th Battalion, accepted the appointment of Honorary Secretary for the purpose of the winding up of the varied activities of the Committee.

POSTSCRIPT

The Northumberland Fusiliers now have a record of nearly 250 years' service as a Regiment of the British Army, and I know that nothing I can say will add to the lustre of the 18th Battalion, who so worthily upheld the proud traditions of the Regiment.

This History has been prepared as a record of this Battalion's various experiences and achievements, also as a token of the high appreciation felt by the Chamber of Commerce for the services rendered by all ranks who so promptly came forward at the beginning of the War.

The Battalion has been fortunate in having the same C.O. almost the whole time, and the graphic narratives contained in this volume are, I believe, the first published records of a " Pioneer " Battalion, and will enable the student of the history of the Great War to understand and appreciate the useful, arduous and necessary work of such units, which are a recent addition to the technical troops of the British Army.

All ranks will be glad to hear that, at the request of Major-General Nicholson, Colonel Shakespear has undertaken to write an account of the doings of the whole of the 34th Division ; also that it has been decided to erect memorials to the 34th Division on the battle-fields of La Boisselle and Mont Noir, thus commemorating the Somme battle of July, 1916, and the Lys battle of April, 1918.

On behalf of the Chamber, I wish heartily to thank all who have assisted in the preparation of the volume, particularly Colonel Shakespear and his " various hands " who have written the narrative, Captain Nixon for his helpful and specially drawn maps, and Lieut. Lawrence of the 19th Battalion for his artistic drawings, " The Pioneer," " The Dedication " and the headpiece to Chapter I. For permission to produce photographs I am indebted to the courtesy of Lieut. Webb, Messrs. Bacon and Sons, Newcastle, and the Proprietors of the " Newcastle Chronicle."

In my search for particulars I have had the ready assistance of the War Office and the O.C. " Records," York, to whom my thanks are due for information given.

In the compilation of the Embarkation and other Rolls I have been guided by Mr. McBryde, late secretary, and many members of the 18th Comrades' League ; every care has been taken to place men in their original platoon and also to trace promotions, honours, etc. ; for any errors or omissions I express regret to those concerned, and can only trust that the pages provided for " personal notes " will be made of use by bringing the owner's copy of History more up to date. If any reader will send me further information of " happenings " to any member of the Battalion, this will be noted and, if thought acceptable, pages of corrigenda and addenda will be distributed in due course.

I have much enjoyed working at my portion of this History, and would be pleased to receive portraits of all members of the Battalion together with full regimental particulars. These portraits would be bound up with a copy of this volume which I would, in due course, hand over to the care of any institution connected with this Battalion or to any memorial founded locally to perpetuate the doings of the "Ever-Fighting, Never-Failing Fifth."

ALFRED BREWIS,
Hon. General Editor.

20 GRANVILLE ROAD,
NEWCASTLE-UPON-TYNE,
25th November, 1919.

INDEX

A

"A" Co.—
  moves to Armentières, 27
  quarters in B.G. line, 28
  work at Armentières, Feby., 1916, 31, 57
  contribution from, 34, 35
  moves to Henencourt Wood, 34
  moves to "Ovillers Post" and to Albert, 35
  takes over 101st Brigade dump, 42
  special party of, dig T.M. emplacements in No Man's Land, 43
  ordered back 4th July, 1916, 47
  in Zouave Valley, 51, 52
  moves to Villers au Bois, 52
  arrives at St. Catherine, 59
  work at St. Catherine, 60
  in operations of 9th April, 1917, 61, 62
  at Houvin-Houvigneul, 63
  at St. Leger, 78
  during retirement from Armentières, April, 1917, 79, 80, 82, 83
  at Nieppe and in retirement from, 87, 88, 89
Abancourt, 97
Achiet-le-Grand, we detrain at, 70
Air raids, 63, 65, 69, 70
Albert—
  we move to, 33
  description of, and neighbourhood, 34, 35, 36
  we vacate our billets in, 41
  we return to, 54, 55
  M.O. revisits, 93
Alincthun, 93, 96, 97
America enters the War, 64
American troops, we instruct, 96
Amiens, attractions of cathedral at, 72
Ancre River, 36
Angel's Tears, 10
"Archie," surprising success of, 62
Armentières—
  "A" and "C" Cos. move to, 27
  description of, in 1916, 31
  we return to, 56, 79
  condition of, in 1918, retirement from, 80–86
  M.O. revisits, 98
Armistice night, 98
Armstrong, Lord, kindness of, 8, 9
Armstrong, Lieut., 31
Army, 5th, letter from, 70

Arras—
  our march to and stay near, 59 et seq.
  battle of, 60
Ashwell's, Lena, concert party, 26
Assault on 1st July—
  plans for, 42
  our duties in, 42
  story of, 43 et seq.
Assault on 31st July, 1917, 67
Assault, Boche, 21st March, 1918, 76, 77, 78
Athies, 65
Aubers Ridge overlooks our lines, 27
Aubigny, 65
Australian, 1st Division, Pioneers, relieve us, 32

B

"B" Co.—
  work in Feby., 1916, 31
  moves to Henencourt Wood, 34
  work in Albert, 35
  special party constructs trench mortar emplacements, 39
  takes over 103rd Brigade dump, 42
  two platoons called to reinforce in La Boisselle, 47
  holds line at Bienvillers, 50
  in Villers au Bois, 51
  moves to Zouave Valley, 52
  work at Armentières, 57
  goes to Nooteboom to train, 58
  work at Etrun, 60
  in operations of 9th April, 1917, 61
  at St. Leger, attached to 102nd Brigade, 75
  experiences in Boche offensive, March, 1918, 76–77
  during retirement from Armentières, 79, 83
  during retirement from Armentières, April, 1918, 81, 82, 83
  at Nieppe, and in retirement from, 87, 88, 89
Bailleul, 89, 90
Band—
  instruments given by Mrs. Renwick, 6
  becomes Divisional band, 24
  fate of, 30
  at St. Catherine, 60
Bapaume Road, dump near, 40, 42
Barrow, Dr., attends our sick, 8

197

Index

Bean, Lieut., 46
Bebby, Mr., entertains Battalion, 13
Becourt—
    Châteaux and Wood, 36, 37, 54
    dump in, 40, 42
Bell, Major P., 65, 73
    commands Depot, 15
    rejoins Battalion, 57
    commands Battalion, 60
Beaudricourt, 62, 65
B.G. line, description of, 28, 29, 30, 56
Bienvillers, we move to, 50
Birthday, our first, 20
Blackett Orde, Canon, kindness of, 8
Blendecques, detrained at, 23
Bœschepe, 91, 92
Bois de Bouvigny, our sojourn in, 51
Boisdinghem, our stay at, 33
Bois Grenier, description of, 29
Bombardment—
    prior to 1st July, 1916, 41
    on Arras front, 60
Bomport's, Mons., house, Albert, 93
Boque Maison, 62, 65
Boyelles, 75
Break-up of Battalion, 93, 95
Bresle, our stay in, 34
Brewis, Mr. Alfred, 21
Bridge No. 4, 67
Brigade, 101st—
    we make friends with, 19
    takes over 8th Division line, 31
    parts of, established in Scots redoubt, 46
    head-quarters, and two companies attached to, 62
    we are attached to, 87, 93
Brigade, 102nd 87
    severe losses of, 47
    two companies attached to, 62
Brigade, 103rd—
    advance of, on 1st July, 1916, 44
    parts of, established in Scots redoubt, 46
    severe losses of, 47
    we are attached to, head-quarters in Contalmaison, 54
    "A" and "B" Cos. attached to, 61
    we are attached to, 93
Brigade, 116th, 98
Brigade, 122nd—
    composition of, 7
    break-up of, 14
Briggs, Lance-Corporal, 24
Brown, Lieut., killed, 74
Buckle, Captain, 122nd Brigade, 9
Bunks, the joys of living in, 34
Burton, Major-General B., inspects Battalion, 15
Burnt Farm, 67

C

"C" Co.—
    moves to Armentières, 27
    shifts quarters; its work at Armentières. Feby., 1916, 31

"C" Co.—
    reopens Greatwood Avenue, 31
    marches to Albert, sustains severe casualties, 34
    work in Albert, 35, 38
    moves into the "Glory Hole," 40, 41
    ordered to capture La Boisselle, 45
    ordered back, 4th July, 1916, 47
    at Ablain Nazaire, 51, 52
    moves to Villers au Bois, 53
    work at Armentières, attached to Franks' Force, 57
    at Moyenville, 75
    billeted in Erquinghem, 79
    during retirement from Armentières, April, 1918, 80, 82, 83, 84, 85, 86
    at Nieppe and in retirement from, 87, 88
    casualties, 91
    billet in Armentières, 93
Cabaret Rouge, 51
Calonne Ricourt, we entrain at, 53
Cambrai, 71
Cameron, Brigadier-General —
    wounded, 50
    meeting with, 55
Canadian, 7th Railway Battalion, we work with, 68
Candas, 62
Casualties in April, 1918, 91
Chalk Farm, 63
Chamber of Commerce, Military Committee of, actual raisers of Battalion, 1
Chambers, Major, second in command, appointed to command 12th K.O.Y.L.I., 19
Chapes Spur, our head-quarters, 45
Chaplin, General, 103rd Brigade, 87
Chapman, Captain, Chaplains' Department, 68
Chemical Works, 62, 65
Chinese Labour Corps, 69
Christmas, 1916, 57
C.-in-C., telegram from, 92
C.O. wounded, 90
Colours—
    we receive, 98
    received in Newcastle, 99
"2nd Commercials" alias 18th Northumberland Fusiliers, 2
Collins, Lieut.—
    rescues civilians, 81
    death of, 89
Composite Battalion, formation of, 4
Contalmaison—
    objective of 103rd Brigade on 1st July, 1916, 42
    head-quarters of 103rd Brigade, 54
    graves of men of 103rd Brigade in, 55
Cook, Lieut., wounded, 44
Coombs, Lieut. W. H.—
    appointed machine-gun officer, 33
    mortally wounded, 44
18th Corps, we work for, 66
Courcelles, 54

Index 199

Cowell, Corporal, 75
Cowie, Private T., falls from train, 23
Cramlington—
 Battalion moves to, 11
 preparation of defensive position at, 12
 Zeppelins over, 13
 Battalion leaves, 18
Crelin, Corporal, 91
Croisilles, quarries, 71
Croix de Poperinghe, 91
Crombalot, 29
Crombeke Wood, camp in, 66, 67

D

" D " Co.—
 moves to Forest of Nieppe, 27
 moves to Rue de Bruges, 27
 located in La Vesée and Rue Fleurie, 30
 work at Armentières, Feby., 1916, 31
 work in Bresle, 34
 work in Albert, 35, 38
 takes over 102nd Brigade dump, 42
 holds line at Bienvillers, 50
 in Villers au Bois, 51
 relieves " C " in Ablain Nazaire, 53
 at Martinpuich, 55
 work at Armentières, 57
 arrives at St. Catherine, 59
 work at, 60
 in operations of 9th April, 61
 at Penin, 65
 broken up, 74
Dawson's Corner, our stay at, 67–71
Dean, Private, 96
Demobilisation, 98
Depot Companies raised, 15
Dernancourt, 36
4th Division, we are attached to, 61
8th Division—
 " B " Co. works for, 31
 moved to the Somme, 31
 Battalion attached to, April, 1916, 34
9th Division, we are attached to, 54, 59
12th Division, M.O. posted to, 93
15th Division, we are attached to, 54
19th Division, in reserve at Albert, 40
23rd Division—
 Battalion attached to, 28
 relieved by 34th, 30
34th Division—
 arrives at Albert, 37
 we rejoin, 54
 attacks, 65
 we rejoin, 70
 we are detached from and rejoin, 71, 73
 detached from and rejoin, 74
 uncomfortable position of, April, 1919, 79
 head-quarters in April, 1919, 79, 82
 to be broken up, 93
37th Division—
 we are transferred to, 47
 relieved by 9th, 52

50th Division, we meet, 55
51st Division relieves us, 61
59th Division hold Bullecourt, 75
63rd Division, we are attached to, 51
Divisional Theatre, pantomime, 57
Doc. See Captain Graham
Dodds, Lieut., wounded, promoted to 25th Battalion, 56
Dodsworth, Captain, in charge of Divisional bomb store, 42
 takes command " A " Co., 48
 63
 Major, announces Armistice, 98
Doullens, 62
Draper, Lieut. A. R. O., joins Battalion, 20
 his good service, 33
 arrives at Pas, 50
 dinner with, 64
 66, 67, 69
 87
 death of, 89
Dug-out at Étaples, rescue from, 25
Dumps at Albert before 1st July, 40, 42
Duncan, Captain, M.C., Chaplain's Department, 56
18th Durham Light Infantry—
 posted to 122nd Brigade, 7
 joins 93rd Brigade, 14
Dyer, Major, Brigade Major 122nd Brigade, 9, 11

E

" E " Co.—
 moves to Wreighburn-Thropton, 8
 training of, 10
 moves to Framlington, 11
Ecoivres, 63
Elswick, possibility of raid on, 12
Embarkation for France, 22
Emergency Battalion. See Composite
Erquinghem—
 27
 we rendezvous at, 32
 53, 54, 79, 80, 81, 84, 85
Ervillers, 76
Étaples, life at, 25, 26
Etrun, 59

F

Fenwick, Dr., kindness of, 11
Finlay, Sir Kirkman, arrival of, 3
 hands over command, 7
Fitton, Brigadier-General, death of, 24
Flag, presented by Mr. R. Robson, subsequent history of, 18
Football, 95, 96, 97
Footbridges over River Lys, 80, 82, 84
Fouguereuil, 59
Francis, Lieut. C., commands " E " Co., 8
 complimented by G.O.C., 41
 acts as second in command, 60
 appointed second in command 25th Northumberland Fusiliers, 72

Index

Francis, Major C., 86
  takes command, 90
Franks' Force, 57
Fremicourt, 73
French, calmness of, 88
Furse, Major-General W. T., letter from, 54

G

Gas attack at Bienvillers, 50
" B " Co. suffers from, 81
Germany, we nearly visit, 71
Gibson Smith, Revd., 10
Gleichen, Major-General Count, commanding 37th Division, 50
  letter from, 53
" Glory Hole," 37
  " C " Co. occupies, 40, 41
Gloucester Pioneers, we work with, 66
  casualties of, 67
Godley, Sir A. J., commanding 22nd Corps, visits us, 59
Gore, Brigadier-General, letter from, 49; on 87, 88
  death of, 90
Graham, Lieut. Joseph, joins as M.O., 8
  leaves Battalion, 14
  tale of on 1st July, 1916, 45
  rejoins Battalion, 37
  provides Christmas dinner, 57
Greatwood Avenue, reopening of, 31
Grispot, A., head-quarters of machine-gunners, 30
Guards, the, relieve us, 76

H

Halfway House, our billets in, 56
Hall, Lieut. R. O., leaves Battalion, subsequent career, 13
Hall, Captain R. O., visits us, 70
Harlettes, 93
Haudricourt, 97
Havery, Private, cuts footbridge, 85
Havre, 98
Havrincourt, our stay at, 71, 73
Hawthorne, Mrs., 10
Henencourt Wood, we revisit, 46, 47
Henin, arrival, departure and return, 71
Henin-Croiselles road, stay at, 71, 72, 73
Henin Hill, 78
Hermaville, Battalion head-quarters at, 63
59
Highland Light Infantry posted to 116th Brigade, 98
High redoubt, 68
Hill Switch, occupation of, 77, 78
Hinchcliffe, Captain, Chaplains' Department, 56
His Majesty the King, review by, 13
  message from, 22
Holbrook, Lieut., 20
Hopoutre, 65
Hunn, Lieut., Transport Officer, 18

Hunter, Brigadier-General J. G., inspects Battalion, 8

I

Ingouville Williams, Major-General E.C., assumes command 34th Division, 18
  letter from, 48
  death of, 51
Inoculation, 10
Inspection—
  by Brigadier-General J. G. Hunter, 8
  by Major-General Lawson, 11
  by Major-General Burton, 15
  by Major-General Ingouville Williams, 18
  by Sir H. H. Paget, 19
  by Lieut.-General Pulteney, commanding 3rd Corps, 26
  by General Joffre, 27
  by G.O.C., 34th Division, 62
  by Corps and Divisional Commanders, 74
  by General Nicholson, 91, 92

J

James, Captain, Trench Mortar Officer, 38

K

Keenlyside, Lieut., 63
King, Lieut.-Colonel, 66, 68
King's Liverpools, 17th, relieve us, 91
Kirkby Malzeard, Battalions stay at, 18
K.R.R.s, 20th, relieve us, 74

L

La Boisselle, 34
  troubles us sorely, 37
  preparations for dealing with, 39
  plans for capture, 42
  " C " Co. ordered to assault, 45
La Conte, 59
La Gorgue, night at, 53
Lauder, Harry, gives us a concert, 63
Laurent Blangy, 63
La Vesée, heroism of farmer and his wife, 30
Laviéville, 55
Les Ciseaux, Battalion arrives at, 26
Lewis gunners, 78, 86, 90, 91
Licques, 97
Light Railway—
  " A " Co. constructs, 60
  work in " Wipers " area, 66-71
Lord Mayor, nominal raiser of Battalion 1
  receives Colour parties, 99
Louez, 64
Lovett, Sergeant-Major, 7
Lys, defence of crossings of, 79-86

Index

M

McBryde, Mr. T., 21
McCrea, Sir George, Scots redoubt, 46
McQuillen, Lieut., 22, 24
Magnicourt, 50
Malcolm, Brigadier-General, reviews Battalion, 20
Martinpuich, 54
Mash Valley, 37
Menin, short stay at, 74
M.O., memories of, 16, 63, 73, 92, 93
Merville, 54
Meteren, hurried move to, 59
Methuen, Lieut.-Colonel J. A., to command Battalion, 96
  farewell order, 99
  in Newcastle, 100
Mines at La Boisselle, 43, 44
"Minnies," 37, 57
Mont Noir, 92
Mont Rouge, 92
Mory, stay at, 72, 74
Moyenville—
  stay at, 75
  Battalion collected at, 79
Munition, men taken for, work, 21
Musketry—
  at Rothbury, 8
  at Totley and Sutton Veny, 19

N

Needham, Captain, Acting Adjutant, 14
Neuville Vitasse, two companies at, 71
Newcastle, Battalion visits, 13
Nicholson, 2nd Lieut., wounded, 44
Nicholson, Major-General C. L., visits us, 54, 64
Nieppe, Forest of—
  "B" Co. moves to, 27
  "D" Co. moves to, 27
Nieppe, Battalion collects at, 83, 86, 87
Night operations, 9, 10
Nixon (Colour-Sergeant J.), 2nd Lieut., 8
  constructs heavy trench mortar emplacements, 38
  opens tunnel on 1st July, 1916, 43
  46
  appointed Adjutant, 58
  Captain, 70
Nooteboom—
  training ground, 58
  transport moved to, 82
Northumberland Fusiliers, 16th—
  raising of, 1
  posted to 122nd Brigade, 7
  joins 32nd Division, 14
Northumberland Fusiliers, 17th—
  raising of, 1
  we work with, 66–68
Northumberland Fusiliers, 18th—
  raising of, 1
  posted to 122nd Brigade, 7
  posted to 116th Brigade, 98
  Colours deposited in Newcastle, 99

Northumberland Fusiliers, 19th—
  posted to 122nd Brigade, 7
  joins 35th Division, 14
  befriends us, 19
Northumberland Fusiliers, 23rd—
  posted to 116th Brigade, 98
  Colours deposited in Newcastle, 99
Northumberland Fusiliers, 25th—
  posted to 116th Brigade, 98
  Colours deposited in Newcastle, 99

O

Oil cans, 34, 37
Ostreville, 50
Outerscloore, D.H.Q. at, 82
"Ovillers Post," "A" Co.'s stay in, 35

P

P Camp, 67, 68
Paget, Rt. Honble. Sir A. H., inspects Battalion, 19
Park, Corporal, 65
Parkinson, Lieut., digs T.M. emplacements, 43
Parry, Lieut., 31, 56; (Captain), 85
Pas, we arrive at, 47
Passchendaele occupied, 70
Peselhoek, we entrain at, 70
Petty, Lieut., good work of, 77, 78
Pig and Whistle, 60
Pig Farm, our billets in, 56
Pioneers—
  Battalion becomes, 9
  definition of, 9
Poelcappelle occupied, 70
Pont d'Achelles, 88
Pont de Nieppe, 81, 83
Poperinghe—
  arrival at, 65
  93
Porch, Major C. P., appointed second in command, 19
  21
  rescues party at Étaples, 26
  precedes Battalion to Bresle, 34
  work at Albert, 39
  organises bombing attack, 45
  guides party to Scots redoubt, 46, 47
  taken to command 25th Northumberland Fusiliers, 48

R

Railway cutting, 62, 63, 65
Raisers, our, 1, 7, 8, 13, 15, 20, 35
Ravelsberg, 90
Reay, Captain T., appointed Adjutant, 14
  made Staff-Captain 103rd Brigade, and subsequent career, 33
Renwick, Mrs., gives band instruments, 6
Renwick, Mr. G., addresses the Battalion, 20
  imitated, 41

Renwick, Major G. A., 8
Rest, definition of, 33
Robecq, 59
Robinson, Private, 94
Robson, Mr. Richard, presents flag, 18, 21
Robson, Lieut., 31
Roclincourt, 60
Roeux, 62
Rogers, Captain L., rejoins Battalion, 57
  death of, 61, 64
Rothbury—
  Battalion arrives at, 7
  kindness of people of, 8
  amusements at, 10
Rowe, Lieut., 85
Royal Scots—
  1/8th relieves us, 64
  we work with, 66
  15th, we act with, 88–90
  16th at Scots redoubt, 46
Rue des Acquis, " C " Co.'s billets in, 27
Rue de Bruges—
  " B " Co.'s stay in, 31
  " D " Co.'s billets in, 27
Rue Fleurie—
  " D " Co.'s billets in, 30
  burnt by Boche, 31
Runners, 82
  casualties among, 92
Russian saps, 38

S

St. Aubyn, 60
St. Catherine, 59, 60
St. George's Day, 34, 35
St. Jan Ter Biezen, 91, 92
St. Julien occupied, 67
St. Leger, billets in, 74
St. Leger Valley, " B " Co. evacuate, 77
St. Nicholas, 63
Sausage Valley, 37
Scots redoubt—
  occupied by parts of 101st and 103rd Brigades, 46
  Battalion carrying parties visit, 46, 47
Sensee reserve, 75
Sercus, 33
75's lent to 34th Division, 40
Shakespear, Lieut.-Col. John, takes command, 7
  rejoins Battalion, 65
  wounded, 90
  his farewell, 100
Signallers' casualties, 92
Simms, Teddy, Drummer, 25
Smith, Captain N., takes command of " D " Co., 52
  transferred to R.E., 57
Smith, Lieut. W., machine-gun officer, 30
  appointed Adjutant, 33
  appointed to Tank Corps, 58 64
  wounded, 73
Snaith, Mrs., 16

Souchez, 52
South Staffords, 9th, " A " and " C " Companies attached to, 28
South Wales Borderers, 5th, 40
Spoil, difficulty of disposing of, 38, 39
Sports, at Rothbury, 10
Staple—
  arrived at, 23
  revisited, 33
Steel points as entrenching tools, 59
Steenwerck—
  D.H.Q., 79
  82
  occupied by Boche, 88
Stephenson, Major R., appointed second in command, 48
  appointed to command 9th South Staffords, 52
  Lieut.-Col. R., visits us, 70
Stockley, Colonel, Commandant Emergency Battalion, 5
Stone, Quartermaster-Sergeant, 7
Stores handled by Battalion between 1st and 5th July, 1916, 42
Stuart Wortley, kindness of, 19
Sussex Pioneers, we work with, 66
Sutton Veny, Battalion moves to, 19
Sweet, Captain, called into La Boisselle, 47
  appointed second in command R.W.F., 72

T

Tanks, first use of, 55
  in Wipers area, 70
Temperley, Major R., first C.O. of Battalion, 1
  first C.O. 19th Battalion, 7
  addresses the Battalion, 20
Temple, Major, in Scots redoubt, 46
Thorne, Lieut., 82
Thropton, " E " Co. moves to, 8
Totley, Battalion moves to, 19
Transport, 36
  in retirement from Armentières, 79, 82, 83
Travis, Private, first man killed, 28
Trench mortar emplacements, construction of, 38, 39
Trench system, near Albert, described, 36, 37
Trower, Colonel, 5th South Wales Borderers, 40
Turnbull, 2nd Lieut., made prisoner, 85
  experiences as prisoner of war, 176
Tyne, possibility of raid on, 12
Tyneside Irish, provide company for composite Battalion, 5
Tyneside Scottish provide company for composite Battalion, 5

U

Uniacke, Major-General, presents Colours, 98

Index

V

Vasey, Lieut., 34
  second in command " A " Co., 48
Vaulx Junction, 71
Velu, 73
Verdrel, we march to, 50
Vieux Berquin, 33
Villers au Bois—
  our sojourn in, 51
  hurried departure from, 53

W

Wainman, Private, bravery of, 86, 183
W.O. takes over Battalion, 20
Warwicks, two companies assist us, 39
Watterdal, 93
Webb, 2nd Lieut., 39, 86
Webber, Sister, attends our sick, 8, 16
Wells, Captain, 92
West India Labour Corps, 69
Wilson, Private, extracts from diary of, 48, 54, 72
Windmill Hill, Battalion's stay at, 19

Wipers, 66, *et sq.*
  revisited by M.O., 94
Wolfhoek Wood, 91
Wood, Lieut., severely wounded, 45
Worcesters, 88
Worthington, Captain, leaves Battalion, 14
Wreighburn, occupied by " E " Co., 8

X

X hutments, 60

Y

Yates, Sergeant, 60
Yorks, 6th East, we work with, 66
Ypres. See Wipers
Y sap, 37
  mine under, 43, 44

Z

Zeppelins, experience of, 13
Zouave Valley, description of, 51

INDEX OF NAMES

(EMBARKATION ROLLS, LIST OF OFFICERS, ROLL OF HONOUR, HONOURS AND AWARDS)

A

Abbott, F., 132
Adams, G., 126
Adams, J. N., 134
Adams, L., 146
Adamson, P., 124, 175
Agnew, J., 108, 170
Aikman, D. W., 126, 175
Aiston, A., 104
Aitchison, W. J., 160, 170
Akers, J., 132
Alderson, A., 124
Alderson, D., 156
Alexander, J., 146
Allan, G., 110
Allan, H., 104
Allan, J. W., 170
Allsopp, J., 146
Allsopp, N., 134
Ambler, J. J., 152
Anderson, A., 158
Anderson, J., 146
Anderson, J. R., 158
Anderson, L., 154
Anderson, R., 170
Anderson, W., 120
Angus, J. T., 156, 170
Archer, H., 156
Arkless, H., 104
Arkley, J. E., 132
Armstrong, A., 140, 174, 175
Armstrong, E., 146
Armstrong, H., 146
Armstrong, H. J., 128
Armstrong, J., 108
Armstrong, J. W., 156
Armstrong, M., 104
Armstrong, R., 134
Armstrong, T., 118, 154, 170
Arnison, F., 108
Arnison, S., 126
Arnold, J., 114
Arrowsmith, G., 124
Arthur, W., 110
Ash, C., 122
Ash, O. C., 170
Ashton, J. W., 116, 170

Ashworth, C., 110
Askew, J., 108, 110
Asprey, V., 140
Atkinson, A., 134
Atkinson, A. T., 154
Atkinson, D., 154
Atkinson, H., 118, 170
Atkinson, R. (839), 138, 170
Atkinson, R. (237), 152
Atkinson, T. R., 170
Atkinson, W., 116, 160
Avery, R., 116, 170
Ayre, W. H., 118

B

Bailey, C., 110, 171
Bailey, N., 126
Baillie, D. T., 126
Baillie, G. G., 146, 175
Baker, A., 126
Baker, G. W., 116
Baker, W., 118, 171
Balmain, H., 108
Bamburg, C., 104
Banham, T., 126
Banks, W., 158
Baptist, J., 146
Barker, T. P., 122, 171
Barkhouse, R. C., 128
Barnes, J., 138, 171
Barnes, L., 112
Barnes, W., 126
Barnwell, T., 154
Barras, J., 146
Barrasford, G., 110
Barrass, J. H., 154
Barrie, A. J., 156, 171
Barringer, C. A., 138, 171
Barron, W. V., 106
Barry, D., 142
Barwick, H., 128
Bateman, I. F., 140
Bates, J., 122
Batey, W., 132
Bath, W., 158
Batie, J., 138, 140

Batie, F., 171
Barter, T., 146
Beadling, J., 128, 171
Bean, G. W., 132
Bean, H., 108
Beaumont, R., 132
Beavis, George, 171
Beazley, R., 112
Beck, D., 124, 171
Beckworth, E., 132
Begg, L., 132
Bell, A., 138
Bell, A. W., 124, 175
Bell, C., 104, 106
Bell, E. D., 142
Bell, G. (82), 152
Bell, G. (1002), 110
Bell, G. (1222), 108
Bell, J. C., 134
Bell, P., 150
Bell, S., 171
Bell, W., 108
Bell, W. H., 171
Belshaw, W., 154, 171
Bennett, J., 156
Best, W. S., 122
Bewick, W., 104
Binney, W., 156
Blackett, E., 152
Blackley, W., 171
Blackshaw, H., 136, 171
Blake, G., 104
Blakey, C., 142, 171
Blakey, E., 140, 171
Blanch, W. L., 122
Blythman, W., 122, 171
Boaden, E., 134
Boag, J., 126
Bone, G. W., 156
Bone, R. A., 138
Bonner, H. V., 134, 175
Bonney, J. L., 138
Bould, T. N., 134
Bowman, E., 126
Bowman, T., 116
Brabhan, W., 112
Brady, W., 134
Bramble, H., 118
Brand, G., 162
Brannan, J., 112, 171
Brass, A., 116

Index of Names

Bremmer, J. M., 108
Brewis, J., 104
Brewis, J. G., 128
Brewis, J. H., 112
Briggs, E., 118, 171
Brittain, C., 122
Brodie, J., 160
Brogan, J., 136
Brookes, T., 108
Brooks, S., 162
Brown, A., 134
Brown, G., 132, 171
Brown, G. R., 150, 170
Brown, G. W., 171
Brown, J. (1073), 112, 171
Brown, J. (355), 124
Brown, J. (373), 124
Brown, J. (603), 128
Brown, J. R. (1298), 122
Brown, J. R. (832), 146
Brown, J. S., 158
Brown, G. (1488), 158
Brown, G. (1190), 171
Brown, O., 108
Brown, P., 160
Brown, R. L., 156, 171
Brown, S. P., 116
Brown, T., 171
Brown, W. B., 112
Brown, W., 130, 158
Brownless, L. E., 156, 171
Bruce, C., 108
Bruce, G., 152
Bruce, M. T., 171
Brunton, J., 130, 171
Brunton, H., 156, 171
Brydon, N. A., 118
Buchan, J., 160
Burlinson, J., 134
Burn, D. H., 136
Burnell, J., 118
Burns, R. B., 160
Burns, W., 118

C

Cairns, F., 140
Cairns, J., 158
Callaghan, A., 138
Callaghan, T., 138
Canning, J., 158
Carey, F., 116
Carlisle, J., 146
Carr, D. E., 116, 152
Carr, G., 122
Carr, G. B., 130
Carr, G. D., 154
Carr, H., 104
Carr, J., 136
Carr, J. R., 158, 171
Carrot, J., 116
Carter, H., 136
Carter, J. J., 112, 171

Caswell, G. E., 124, 150, 174
Chambers, E. L., 152
Chambers, R., 156
Chandler, T., 162
Chapelow, I., 130
Chapman, W. A., 122
Chapman, W., 154
Charlton, J., 118, 158
Charlton, N., 124
Charlton, R. H., 160, 171
Charlton, T., 138, 160, 171
Charlton, W. (Corpl.), 142
Charlton, W. (1731), 160, 171
Charlton, W. R., 106
Cheesman, W. D., 134, 171
Cherry, W., 146
Chipperfield, D., 158
Chisholm, G. A., 142
Chisholm, M., 116
Churchill, W., 116, 175
Clark, A., 114
Clark, B., 114
Clark, D., 114
Clark, J., (195), 114
Clark, J. (205), 114
Clark, J. (148), 152
Clark, G. (1005), 144
Clark, G. (887), 171
Clark, G. W. W., 144
Clarke, G. A., 126
Clarke, R. J., 118
Clarkson, J. H., 138
Clasper, John, 171
Clements, J. S., 150
Clennan, J. R., 118
Clennan, W., 118, 171
Clough, J. R., 134
Clough, R., 156, 171
Clydesdale, W. L., 146, 171
Coakley, J., 160
Cockerton, W. G., 136
Cole, F., 154
Cole, S. J., 152
Coleclough, W., 154
Collings, W., 130
Collins, C. H. T., 150, 170
Collinson, J., 146
Connell, J., 142
Cook, J. S., 108
Cook, P. S., 144
Cook, S. E., 126
Coombs, H., 112, 170
Cooper, R., 144
Cooper, T. G., 146
Corbitt, J. D , 150
Corbitt, R., 136
Corder, J., 156
Cothics, R., 156
Coulson, A., 128, 170, 175
Coulson, A. E., 124, 171

Coulthard, E., 146, 171
Cowan, J., 138
Cowans, A., 132
Cowans, R., 108
Cowell, J. T., 138, 171
Cowell, T. H., 136, 171
Cowen, J., 104
Cowey, T., 142
Cowings, G., 104
Cowlic, A., 160
Coxen, E. H., 156
Coxon, E., 130
Coxon, W., 122
Craig, F., 136, 175
Craig, R., 108
Craigie, B., 108
Crankshaw, R. T., 138
Crawford, F. L., 150
Crawford, W. F., 158
Crellin, G., 106
Crosby, W., 154
Croudace, J., 146, 171
Cubin, R., 124
Cummings, F., 130
Cummins, N., 118
Cunningham, W., 142
Curry, F. B., 118
Curry, R. W., 104, 171
Cutting, J., 122

D

Daley, J., 110
Dance, E., 150
Darmody, J., 162
Davidson, J., 118
Davidson, R. B., 132
Davidson, W., 134
Davies, R., 110
Davison, A. S., 138
Davison, J., 136, 144
Davison, T. R., 134
Dawson, A., 106
Dawson, J., 126
Day, J., 122, 171
Dean, C., 130
Deighton, D., 126
De Leuw, R. H., 114
Dellow, R., 146, 170
Dent, J., 110, 171
Devere, E., 138
Devlin, D., 122
Devlin, J., 130
Dick, J., 142, 171
Dickenson, R., 171
Dickinson, A., 108
Dickinson, J., 142, 171
Dixon, A., 158
Dixon, C., 108
Dixon, F. A., 126, 171
Dixon, G. W., 110
Dixon, J. (179), 108
Dixon, J. (919), 144

Index of Names

Dixon, J. (1004), 144
Dixon, M. B., 122, 171
Dixon, R., 130
Dixon, W., 108, 171
Dixon, W. S., 112
Dobbins, T., 156
Dodd, E., 132
Dodds, F. C., 124
Dodds, S., 154
Dodds, W. M., 140, 170
Dodsworth, P. C., 108, 150, 174
Dolman, E., 142, 154
Donkin, D., 136
Donkin, J. E., 104
Donnelly, F., 154
Dorman, R., 144
Douglas, J., 146, 171
Douglas, W., 118
Douglass, J., 138
Dow, J., 134
Downey, E., 114
Dowson, R. A., 136
Dracup, R. H., 118
Drady, D. R., 126
Draper, A. R. O., 104, 150, 170
Drinkald, G., 104
Drury, P. B., 138, 170
Dufour, G., 136
Dufour, J., 171
Duggin, C. H., 136, 171
Dunn, A. E., 104
Dunn, D., 124
Dunn, E., 116
Dunn, J. B., 116
Dunn, N., 116
Dunn, R., 132
Dunn, W., 116
Dwyer, J., 132

E

Edgar, A., 104, 171
Edgar, T. W., 134
Ekin, J., 132, 171
Elgey, M., 106
Elliott, A., 108, 142
Elliott, E., 116
Elliott, J., 118, 130, 171
Elliott, N. L., 160, 171
Elliott, R., 116, 171
Elliott, R. A., 122, 171
Emerson, J. W., 122
Emmerson, A., 160
Emmerson, A. G., 130
Emmerson, G., 108
Emmerson, J., 122
Emmerson, S., 171
Emslie, G., 158
England, H., 112
Ensell, E., 118
Errington, P., 144

Errington, R., 110
Everson, R. L., 138

F

Fairbairn, T., 132, 171
Fairless, F., 110
Falcus, J., 126
Fall, A., 156
Farbridge, A., 136
Farrage, C., 118
Farrar, W., 122
Farrell, E., 126
Farrell, M., 136, 175
Fawcett, B., 132
Featherstone, J., 130
Fenn, R. W., 118, 171
Ferguson, D., 154
Ferguson, W., 126
Finlay, W., 122
Finnigan, W., 118
Fisher, F., 136
Fisher, N. (902), 146
Fisher, N. (1180), 156
Fisher, W., 171
Fitzpatrick, J., 160
Fletcher, J., 106
Fletcher, L., 116, 175
Fletcher, Lieut. L., 174
Foreman, W., 114
Forrest, J., 122
Forrest, T., 134
Forster, G., 110
Forster, G. H., 132
Forster, J. J., 162
Forster, L., 171
Forsyth, C. N., 160
Forsyth, J., 108, 175
Fortune, G. S., 138
Foster, L., 106
Foster, T., 124
Fox, T., 146
Frampton, J. S., 138
France, W. P., 110
Francis, C. J., 128, 150, 174
Franklin, T., 142
Freeman, G. E., 122, 171
French, A., 144
French, J., 124
French, W., 136, 171
Friend, J., 114
Furness, J., 154
Futers, N., 150, 170

G

Gair, E., 124
Gair, J. E., 160, 171
Gair, W., 124
Gallagher, J., 160, 171
Gallirher, G. W., 160, 171
Galloway, J., 106

Garbutt, R., 142
Gardiner, A., 116
Garrity, J., 126, 171
Garthorne, J. G., 134
Gavine, P., 114
Gaynor, J., 106
Gentles, W. S., 116
Georgeson, H., 132
Georgeson, J., 134
Gibbon, G., 126, 156
Gibson, A., 120, 132
Gibson, J., 156, 171
Gibson, R., 160, 171
Gibson, S., 140
Gilbert, M., 158
Gilhespy, S. K., 114
Gill, E., 114
Gillait, F., 112
Gleghorn, J. A., 134
Glen, J. A., 144, 171
Good, R., 132
Goodfellow, G., 124
Goodman, R., 144
Goodrich, A., 158
Goodwin, J., 110
Gowland, R., 106, 136
Graham, Capt. J., 152
Graham, J., 120, 171
Graham, W. T., 120, 154
Grainger, W. T. A., 142
Gray, A. D., 108
Gray, Lieut. J., 108, 170
Gray, J. (1069), 134
Gray, J. (904), 144
Green, E., 140
Green, J., 136
Green, P., 116
Green, R., 144
Green, R. B., 140
Greenhall, W., 122
Greenwell, A., 136, 171
Greenwell, T., 122
Greenwell, W., 122
Gregan, C., 120
Gregory, C., 160
Gregory, R., 156
Grey, A. E., 112
Grey, W. J., 112
Gribbon, B. R., 152
Gunn, B., 158
Gustard, T., 120, 171
Guthrie, G., 124, 156
Guy, R., 144

H

Hadaway, J. W., 162
Haddon, H., 124
Haley, F., 140, 172
Hall, A., 112, 172
Hall, G. (473), 124
Hall, G. A. M., 130
Hall, H., 140
Hall, J. (774), 134, 172

Index of Names

Hall, J. (625), 130
Hall, J. (321), 154
Hall, N., 136
Hall, R. (322), 122, 172
Hall, R. (333), 154
Hall, R. (1456), 158
Hall, R. O., 174
Hall, T. L., 154
Hamilton, D. M., 122, 172
Hamilton, R., 160
Hammell, G., 140, 172
Hancock, T., 158
Handcock, T., 134
Hands, J., 112
Harbit, J. W., 146, 172
Harding, T. O., 152
Hardwick, E., 142
Hardy, A., 106
Hardy, G., 108
Hardy, J., 132
Hardy, J. R., 154
Hare, J. M., 144
Hargreaves, J., 114
Harley, W. S., 108
Harmison, W., 124
Harper, S., 126
Harris, E., 140
Harris, T. W., 126
Harris, W., 120, 170
Harrison, E. W., 142
Harrup, J., 142
Hart, J., 160
Hart, G., 172
Harvey, A., 154
Harvey, W., 142
Havelock, J. A., 132, 172, 175
Hawson, W. B., 138
Heads, T. C., 134
Healey, J., 126
Hedley, J. W., 146
Hedley, W., 112
Helsby, R. G., 152
Henderson, G., 126
Henderson, L., 114
Henderson, T., 110
Heron, F., 114
Heron, J., 112, 172
Heron, O., 106
Heslop, G., 146
Heslop, R., 134
Hetherington, R., 160
Hewitt, I., 116
Hey, L., 142
Hiftle, J., 142
Higham, J. S., 158
Hill, A., 142
Hill, R., 136
Hill, W. A., 146
Hillhouse, J. P., 150
Hind, J., 110
Hindmarsh, J., (1316), 134
Hindmarsh, J. (1048), 112
Hindmarsh, J. (873), 142
Hindmarsh, R., 136, 172

Hindmarsh, T., 112
Hinds, G. E., 160
Hinton, J., 110, 172
Hird, J., 114
Hitcham, S. P., 112, 172
Hobson, A., 144
Hodge, J., 144
Hodgin, J., 126
Hodgkinson, J., 128, 150, 170
Hodgson, J., 144
Hodgson, R., 144
Hogg, C. E., 116
Hogg, J., 106, 124
Holbrook, W. S., 134, 150, 174
Holland, J. E., 106
Holmes, F. W., 116
Holmes, G., 134
Holmes, T., 124
Home, W., 134, 172
Hooker, B., 124
Hooker, R., 124
Hope, E., 136
Hope, T. T., 160
Hopson, J. E., 158
Horan, I., 132
Horn, G., 108
Hornsby, J., 146
Hough, D., 110
Howarth, A., 144
Howarth, R., 144
Howe, T., 128
Howorth, R., 154
Hudson, T., 130
Hughan, H., 146
Hughes, J., 128
Hughson, S., 130
Hulbart, A., 172
Hunn, Lieut., 152
Hunter, A., 144
Hunter, C. S., 156
Hunter, C. W., 106
Hunter, J., 136
Hunter, N., 116, 156
Hunter, R., 154
Hunton, J., 136
Huston, A., 158, 172
Hutchinson, R. W., 122
Hutchinson, S., 140
Hutchinson, W., 120

I

Imeson, E., 124, 172
Imeson, J. B., 122
Innes, J., 140
Irving, J., 140
Irving, W., 124

J

Jackson, H., 158

Jackson, J. W., 142
Jackson, J., 150
Jackson, T., 130
Jackson, T. W., 160
Jackson, W., 108, 170, 174
Jacques, S., 124
Jameson, J., 132, 172
Jee, A. A., 172
Jefferson, T. E., 106
Jeffrey, J., 140, 172
Jeffrey, R., 114
Jeffrey, T., 158, 172
Jenson, J. L., 160
Jobling, D., 116
Johnson, A., 156, 175
Johnson, A. G., 146
Johnson, D., 120
Johnson, I., 116, 156
Johnson, J., 158, 172
Johnson, J. J., 120
Johnson, J. M., 150
Johnson, J. S., 146
Johnson, J. W., 140
Johnson, R., 106
Johnson, R. J., 124
Johnson, S., 144
Johnson, W., 144
Johnson, T., 106, 136, 172
Johnston, C., 156
Johnstone, T., 136
Jones, E., 136
Jones, E. E., 175
Jones, H., 134
Jones, N., 160
Jopling, G., 140
Jude, E. J., 158, 172

K

Kay, E., 106
Kay, J., 106
Keeghan, H., 146
Keenlyside, T. E., 150, 170
Keigham, G. A., 158
Keir, O. L., 116
Kelly, J. W., 154
Kennedy, J. H., 152
Kennedy, W. B., 160
Kennedy, W. H., 154, 172
Kershaw, E., 106
Kidd, M., 104
King, D., 132
King, D. R., 154
King, G., 154
King, J. E., 158
Kirsop, A., 120
Kirtley, A., 144
Knight, S., 114
Knox, H., 108, 116
Kyle, J., 106, 172

Index of Names

L

Labbett, T. G., 172
Laben, C., 160
Laing, P., 162, 172
Lambert, J., 130
Lamberton, J., 130, 172
Lamming, W., 134
Lancaster, W., 132, 172
Lathey, W., 172
Laverock, N., 162
Law, A., 136
Lawes, M. R., 114
Lawson, E. G., 154, 170
Lawson, T., 112
Leach, J. G., 134, 172
Leblique, L., 116
Lee, E., 122
Lee, J. H., 146
Lee, J. T., 154
Lee, S., 108
Levitt, T., 172
Lewis, R., 140
Lewis, T., 122
Liddell, J. T., 130
Liddell, T. J., 172
Liddle, G., 114
Liddle, W., 140
Lightfoot, T., 158, 172
Lillice, J., 154
Lillicoe, A., 136
Lillicoe, J. H., 136
Lincoln, C., 140
Lishman, J., 136
Lister, J., 122
Little, G., 152
Lobley, A., 140
Lock, J. S., 114
Logan, C., 152
Logan, J., 130
Lombard, E., 112
Longstaff, G., 122
Longville, J. B., 128
Lough, J., 130
Lovett, J. R. C., 172
Lowe, S., 114
Lowe, W., 114
Lowery, W. E., 172
Lowes, C., 144
Lowes, G., 134, 172
Lowes, W., 114
Lowry, A., 142
Lowry, J., 124
Lowry, W., 140
Luke, T., 124
Lumsden, J., 134, 172
Lyall, G., 130
Lyon, W. M., 128

M

McCallum, J. H., 132
McCaulay, T., 134
McCormick, F. P., 152, 170
McCourt, T. L., 142
McCutcheon, T., 132
McDermott, G., 116
McDonald, J., 154
McDougall, R., 142, 154
McDougall, T., 116
McElwaine, E., 140
McFarlane, G. F., 104
McGowan, J., 110, 172
McGuire, G., 138
McInnes, R. D., 130, 170
McKay, E., 124
McKay, J., 112
McLaren, H., 132
McLaurin, A., 128
McLean, W., 106
McMahan, M., 154
McManus, J., 134
McParlin, W., 146
McPeak, A., 160
McPherson, James, 172
McQueen, R., 112
McQuillen, W. T., 118
McTaggart, A., 158
Mafhan, J., 146, 172
Makepeace, F. G., 152
Malone, T., 138, 172
Malone, J., 138, 172
Maltby, T., 120, 172
March, W., 134
Margetson, F. A., 138, 172
Marley, J., 114
Marr, R. S., 144
Marshall, J., 160
Marshall, J. W., 122
Marshall, W., 106
Martin, C., 134
Martin, J., 130
Mason, N., 120
Mason, T. R., 110, 132
Mather, J., 134
Matthew, E. G., 120
Matthews, P., 110
Mawston, A., 110
Meadows, W., 150
Meggison, J., 144, 172
Mercer, J., 132, 172
Merrilees, S., 158, 172
Methuen, J. A., 174, 175
Milburn, T. W., 156, 172
Milburn, W., 116, 172
Miles, E. W., 156
Miller, R., 138
Mills, W. J., 152
Milne, A., 130
Milne, D., 158
Milne, F. B., 146
Miners, G. A., 172
Minto, G., 134
Mitchell, A., 122
Mitchell, G., 146

Moffitt, J., 154, 172
Moffitt, W., 152
Mole, A., 138, 172
Mole, W., 150
Moll, E., 108
Monaghan, P., 122
Monkhouse, T., 158, 172
Mooney, J., 124
Moore, A., 160
Moore, C., 116
Moore, G., 116, 154
Moore, H., 156, 172
Moore, W. T., 116
Mordue, W. S., 106
More, J., 124
Morpeth, A., 144, 172
Morris, C. F., 172
Mortimer, A., 120, 172
Mortimer, G. H., 116
Morton, G., 152
Mounsey, J., 124
Moyes, R., 112
Muirs, G. E., 106
Murphy, J., 122
Murray, A., 144
Murray, C. A., 150
Musgrove, J. W., 144

N

Naylor, R., 116
Needham, J. M., 152
Nelson, J. R., 112
Nesbitt, E., 156
Newall, A., 156
Newman, S., 122, 175
Newton, H., 160
Newton, R., 120
Nichol, J., 120
Nichol, W. J., 106
Nicholls, J. H., 112
Nicholson, A., 132
Nicholson, J. H., 152
Nicholson, R., 122
Nicholson, S. R., 146
Nicholson, W. E., 104
Nisbet, J., 146
Nisbett, G. C., 134
Nixon, J. B., 120 150, 174
Nobes, E. G., 112
Noble, J., 128
Noble, W., 106
Norman, F. R., 172

O

O'Connor, R., 112
O'Neil, A., 128
O'Neill, R., 172
O'Neill, S., 144

Index of Names

Ormston, W., 110
Ostle, R., 120
Oxley, J., 116, 172

P

Palmer, A., 114
Palmer, J., 138
Palmer, R. R., 160
Pargeter, T., 142
Parker, G. P., 138
Parker, J. T., 130
Parker, W., 112
Parkin, J., 120
Parkin, F. W., 158, 172
Parkinson, E., 114
Parkinson, P., 110
Parmley, J. H., 112
Parry, G. H., 142, 150
Partis, T., 110
Patterson, J., 122
Patterson, T., 140
Paumier, A. W., 172
Peacock, J. C. M., 128, 170
Pearcy, G. W., 138
Pearson, F., 156
Pearson, J., 122
Pearson, J. F., 114
Pearson, H. E., 114
Pearson, P., 110, 172
Peart, G. R., 175
Peel, J., 160
Percival, A., 112
Petrie, J., 124
Petty, J. T., 150
Philips, G. S., 158
Philipson, N., 142
Phillipson, T. H., 140
Phillips, J., 112, 175
Phipps, A., 124
Pigott, L., 152
Pinckney, T., 134
Pinkett, T., 154
Plantin, R., 132
Platten, H., 156
Poctrous, W. H., 154
Porch, C. P., 104, 174
Porteous, J., 110
Potts, J. W., 110
Potts, W., 124, 172
Powell, R. D., 122
Preston, R., 172
Price, J., 156
Price, R. G., 116, 152
Price, W., 130
Prim, R., 144
Pringle, W. H., 150
Pritchard, T., 138, 154
Proud, J. (1116), 142
Proud, Jos. (1117), 142
Proud, T., 156
Proudfoot, A. S., 140, 172
Proudlock, R., 140, 152

Proudlock, T., 124
Prower, F., 144
Prower, W. A., 144
Puddicombe, F. W., 172
Purvis, G. S., 142
Purvis, J., 132, 142
Purvis, W. P., 114
Pybus, C., 130
Pyle, J., 140
Pyle, S., 114

Q

Quickmire, A., 140
Quickmire, J., 120
Quinn, G., 112
Quinn, J. E., 110, 170

R

Railston, W., 130
Rainey, C. G., 104
Rawson, W., 158
Read, J., 124
Reay, J., 106, 124
Reay, G. J., 175
Reay, G. T., 158
Reay, R. E., 106
Reay, T., 104, 174
Reay, W., 132
Reed, C. E., 146, 172
Reed, E., 134
Reed, J. S., 146
Reed, R., 138
Reed, W., 138
Rees, W. H., 136
Relph, J., 110
Renton, A., 138, 150
Renwick, G., 134
Richardson, D., 146
Richardson, E., 130, 134
Richardson, H. W., 130
Richardson, H., 116
Richardson, N., 146
Richardson, P., 124
Richardson, R., 116
Richardson, W., 128
Ridd, R., 134
Riddle, C. W., 172
Riddle, W., 134
Riddle, W. H., 134
Ridley, C., 144
Ridley, J., 122, 130
Ridley, O., 106
Ritson, J., 144
Roberts, H., 106
Roberts, T., 106
Robertson, J. (596), 136, 152
Robertson, J. (1320), 146
Robertson, J. W., 158, 172
Robinson, A., 130

Robinson, H., 122, 160
Robinson, J. (152), 116
Robinson, J. (285), 120, 154
Robinson, J. (847), 140
Robinson, J. (567), 132
Robinson, R. V., 132
Robinson, R. (1096), 142
Robinson, R. (258), 116
Robinson, R. (1356), 116
Robinson, W. A., 146
Robson, A., 160
Robson, C., 128, 152, 170
Robson, C. J., 146
Robson, E., 122
Robson, F., 172
Robson, J., 116, 146
Robson, J. E., 146, 150
Robson, J. W., 146, 156
Robson, M., 126
Robson, P. J., 144, 172
Robson, P., 128
Robson, R. (1239), 126
Robson, R. (709), 126
Robson, R. (1415), 130
Robson, R. (515), 128
Robson, R. (950), 142
Robson, R. (711), 106
Robson, S., 112, 122
Roche, R., 136
Rodham, J., 160, 172
Rogers, L. N., 152, 170
Rogers, V. B., 174, 175
Rogers, W., 126
Rogerson, R. D., 136
Rolls, G. F., 172
Roper, J. H., 126, 172
Ross, H., 118, 126, 172
Ross, W., 140
Rough, W., 152
Roughton, L., 144
Routledge, B., 104
Rowbotham, E., 146
Rowe, A., 114, 150
Rowell, E., 142
Rowell, P., 112
Rowntree, M., 148
Roy, E. G., 134
Roy, J. T., 132
Rush, F., 172
Russell, C. S. C., 152
Russell, E., 110, 170
Russell, J. F., 112
Russell, R., 112, 172
Ruth, T., 128, 154
Rutherford, F., 112, 172
Rutherford, W. (1291), 110
Rutherford, W. (1538), 158
Rutherford, W. C., 156, 172
Rutter, F. W., 152
Rycroft, J., 140
Ryder, G., 120

Index of Names

S

Salkeld, M., 114
Salkeld, R., 116
Sanderson, G., 106
Sanderson, R., 106
Sanderson, W., 116
Savory, W., 116
Saxby, F., 120
Schooling, G. R., 152
Scorer, J. A., 108, 174
Scorer, T. L., 148
Scott, A. (317), 120
Scott, A. (1167), 120
Scott, B., 120
Scott, J. H., 144, 154, 173
Scott, F. H., 138
Scott, H., 114
Scott, T., 138
Scott, W. J., 138
Scribbins, F., 152
Sewell, A., 154
Shakespear, J., 104, 150, 174
Shanks, J., 120
Shannon, D., 132
Shannon, T., 132
Sheader, H. J., 120
Sheader, R. A., 120
Shegog, R. W., 104, 170
Sheperd, R., 104
Shepherdson, S., 144
Sherrington, J. N., 156
Shiel, A. C., 116
Shipley, A., 140
Short, J., 120, 173
Short, W., 112, 173
Shotton, J., 120
Sibbit, G. B., 136, 170
Silk, R. W., 152
Simm, D., 138, 175
Simm, E, 120
Simms, D., 136
Simpson, W., 110, 114, 152
Singer, F., 173
Skeoch, N., 152
Skeock, A., 128
Small, E., 106
Smith, A., 128
Smith, C. M., 126
Smith, E., 106, 173
Smith, J., 110
Smith, J. H., 130
Smith, J. R., 128
Smith, J. W., 126, 173
Smith, H., 132
Smith, H. B., 114
Smith, N., 128
Smith, R., 126, 154
Smith, T. B., 122
Smith, T. H., 148
Smith, W. (1322), 122
Smith, Lieut. W., 104
Smurthwaite, O., 150, 170
Snaith, R., 130
Snowdon, A., 126
Snowdon, G., 138
Snowdon, R., 138, 173
Spain, I., 152, 175
Spencer, R., 136
Spiller, H., 152
Spoors, R., 152
Spraggon, A. E., 108
Stanley, G. S., 160
Steel, G., 148
Steele, J. T., 132
Stephenson, E., 152, 156
Stephenson, J., 106, 114, 173
Stephenson, J. G., 126
Stephenson, J. H., 114
Stephenson, J. W., 130
Stephenson, P., 120
Stephenson, R., 108, 174, 175
Stephenson, T., 173
Stephenson, W. N., 108
Stewart, J., 138
Stewart, T., 112
Stewart, T. S., 110
Stobbs, D., 112
Stobes, J., 142
Stokoe, T. D., 126
Stoker, R., 116, 152
Stonehouse, D., 108
Storey, A. B., 120
Storey, A. G., 126
Storey, E., 110, 175
Storey, E. G., 120
Storey, H., 110
Storey, R., 136
Storey, T. W., 108, 173
Stott, J. T., 114, 173
Stott, J. W. D., 114
Stoves, A., 140, 173
Stoves, J., 126, 173
Straughan, J., 106, 160
Straughier, R. H., 173
Strawbridge, W., 118
Sunter, S., 140
Surtees, F., 175
Surtees, W. M., 128
Sutherland, D., 130
Sutherland, J. (286), 120
Sutherland, J. (458), 126, 173
Sutherland, R., 128
Sweet, F., 118, 174
Swift, J., 118
Symonds, W., 144

T

Tait, M. S., 118
Tait, R., 160
Tallant, J. W., 128
Taylor, J., 128
Taylor, J. F., 140
Taylor, G., 156
Taylor, R., 138, 173
Taylor, T., 144, 173
Teasdale, J., 158
Telford, F., 126
Telford, J., 110
Telford, N., 142
Temperley, G., 140
Temperley, J. W., 140
Temple, T. S., 114
Tennant, J., 108
Thirlwall, T., 136
Thomas, J. G., 160
Thompson, F., 148
Thompson, G., 160
Thompson, G. R., 148
Thompson, J., 110, 160
Thompson, J. B., 142, 173
Thompson, J. D., 173
Thompson, M. W., 130
Thompson, R. (112), 106
Thompson, R. (997), 118
Thompson, R. (1163), 126
Thompson, R. (1186), 156
Thompson, R. B., 118
Thompson, S. R., 134
Thompson, T., 130
Thompson, T. A. (518), 130
Thompson, T. A. (514), 128
Thompson, T. G., 173
Thorne, C. E., 150
Tilney, F., 132
Tindle, E., 110
Todd, F. D., 118
Tomilson, T., 158
Tomlinson, F., 126, 175
Tomlinson, J., 118, 160
Tones, J., 112, 173
Toole, E., 140
Totton, P., 142
Totton, W., 148
Tozer, T., 130
Travis, W. H., 110, 173
Tully, S., 128
Turnbull, C. R., 152
Turnbull, E., 150
Turnbull, G., 154
Turnbull, J., 154
Turnbull, R. H., 106, 130
Turnbull, S., 132
Turnbull, S. R., 136
Turner, T. S., 160
Tweddle, W., 112
Tynemouth, W., 140

U

Ullathorne, G., 144
Urwin, A., 156, 173
Urwin, F., 142, 156
Urwin, J. C., 160

V

Van Hee, R. H., 150
Varty, A., 128

Index of Names

Vasey, J. R., 120, 173
Vasey, J. W., 136, 150, 174
Veitch, E., 150, 170
Vost, J., 158
Voyzey, G., 140

W

Waddell, J., 136
Waddington, J., 114
Wailes, S., 106
Wainman, J. W., 175
Waite, J., 132
Wake, H., 148, 173
Wake, R., 138
Waldie, H., 122
Walker, J. (389), 122
Walker, J. (509), 130
Walker, J. N., 108
Walker, W., 122
Wall, E., 173
Wall, F., 114
Wallace, B., 132
Wallace, R. W., 140
Walpole, B., 148
Walsh, J. M. P., 118
Walton, A., 160
Walton, F., 144
Walton, I. G., 120, 173
Walton, J., 120, 142
Walton, S. W., 108
Walton, W., 112, 173
Wand, A. B., 106
Wann, A. G., 128
Wannop, W. D., 140
Ward, J., 148
Ward, J. R., 148
Ward, M., 158
Ward, W., 118, 128, 175
Wardhaugh, T., 112
Wardle, H., 122
Wardle, J., 160
Warren, A., 120, 154
Watson, A. S., 154
Watson, G. A., 118

Watson, H. W., 158
Watson, J., 140
Watson, M. L., 132, 173
Watson, R., 128
Watson, S., 142
Watson, S. T. (220), 152
Watson, S. T. (230), 118
Watson, T., 118, 173
Watson, W. (146), 106
Watson, W. (263), 120
Watson, W. (527), 128
Watson, W. H., 160
Watts, C., 130, 140, 154
Weatherhead, H., 156
Webb, F. R. G., 150, 174
Weddell, W., 112, 173
Weir, G. T., 130
Weir, H. W., 128
Welch, J., 136
Welch, R., 132
Wells, D., 120
Wells, G. W., 173
Welsh, J. R. F., 152, 175
Welsh, R. J., 120
White, B., 158
White, J. R., 124
Whiteman, R., 162
Whiteside, J. T., 144
Wiffen, G., 144, 173
Wilde, H., 148
Wilde, J., 154
Wilde, T. H., 148
Wilkie, J. T., 160
Wilkie, W. S., 142
Wilkinson, R. D., 144
Willey, C., 140, 158
Willey, W., 104
Williams, J. H., 106
Williams, T., 114
Williams, W. A., 160, 173
Willis, E., 106
Wills, J., 156
Wills, S. C., 152
Wilson, F. G., 118, 174
Wilson, G. C., 173

Wilson, G. T., 148, 156
Wilson, H., 110
Wilson, H. H., 173
Wilson, I. (1413), 132
Wilson, I. (1288), 128, 173
Wilson, J. S., 150
Wilson, M. H., 150
Wilson, R., 162
Wilson, T., 158
Wilson, T. J., 112, 173
Wiltshire, V., 173
Winship, S., 114
Winwood, J. 124, 173
Witherley, J., 128
Wonnocott, W. G., 124
Wood, C. C., 144
Wood, E., 126, 173
Wood, E. E., 154
Wood, J. (435), 128
Wood, J. (437), 128
Wood, W., 128
Wood, J. F., 148
Wood, J. T., 114
Wood, R., 110
Wood, R. W., 110, 114
Woodhead, C. M., 130
Woodhouse, J. W., 142
Worthington, R., 170
Wright, G. T., 120
Wright, J., 120, 142, 152
Wright, J. R., 142
Wright, J. W., 156
Wright, O., 138
Wrightson, F. S., 114

Y

Yarrow, E., 106, 173
Yates, G., 104
Yeeles, W., 136
Yendell, J. H., 136
Young, A., 108, 104
Young, G., 158
Young, J., 130, 140

Sketch Map of Somme Sector

shewing lines held on July 1st 1916, and Trenches in 34th Division Sector.

MAP 1.

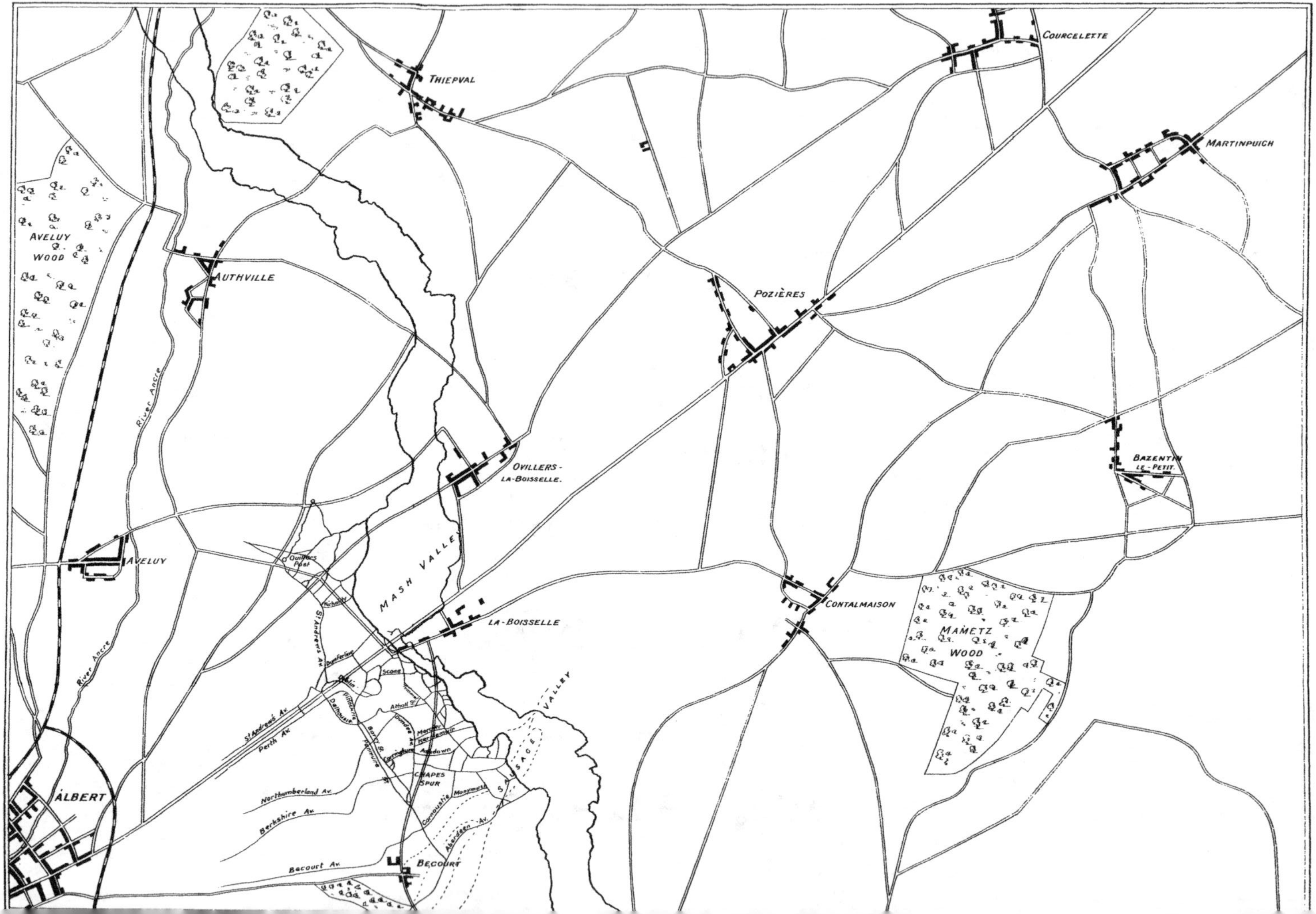

SKETCH MAP OF

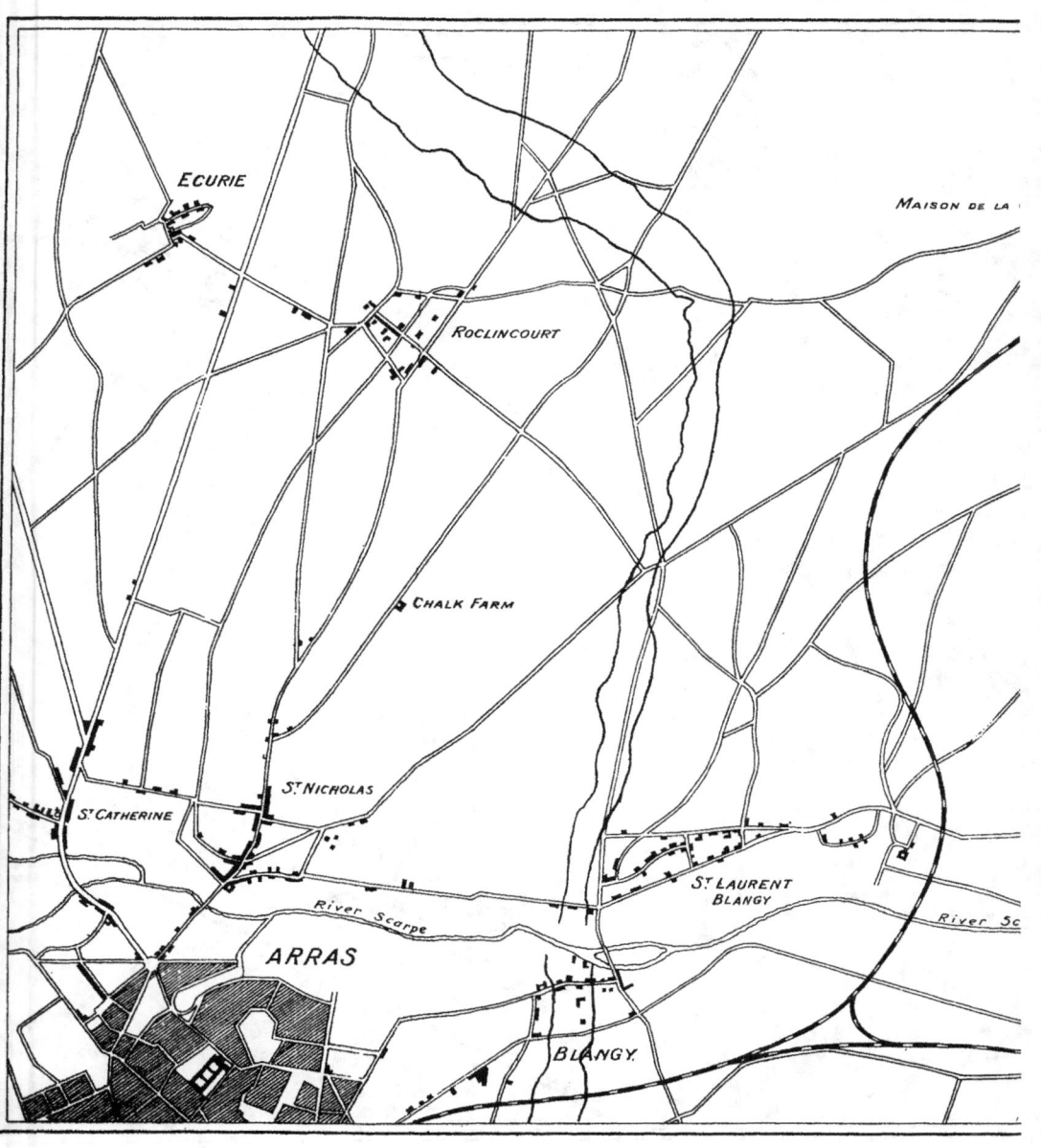

ARRAS SECTOR. MAP 2.

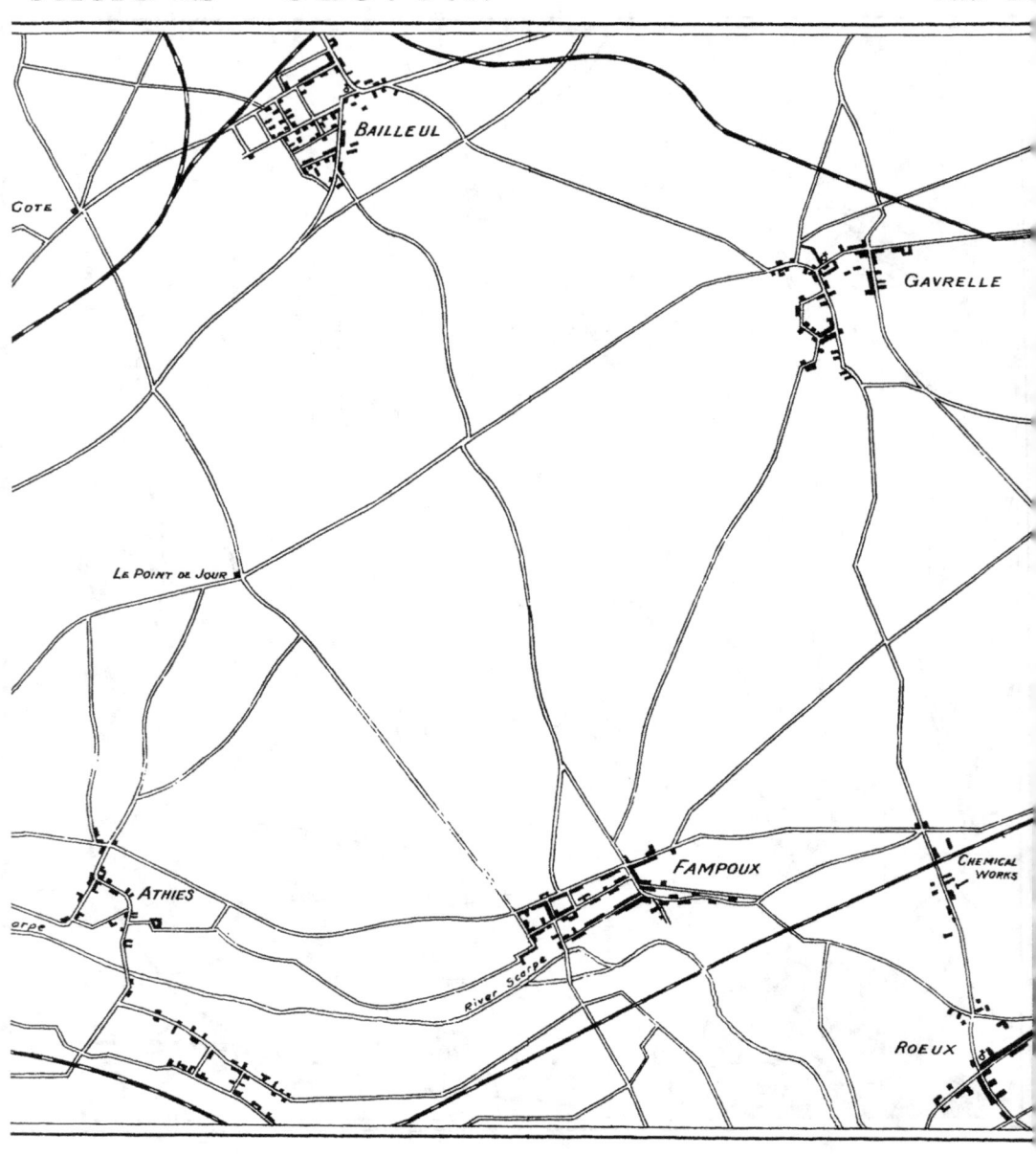

Sketch Map of Lys Sector

showing enemy advances and positions taken up by 18th Battalion Northumberland Fusiliers.

10th to 14th April 1918.

Companies shown ⊠ ⊠ ⊠ ⊠

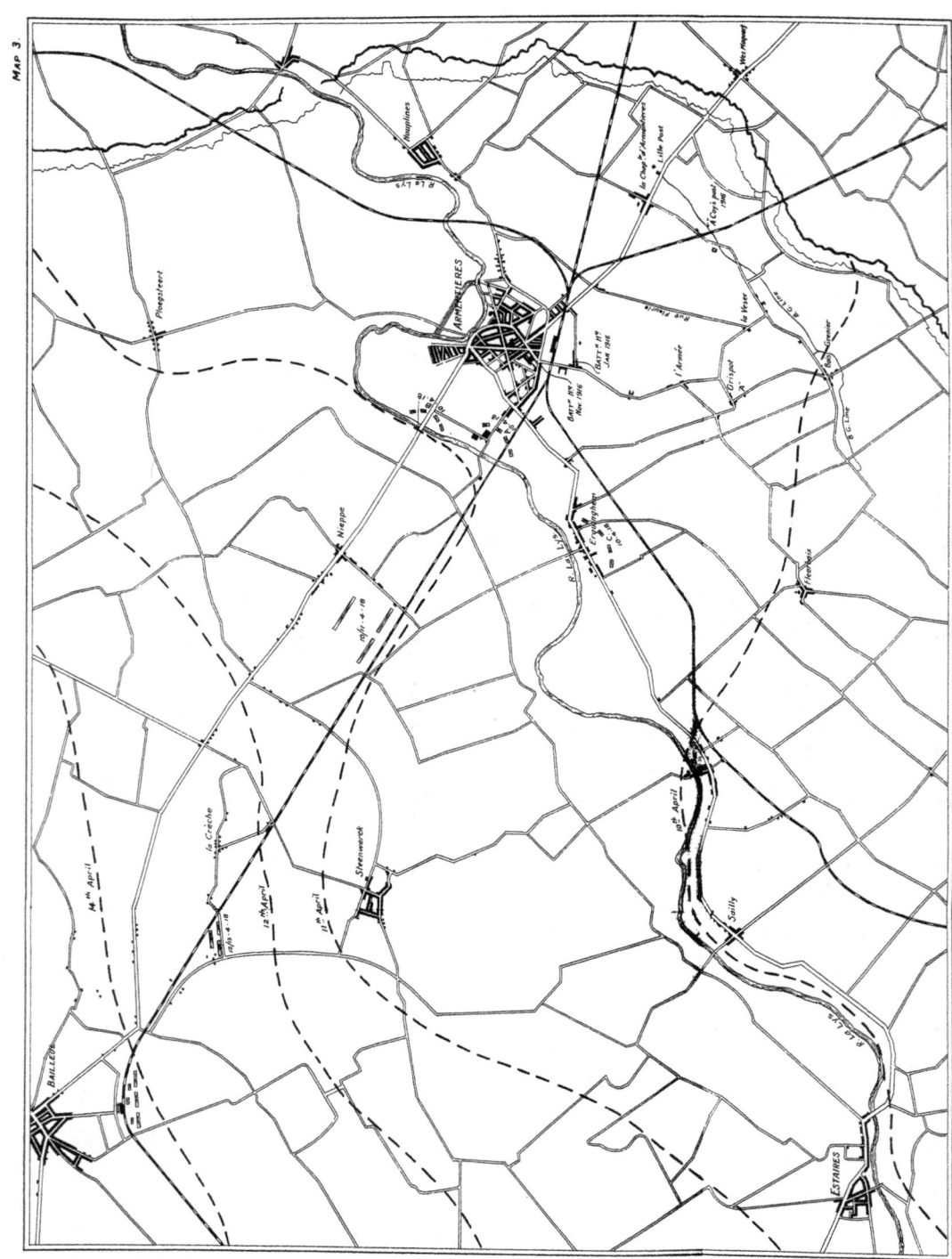

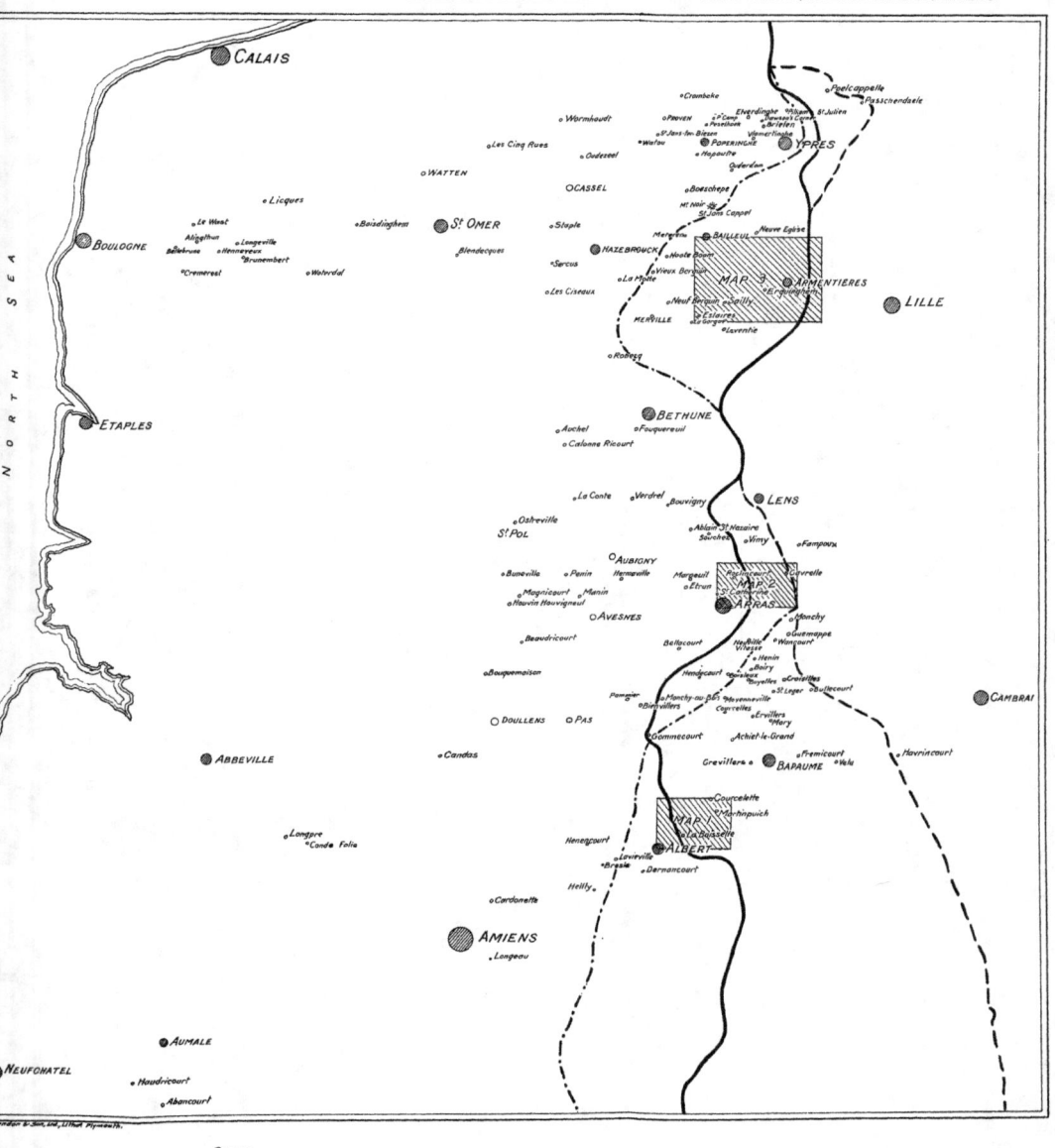

www.ingramcontent.com/pod-product-compliance
Lightning Source LLC
Chambersburg PA
CBHW060558230426
43670CB00011B/1881